MONEY & WORK: An Essential Guide

by

Wyn Derbyshire
Stephen Hardy and
David Wicks

2007

Published by Spiramus Press
September 2007

© Spiramus Press Ltd 2007

ISBN 978 1904905 48 6

British Library Cataloguing-in-Publication Data.

A catalogue record for this book is available from the British Library.

Typeset and cover design by: Spiramus Press Ltd

Printed in Great Britain by: Biddles, King's Lynn, England

Dedications

For Clare and Elizabeth	-	WD
For Louise, Dominic and William	-	SH
For Tamsin, Lucy and Anneka	-	DW

Acknowledgements

With thanks to Helen Cobby, Robert Gaines and Jill Hallpike.

About the authors

Wyn Derbyshire is a Partner at SJ Berwin LLP, Solicitors, where he is Head of the Pensions Group. He has written numerous articles, commented in the media on various pensions issues and with Hardy and Maffey has co-written 'TUPE: Law & Practice', 2006 (Spiramus). Along with Stephen Hardy, he is also co-editor of Sweet & Maxwell's 'Doing Business in Europe' looseleaf (2 volumes), as well as being legal consultant to Gee's "The Pensions Factbook".

Stephen Hardy is a Barrister, and was formerly Professor of Law at the University of Manchester where he researched in EU and employment law. He is currently co-editor of Sweet & Maxwell's 'Doing Business in Europe' and General Editor of Sweet & Maxwell's 'Employment Encyclopaedia', as well as widely published on employment-related matters.

David Wicks entered the financial services industry in 1971, and has held a variety of Marketing, Technical and Developmental roles with life assurance companies. As Managing Director of Finance Industry Training Limited (FIT), he provides various consultancy services to Insurance Companies, IFAs and other institutions in the financial world, and writes extensively on a range of financial topics.

Foreword

By Cherie Booth, QC

Thirty years ago, being in employment was a relatively straightforward business. An employer would engage an employee, who would slot into the workforce and get paid for getting the job done. Employers didn't ask too many questions of their employees, who, in turn, didn't ask questions of their bosses. And when disputes occurred, both parties would head off for to the relatively unsophisticated industrial tribunal, as they used to be known, give evidence without first exchanging witness statements and then await the tribunal's determination. The tribunal hearing would take place in a cold, barely furnished room, which alone was sufficient to keep the press from the door.

As readers of this book will discover, social and technological advances and legislative changes have propelled us all into a far more complicated far more regulated world of work. Most young people whilst in full time education have benefited from other people's taxes but now on the threshold of work, its payback time and for many the plethora of rules governing tax are not only incomprehensible but are often remote from the benefits for which they pay. This book provides essential insight into what taxation is all about.

Domestic employment legislation has mushroomed at an astonishing rate, often driven by European directives. The primary purpose of these developments has been to develop the protection of individual and collective employment rights. These reflect the changing nature of our society and its current preoccupations. Glancing at the chapter headings in the work section of this book confirms that the world of work in the 21st century is multifaceted, complex and full of pitfalls for the unwary. Certainly the old assumptions about the role of men and women in the workforce and the pattern of working life whether in respect of work/life balance or retirement are no longer valid. This book provides a quick and accessible overview of what to look for and where to go if things go wrong and is an essential signpost for all those new to the world of work.

Cherie Booth

Cherie Booth QC
Matrix
Grays Inn
London

Contents

CONTENTS

CONTENTS

CONTENTS

CONTENTS

CONTENTS

Preface

Levels of personal debt in the United Kingdom – recently estimated to be as high as £1.3 trillion – have never been greater. The range of available investment products steadily increases – as do the potential risks of poor investment. House prices have soared over recent years, making it harder for first-time buyers to acquire even a modest property of their own. We're all living longer and yet the pensions system gets steadily more difficult to understand. The working environment becomes ever more complex as new employment laws and practices emerge and the old certainties (good and bad) about the working world disappear, creating a confusing tapestry of rights and obligations.

All in all, life (at least those aspects of life relating to work, savings, debt, pensions, mortgages and so on) is complicated today. Hence the reason for this book, the aim of which is to demystify at least some of the confusion which can exist in relation to financial and employment matters. It is aimed primarily at people who are commencing work for the first time or starting college or going to University – in other words, it's a book for people who are taking personal responsibility for their working and financial lives for the first time. Having said that, it isn't just for them; we hope that there will be something of interest for everyone who is keen to avoid the potential financial pitfalls and workplace difficulties which can be encountered in modern life, regardless of how long they may have been earning a living.

If there is one lesson that has been driven home to each of us whilst writing this book, it's the lesson that teaches us that nowadays – and we suspect, this will increasingly be the case in the future – the only person any of us can really count on if we want to minimise financial concerns and workplace problems is ourself. Our employers, our families, the Government and other public bodies can help to a degree, of course, but at the end of the day, it is up to each of us to recognise the choices and opportunities which exist and the traps that can potentially ensnare each of us. We hope that this book is of at least some help in this regard.

WD, SH and DW – the authors
June 2007, London

PART ONE: MONEY

1 Handling money

Although, as is often said, money is not everything in life, it is an important aspect of everyday activity, and handling money sensibly and with confidence is important. In this Chapter, we look at some of the basics, including running a bank account.

1.1 Current accounts

A current account is a basic account intended to deal with your normal cash flow. Typically, money from your job, whether weekly or monthly paid, will be credited to your current account, and you can then use that money in various ways. For example, you can draw cash, or use other methods such as cheques or debit cards to pay bills.

1.1.1 Who offers current accounts?

Banks and many building societies offer these accounts, and terms vary, so it is worth shopping around. Accounts may be based at a branch in the high street, but increasingly, we are being encouraged to run our accounts at long range, via the telephone or internet. This is an efficient way for the banks and building societies to operate, because branch networks involve substantial costs, whereas the cost of running a telephone or internet banking operation is much less.

1.1.2 Depositing money

Putting money into the account is straightforward. The money might be in the form of cash or cheques, which can be paid in at your branch or other branches of the same or another bank or building society. The institutions offering accounts of this sort belong to or subscribe to a central organisation (the Cheque and Credit Clearing Company) which facilitates this clearing process.

Some banks make a charge for dealing with credits to accounts at other banks and some may refuse to deal with some transactions.

If you pay into a branch of your own bank or building society, cash is generally cleared straight away so that you can draw on it when you wish. Cheques take a few days (generally at least three working days and sometimes longer) to clear – in other words to pass through the clearing system so that the money is actually transferred. You cannot draw on the money until it is cleared.

Sometimes a cheque is not honoured (often referred to as the cheque 'bouncing'). This will usually only happen if the person who wrote the cheque does not have sufficient money to cover the cheque, and has not arranged an overdraft (see below) to cover it either.

This is one of the reasons that it takes some time for a cheque to clear. Your bank needs to be sure that it will receive the money it expects from the account of the person who wrote the cheque, before it allows you to draw on it. If you pay in a cheque which bounces, you may be asked to present the cheque again i.e. pay it in again, in the hope that there will then be money in the cheque writer's account to cover it. This may happen if the situation is expected to be temporary, for example where there should be another regular salary payment into the account soon.

Sometimes you will be told to 'refer to drawer' in which case you must go back to the drawer (the person who wrote the cheque). The drawer may pay you in another way, or may tell you to represent the cheque if he has paid more money into his account.

As a general rule, you should not give the cheque back unless you are paid in another way. If the cheque is not eventually honoured, the bounced cheque can be the basis of a legal action against the drawer.

1.1.3 Drawing money out

There are a number of ways of using the money in your current account to pay for things. Traditionally, the most common way of doing this has been to write a cheque. The recipient then pays this into his account and the money is transferred through the normal clearing process.

Cheques are being replaced by debit cards to a large extent and indeed many petrol stations and, increasingly, shops no longer accept cheques. Debit cards allow such payments to be made electronically, which is quicker and cheaper. Generally if you use a debit card, you must have a PIN (Personal Identification Number) which you must input to a numeric pad to confirm the transaction. Because the PIN should be known only to you, this is more secure – someone stealing a debit card could forge a signature, but it would be much harder to find out someone's PIN.

It follows that you need to be careful with your PIN. You should not write it down in a recognisable form, and preferably should memorise it so it is not kept in writing at all. You should never let anyone know your PIN either, even if they claim they work for the bank or building society. This information is never requested by bank or building society staff, and they will not contact you to ask for it.

You can also use a debit card to buy goods over the phone, via the internet or by post. You provide the details of your card (your PIN is not required, but instead you will often be asked for the security number printed on the card – usually a three digit number on the back of the card, but there are different configurations).

You should only give these details if you are sure that you are dealing with a bona fide person or organisation. Otherwise, those same details could be used by a fraudster to buy goods using the money in your bank account. We discuss fraud and scams in Section 1.4 of this Chapter.

Note that debit cards are not the same as credit cards (see below), and they create an immediate debit directly against your bank account. You need to be sure you have enough money in the account, or an overdraft arranged to cover the debit. Otherwise the transaction may be refused, or you may be faced with substantial extra charges on your account.

Alternatively, you can draw out cash, either by presenting a cheque over the counter at your branch, or by using your debit card over the counter or in a cash machine. These are more correctly known as ATMs – Automatic Teller Machines. Generally, cash machines in, or outside branches are free of charge, even if you bank elsewhere. However, some machines in other places, such as shops or garages, charge a fee for withdrawals.

You can also use these cash machines to change your PIN from that which applied to the card when first supplied to you. This is simply done by following the on screen instructions. The intention is that you should choose a sequence you can remember, but you should avoid the obvious, such as 1234, 1066 or something relating to your address or birthday. If your card is stolen, there is a good chance that the thief could steal other information including your birthday and address and so could guess your PIN.

1.1.4   Direct debits and standing orders

You may want to establish a regular arrangement to make payments from your account. For example, many people pay their gas, electricity and phone bills by regular instalments each month, because this is easier to budget for than (for example) large quarterly amounts.

Direct debits involve your giving the organisation you are paying the details of your bank account and authorising them to take payments direct from the account. Direct debits are usually variable – the amount taken can be varied by the recipient without their having to get a further authorisation from you. This simplifies administration and is a useful facility. For example, if you pay your gas bill by direct debit and prices increase, the amount you pay will need to increase, so your gas supplier can handle this automatically.

This sounds a little bit risky, in the sense that the person to whom you give a variable direct debit has a lot of control over your account. Because of this, some people will not agree to pay bills in this way. However, in reality, there is a high degree of protection under the Direct Debit Guarantee. The guarantee provides that:

- If there is a change to the amount of the direct debit, or the payment date, you will be given notice by the organisation collecting the payment. The notice is normally at least 10 working days, unless it has been agreed otherwise.
- If an error is made by the organisation collecting the payment, or your bank or building society, you will receive a full and immediate refund from your own branch.

This means that if any problems arise, you can contact your own bank or building society who will sort out the problems, rather than having to deal with the recipient organisation. Banks and building societies only allow reputable organisations to be recipients of direct debits, and monitor the arrangements carefully, otherwise they could not offer such a strong guarantee.

You can also cancel a direct debit at any time, by instructing your bank or building society to stop meeting the payment requests from the recipient. You should tell the recipient too, and make other payment arrangements where necessary, otherwise you could face legal action in respect of any money you owe.

Standing orders are paid by your bank or building society rather than being collected by the recipient, and are fixed in amount, unless or until you tell the bank or building society to change the payments. Standing orders are less convenient for the recipient and are becoming less common, though some people feel that this basis gives them more control over their bank account than if a direct debit arrangement is in force.

Some recipients use standing orders because they cannot collect direct debits. If you rent your home, your landlord may insist that you pay your rent by standing order. (Landlords often do not receive enough payments for their bank or building society to be prepared to allow them to collect direct debits.) If it is part of your rental agreement to pay in this way, then you must do so.

Other recipients may insist on a direct debit. For example, this is usually true of a mortgage lender if you buy a property.

1.1.5 Paying bills

Direct debits and standing orders are a convenient way to pay many bills. They allow you to spread costs over time, often by making monthly payments of a constant amount. This usually applies for costs such as gas, electricity and landline telephone charges. Council tax is also generally paid on this basis.

Paying monthly means that you can plan for your liability much more easily than if you wait for a bill to arrive, perhaps every three months. These bills can be hard to pay, particularly if the bill is larger than usual – perhaps the heating bill for a cold winter quarter.

Providers of gas, electricity and telephone services usually help you to estimate what your payments should be, and then they collect the same amount each month, carrying forward any positive or negative balance to the next month. They send regular statements and will suggest an adjustment to your payments if the balance being carried forward is getting too great (whether positive or negative).

Council tax and water supply bills (usually known as water rates) can be paid by direct debit too, but the cost is known in advance for the year, so the payments (which may be spread over a number of months rather than the whole year), are set in advance and you receive notification of them.

Some other bills vary from month to month, for example, mobile phone costs, but you are told the amount that will be taken from your account well before the deduction is made.

If you choose not to pay by direct debit, you must make payments as they fall due. As already mentioned, this can sometimes be difficult, particularly when they are larger than expected or a number of bills fall due at the same time. It is a good idea to put some money aside so you are not trying to meet three months' costs from one month's income. You could put this money in a deposit account (see Section 1.2 below) so it earns interest, but although this sounds a good idea, many organisations give a discount to customers who pay by direct debit (or charge an additional amount to those who do not). This will probably more than equal the interest you earn.

You can pay your bills in many different ways. Putting a cheque in the post has been most common in the past, but often, you can pay directly into the recipient's bank account, either at your bank or building society, or electronically via the internet.

It is useful to keep records of your expenditure, in case a recipient cannot trace receiving the money. The more information you have, the easier it will be to show that you have paid what you owe.

1.1.6 Overdrafts

Current accounts often have overdraft facilities, but these should be used with care. Some accounts offer a free overdraft, up to a certain limit – these include many student accounts (the bank hopes to retain former students as customers and may make a loss on the student account but aims to make profits on services provided later).

In general however, banks charge interest on overdrafts in the normal course of business. Most banks charge a much higher rate of interest on unauthorised overdrafts than on authorised overdrafts, so this distinction is an important one.

If you know you are going to need an overdraft, you should approach your bank as soon as you can. This may not be a task you are enthusiastic about, but if you delay, or avoid approaching the bank, the situation will not improve. The bank will want to know how much you need, why you need it and how you will pay it back, so you should think through these points in advance.

If the bank agrees to the overdraft, it will specify the terms, including the interest rate and often there will be an initial arrangement fee. This is an authorised overdraft. Generally, they will expect the overdraft to be repaid over a period of a few months.

If you do not approach the bank, but continue to write cheques or use your debit card, the bank may decide not to honour the transactions, so your cheque may bounce or your debit card may be declined when you try to use it. You will then be forced to contact the bank to discuss the position and you may find them less accommodating than if you had approached them in the first place.

Alternatively, they may decide to honour the transactions that take you into an overdrawn position, and they will then treat the overdraft as unauthorised. As already mentioned, this is likely to attract higher interest charges than an authorised overdraft.

There may also be other charges involved, including charges where transactions are refused, and sometimes for writing to you about the situation. All these charges will only make the situation worse, and so it is much better to contact the bank early on. After all, the bank's business is to lend money, so you may find them more willing than you expect – provided you have thought through how you will eventually repay.

1.1.7 Charges and interest

It is up to the institution offering the current account to determine what charges apply and what interest is credited. This is a competitive area, and it can pay to shop around.

In recent years, many current accounts have been operated without charges, subject to certain conditions. These may include a minimum balance being maintained for example, or simply that the account does not become overdrawn. There does however appear to be a move towards introducing charges and this may be an area of change over the next year or two.

Interest is sometimes not paid at all on current accounts, or may be credited at a low rate which may be almost negligible. If you generally do not have a substantial credit balance in your account, this may not matter very much, but if you often do have a high balance, you should consider accounts which offer a better rate of interest.

1.2 Deposit accounts

Although current accounts are useful – probably indispensable for most of us – they generally pay little interest. Deposit accounts of various sorts are offered by most banks and building societies and interest rates are better. They do not have cheque book or debit card facilities and do not permit standing orders or direct debits. They are intended for money which will be held on deposit for some time, rather than money which is paid in and drawn out on a rapid cycle.

1.2.1 Special terms

Many accounts have special terms applying to them and where these restrict the way in which the account operates, they generally also result in an improved interest rate. When you select an account, you need to find the best combination of interest rate and terms for your particular needs.

Examples of special terms include:

- **Limited withdrawal facilities**: for example, you may not be able to make withdrawals at all for a certain period, or may be restricted to one or two each year.

- **Fixed term**: in other words, you commit your money for a known period, of perhaps one or two years, but sometimes longer. Where the account has a fixed term, it may offer a guaranteed interest rate too, which will work in your favour if interest rates in the market generally go down, but not if they go up and you could have done better elsewhere.

- **Minimum investment**: it is cheaper for institutions to handle a small number of large transactions than a large number of small transactions, so if you have a large amount to invest, you may be rewarded with a better interest rate.

- **No branch service**: even though the institution may have a network of high street branches, the account is not handled through them, but can be accessed only by remote means, such as telephone, internet or post.

This is a competitive market place, so many different accounts are available, and the range changes constantly. You can research what is available via the internet, in the money sections of weekend newspapers, or you can simply take a walk down the high street and look at what the various banks or building societies can offer.

You should decide how much you want to invest and for how long before you start your research. This way, you avoid wasting time finding out about unsuitable accounts.

1.2.2   Stockmarket-linked accounts
Some accounts, which will always be for a fixed term, offer interest linked in some way to stockmarket performance, measured by means of an index based on certain share prices. For example, the FTSE 100 index reflects the performance of the largest 100 companies on the London Stock Exchange.

Often the account pays interest at a rate slightly more than the increase in the index, and guarantees that you do not lose anything, even if the index falls over the relevant period. This sounds an excellent arrangement, and it can suit many people, but it is important to be aware that the detailed terms can be complicated. The comparison with direct investment in the stockmarket is not as straightforward as it might appear.

For example, often these accounts measure the index not on the day you invest, but over a period of several months after investment. Similarly, at the end of the fixed term, the index is averaged over several months prior to the day the account pays out. This reduces risk, because it lessens the effect on your investment of fluctuations in the index. However, if stockmarket performance is generally positive, it is likely to reduce the interest paid over the term.

Also, the index is not adjusted for the income that you would have received if you had invested in the shares that make up the index. As discussed in Chapter 2, when you invest in shares, you hope to benefit from both an income stream and an increase in the value of the shares. Because the index is based only on the latter, it does not reflect the total return a stockmarket investor would achieve.

The term is fixed, and if you want to access your investment early, you may not be allowed to, or you may get back less than you invested. You should therefore only commit amounts which you are as certain as possible will not be needed until the end of the fixed term. Investors in shares can sell at any time, although they must accept that they may lose money if share prices are low when they do so.

Another point to bear in mind is that the return on these accounts is generally regarded as interest and is therefore subject to income tax. Investors in shares pay income tax on the dividend income they receive, but are subject to capital gains tax (see section 7.2.2) on increases in the value of their shares. Capital gains tax is generally less onerous than income tax, because of the annual exemption available and also because there are various tax reliefs available.

These points do not mean that these stockmarket-linked accounts are poor, and indeed there are clear advantages in the guarantee of no loss or a limited loss, the lack of costs involved (everything is usually allowed for in the structure of the product) and the likelihood of a gain in excess of the growth in the index. However, as always, investment decisions must be considered carefully, and all aspects must be taken into account.

1.2.3 Demutualisations

Building societies differ from banks in that they are 'mutual' organisations – in other words they are owned by their members (i.e. their investors and borrowers), and have no shareholders. Banks do have shareholders, who receive a share of the bank's profits through the payment of dividends on their shares.

Societies are often keen to promote the benefits of being mutual, in particular that all of their profits can be used for the benefit of their members rather than being paid out to shareholders. On the other hand, opponents of mutual status argue that having shareholders keeps a bank 'on its toes' by providing an external influence, particularly if the bank is not performing well, or seems to be falling behind the times. Also it is shareholders who initially put capital into the business, and who therefore provide the money that it needs to grow.

Both views have merit, and perhaps in the final analysis, it is less important how a bank or building society is structured than how good its management is.

It is a fact that in recent years, a number of building societies have 'demutualised' and have become banks. Shares are issued to new shareholders and this raises capital, which is available for the business to use. However, if the society belongs to its investors and borrowers before demutualisation, it is right that those investors and borrowers are compensated for the change in status. This compensation may be in the form of a cash payment and/or free shares.

There is often an opportunity to buy further shares too, sometimes on favourable terms. Investors and borrowers must be consulted and must vote in favour of demutualisation if it is to go ahead, so the terms must be sufficiently attractive to persuade them to do so.

Investors and borrowers have therefore received an unexpected 'windfall' profit on demutualisation. Some people decided that it would be a good idea to place small sums in a large number of building societies in order to benefit if one or more of those societies demutualised, and this proved a successful strategy for many.

However, this was a damaging development for the societies themselves, largely because they had to handle a lot of small accounts which could put their costs up quite considerably. Most have therefore made this practice (often referred to as 'carpet-bagging') unattractive for new investors. They have taken various actions to achieve this including:

- paying very low rates of interest on small balances
- requiring a high minimum initial investment
- restricting the availability of accounts which carry membership (i.e. partial ownership of the society) and offering other accounts with no ownership rights
- requiring new investors and borrowers to agree to donate anything they would otherwise receive on demutualisation to a charity

In general, this means that carpet-bagging is much less likely to be a good strategy, but if you have a long-standing building society account, you could be fortunate. However, although for a period in the 1990s, demutualisations were common, this is no longer so.

On occasion however, a society might be taken over by a bank, or a larger building society, and this will also generally result in similar payments being made to existing investors and borrowers.

1.3 Loans and credit

Most people need to borrow money at various times in their lives, sometimes for a specific purpose, sometimes to boost their cashflow for a period. Two things are certain with loans – you have to pay interest on the amount borrowed, and you have to pay back the capital at some stage. We have already discussed overdrafts earlier in this chapter and these can provide an effective and useful means of dealing with cashflow problems.

We now go on to discuss other forms of borrowing, the terms of which vary considerably.

1.3.1 Secured loans

If a loan is secured, it means that you give the lender a legal charge over an asset, most commonly a house or flat that you own. The most familiar loan of this type is a mortgage, used to buy a property to live in, and secured against it. (Mortgages are dealt with in Chapter 5.)

However, loans for almost any purpose can be secured against a property, provided the property value is high enough. Often there is more than one loan secured against the same property – the first is known as first charge, the next a second charge, and so on.

Lenders are protected in the case of a secured loan because the legal charge allows the lender to claim against the value of the property, and a secured loan has priority over any unsecured loans if you become bankrupt (see below).

For example, if you buy a house with a mortgage, and do not make the repayments required of you, the lender can take possession of the property and sell it. From the proceeds of the sale, it can retain the amount you owe, including interest and any charges, and only any excess is returned to you.[1] This is why advertisements for mortgages must always include the statement 'Your home may be repossessed if you do not keep up repayments on your mortgage'.

If there is more than one charge against the property, the lender with the first charge sells the property, but any excess after it has taken what is owed is passed to the lender with the second charge, and so on.

The protection for the lender is greatest if the value of the property exceeds the loan by a large margin. Otherwise accumulated arrears and possibly reductions in property prices could mean that it cannot recoup what is owed if it has to take possession of the property. A lender with a first charge has greater protection than a lender with a second charge, because the lenders are repaid in order.

The element of security means that lenders will usually charge lower interest rates for secured loans, and lower interest rates for loans secured by a first charge rather than a second charge.

---

[1] Of course, if the proceeds of sale are less than the amount you owe, the lender can pursue you (through the Courts if necessary) for the balance.

There are costs involved with secured loans. For example, a solicitor will generally be required to draw up the legal charge, and lenders may also charge an arrangement fee at outset. These costs inevitably reduce the advantage of the low interest rate.

1.3.2 Unsecured loans

Unsecured loans are the only option for those who do not have a property against which to take a secured loan, and for those who already have borrowed as much as they can on a secured basis. They are also the preferred choice of many people, particularly for short term loans where the reduced rate of interest which might be obtainable on a secured basis would not compensate for the other related costs.

Interest rates vary widely, but lenders will always want to have some basis for judging whether you can pay back any loan that you apply for. This may require you to fill in an application form, giving details of your income and assets, and you may need to provide evidence of income, perhaps in the form of some recent payslips.

Lenders will often check the credit records of applicants to see if there is a track record of successful repayment of previous borrowings.

You should always remember the basic rule that if you borrow money, you need to repay both interest and capital. Before you enter into a loan, you should be confident of your ability to meet the repayments.

1.3.3 Student loans

You may have experience of a student loan, and if you have, you will see repayments of the loan deducted from your earnings – through the PAYE (Pay as You Earn) system if you are employed.

Interest on student loans is charged at a very low rate, in line with the Retail Prices Index. Currently, this is far below the rates of interest you are likely to have to pay on other borrowing.

Repayments are only required if your income exceeds a certain level (currently £15,000 in 2007/08). The repayments increase if your income increases, but reduce if your income reduces. They stop if your income falls below the set level at which repayments are due. This is a very unusual repayment basis. Usually loans have to be repaid at an agreed rate whatever happens to your income.

If you have capital available, perhaps through an inheritance, it can be attractive to repay the student loan, but because of its favourable terms, it is not as pressing to do so as would be the case with more conventional borrowing. If you have other loans as well as your student loan, it may be best to repay the other borrowing first – generally it is wise to repay loans carrying a high interest rate before those with a low interest rate. You do need to look at all the terms however, because some loans carry additional charges if they are repaid early.

1.3.4 Credit cards

If you have a credit card, or indeed several, you will already know that this is a convenient way of borrowing money to fund everyday purchases. Most shops and restaurants take payment by credit card and if you shop via the internet, or by phone, credit cards are also a straightforward way to pay.

Debit cards and credit cards are used in a similar way, and as discussed with debit cards (see Section 1.1.3 above), you will generally have a PIN which you need to use to authorise a purchase when you are in the shop, restaurant etc when the purchase is made. If you shop via the internet or telephone, you will use the security number printed on the card.

However, the financial effect is different. A debit card uses your own money from your current account, and debits that account with the cost of the purchase.

A credit card is a form of borrowing and when you make a purchase, the amount is added to the amount you owe the credit card provider. You receive a statement each month, telling you the total amount outstanding, and asking you for a payment to reduce the balance.

If you repay the whole of the outstanding balance each month, there will usually be no interest charged. Credit cards used in this way can be extremely convenient, and they cost you nothing in terms of interest. Some cards have a monthly or annual fee, but most do not, so this is attractive. (The credit card issuer charges the seller a percentage fee based on whatever you have bought, so they are not really providing a service for nothing, and in some cases the seller charges you an additional amount to cover the fee.)

If you do not repay in full, interest is charged on purchases, usually from the date you made them, and interest rates are high, often more than 1% per month. There is usually a minimum repayment, which depends on your balance, but you can choose to pay that minimum or anything above it. The less you pay, the more interest you will end up paying, because the debt is outstanding for longer.

It can be very tempting to buy what you want now with a credit card, and aim to repay slowly from your income. The problem that many people have is that instead of paying back what they initially borrowed, they find that the next month, they buy something else, and the outstanding balance starts to increase rather than reduce.

It can mount up quickly. Let us look first at the effect of repaying, but not spending any more. Suppose you buy something for £100 using a credit card. You decide you can repay £10 per month, but the interest is 1% per month on whatever you do not repay. The effect of this is shown in the table below.

Month	Balance at start of month £	Spend £	Repay £	Interest £	Balance carried forward £
1	0.00	100.00	10.00	0.90	90.90
2	90.90	0.00	10.00	0.81	81.71
3	81.71	0.00	10.00	0.72	72.43
4	72.43	0.00	10.00	0.62	63.05
5	63.05	0.00	10.00	0.53	53.58
6	53.58	0.00	10.00	0.44	44.02
7	44.02	0.00	10.00	0.34	34.36
8	34.36	0.00	10.00	0.24	24.60
9	24.60	0.00	10.00	0.15	14.75
10	14.75	0.00	10.00	0.05	4.79

| 11 | 4.79 | 0.00 | 4.79 | 0.00 | 0.00 |
| 12 | 0.00 | | | | |

The detailed terms of credit cards vary, so the above is a simplified example, but it shows how a credit card can be used to spread cost, if you manage your account well. The next table shows what happens if you are tempted to spend a further £50 each month.

Month	Balance at start of month £	Spend £	Repay £	Interest £	Balance carried forward £
1	0.00	100.00	10.00	0.90	90.90
2	90.90	50.00	10.00	1.31	132.21
3	132.21	50.00	10.00	1.72	173.93
4	173.93	50.00	10.00	2.14	216.07
5	216.07	50.00	10.00	2.56	258.63
6	258.63	50.00	10.00	2.99	301.62
7	301.62	50.00	10.00	3.42	345.03
8	345.03	50.00	10.00	3.85	388.88
9	388.88	50.00	10.00	4.29	433.17
10	433.17	50.00	10.00	4.73	477.90
11	477.90	50.00	10.00	5.18	523.08
12	523.08	50.00	10.00	5.63	568.71

It is easy to get into debt, but much harder to get out of it. Also, although the table has shown payments of £10 per month, in fact, minimum payments are usually 3% or 5% of the outstanding balance, so you would, in reality, have to start repaying more each month as the balance climbs.

1.3.5 Comparing sources of credit

Credit providers, whether of loans, credit cards or any other sort of borrowing, are obliged to calculate the APR (Annual Percentage Rate) for the borrowing they are offering. The APR is calculated on a basis set down by legislation, and the intention is that it should provide borrowers with a means of comparing the interest rates charged on different loans.

The idea is that however complicated the terms of the loan, the greater the APR, the more expensive it is.

From a technical point of view, the basis of calculating the APR is not as well-defined as it might be, but the principle remains true. You should use the APR as a measure of how competitive a loan is.

It is a useful exercise if you are considering different forms of credit to get the details of various types and compare the APR. You are likely to be surprised at the range of rates that exists.

1.3.6 Credit standing

The ability of individuals to raise finance through loans, credit cards and so forth, is an important aspect of everyday life. The way you deal with loans that you take, and the way you operate a credit card account or a bank account will contribute to your credit record and standing.

In particular, if you do not keep up the agreed level of repayments, this information will be shared with credit agencies, who maintain these records. This in turn may make it difficult for you to obtain new credit in the future. You therefore need to keep in mind that your current actions will affect not only your current situation but your future situation as well.

1.3.7 Getting into debt

It is easy to overreach yourself and find yourself in a situation where your income does not match your outgoings, and you therefore slide into debt. To some extent this is manageable if temporary, and the availability of overdrafts, loans and credit cards allows us all some leeway to deal with this situation. However anything you borrow does eventually need to be repaid, so these are not permanent solutions. In addition, you need to meet your other obligations, such as telephone, gas and electricity bills.

If you find yourself in a situation where you cannot meet your obligations, it is very important that you take action to reach agreement, if possible, with those that you need to pay. It is not easy to admit that you cannot pay your bills, but avoiding the issue does not improve it, and indeed can make it worse. Often, it is possible to reach an agreement with suppliers, credit card companies and so on, which can help you to discharge your debt at a slower, but manageable rate. Certainly you are likely to receive a more sympathetic hearing if you talk to them as soon as you are getting into trouble, rather than waiting until you have received reminders and threats of legal action. In general their wish is to get the money which is owed to them rather than force you into bankruptcy. This is why they are often willing to enter into an agreement with you.

If you are worried about your debts, for example because you have been tempted to take out a number of credit cards, and have spent freely, and later find that the repayments are too onerous, as well as talking to the credit cards suppliers, you should also seek further advice. A good source of advice and information is the Citizens Advice Bureau, and you can find details of a local bureau via the internet (www.citizensadvice.org.uk) or through the telephone directory.

1.3.8 Bankruptcy

If you are unable to pay your debts, it is possible for your creditors (i.e. those you owe money to) to apply to the court to make you bankrupt. This is an extreme solution, and if you are declared bankrupt, it is likely to have a serious long term effect on your credit standing. It is also an extreme solution from the point of view of your creditors.

Broadly the position on bankruptcy is that your assets will be controlled by a trustee in bankruptcy appointed by the court, who will generally be a specialist in this field. His job is to raise money from your assets in order to pay back your creditors as far as possible.

The rules relating to bankruptcy are complicated, but you will usually be able to keep items which you need for day to day living, for example furniture, bedding, personal effects and so forth, provided that they are necessities rather than luxuries. You will also be allowed to keep items which you need for your job, for example any tools which you use in your job.

A bankruptcy order normally lasts for 12 months, after which you will be discharged. Again there are exceptions to this general rule, particularly if you do not cooperate with the trustee in bankruptcy. It is likely that your creditors will receive only part of the money which is owed to them, but when you are discharged from bankruptcy, any remaining debts which you incurred prior to being declared bankrupt will be cancelled.

In some ways, this seems a good solution for the person who owes the money, because they will not have fully paid back their debts, but the debts will have been cancelled. However the effect on the individual's ability to raise further loans and credit in the future can be extremely damaging, because inevitably banks, building societies, credit card companies and so on will be reluctant to lend to someone who has a past record of not repaying in full.

You can obtain further information regarding bankruptcy from the website of The Insolvency Service at www.insolvency.gov.uk.

An alternative to bankruptcy which is increasingly common is the Individual Voluntary Arrangement (IVA). This avoids a formal declaration of bankruptcy and involves entering into an agreement with your creditors instead, to repay all or part of what you owe them on a negotiated basis. This can be a useful alternative, but you should be aware that if you enter into an IVA with your creditors, this does not prevent them from later deciding to apply to the court to declare you bankrupt. Entering into an IVA will also affect your credit standing and record.

Once again the Citizens Advice Bureau is a useful source of advice and information, and you should discuss your situation with their staff early in the process.

1.3.9 Restructuring debt

It is sometimes possible to restructure debt into a more manageable form, and there are various firms which will offer advice and who specialise in this area. Generally the approach is to consolidate your existing debts into one larger debt, which is usually intended to be repaid over a relatively long term (because this reduces the level of repayments you need to make).

Although this is a possible route, you should consider carefully before embarking on such a solution. There are drawbacks, in particular because if the term of the loan is increased, you will end up paying more interest than you would over a shorter term. Also, in some cases, the firms involved charge substantial fees. Even if these are added to the amount of the debt, so that you do not have to pay them as a lump sum initially, you should be sure that the amount you pay is reasonable in relation to the help and service which you receive.

In some cases, if you own a property, it may be suggested that existing borrowings which are unsecured, are restructured into a loan which is secured against your property. This will usually allow a lower interest rate to be charged than the interest rate on your unsecured borrowings, but once again the term of the loan will usually be longer, and therefore the interest you pay over the term is likely to be substantial. You need to bear in mind that if you are unable to keep up the payments on a secured loan, you may be in a situation where your property is taken into possession by the lender and is sold to repay the debt, leaving you in a situation where you have to find somewhere else to live.

1.4 Scams

Part of handling money successfully is to ensure that your assets remain secure. However there are many fraudsters who find ever more inventive ways of trying to part you from your hard earned cash.

In this section we discuss some of the scams which are commonplace these days, but there is an overriding rule which says that if something appears to be too good to be true, it probably is. You should be wary of anything which appears to promise you high returns for little effort or risk, because in many cases these offers disguise an attempt to defraud you.

1.4.1 Emails

Many scams start with the receipt of an unsolicited email. These take various forms, and they often sound enticing, but should always be treated with extreme caution.

A common approach is to claim that the sender has access to a large sum of money, generally in a foreign country, and often in a major currency such as dollars. The sender will claim to be authorised to access this money, but in order to do so, it will be claimed that he needs to transfer the money to a bank account outside of his own country. The offer to you may be along the lines of a substantial share in the money available in return for you providing access to your bank account in order to allow the transfer of money to take place.

If you respond to the email, you are likely to be asked to provide details of your bank account, which in turn can be used by the fraudster to take your money out of the account rather than pay their money in. In addition, in many cases, prior to this taking place, you may receive further emails stating that certain fees need to be paid before the transfer can take place, and suggesting that you make this money available in some form.

Inevitably, the anticipated transfer into your account will not occur, but the losses which you incur can be very substantial. You should of course ignore these emails when they arrive.

Other scam emails often advise you that you have won a prize, perhaps in a lottery in an overseas country, and again your bank details will be required in order to allow the prize to be transmitted to you. There will also often be requests for sums of money for reasons such as customs clearance or security checking. The lottery referred to may be a real lottery or a fictitious one, but it is certain that the supposed prize for which you have qualified is not real, and the objective of the email is in fact to elicit your bank details and/or take cash sums from you.

Sometimes, if you respond to such an email, you will receive follow up telephone calls, often from individuals who are very persuasive and sound very plausible. You should avoid any such contact.

1.4.2 Phishing and Hoax Websites
Some scams invite you to follow a link to a website. These will often appear to be the website of a bank or other financial institution. The email may claim to be from the bank's security department and may say that in order to activate or reactivate your account, you need to follow the link and enter your personal details.

The link is not to your bank's real website but to a scam website and the intention is to obtain your details so that your account can be raided.

Often emails of this sort are received by individuals who do not have an account with the institution from whom the email is purported to come, in which case it is clear that it is a scam. However, even if you do have an account with the institution named, you should be aware that banks do not send unsolicited emails of this sort asking for personal information. You should therefore not respond, and indeed it is useful if you report the email to the institution concerned. This type of fraud has become known as "phishing", using the internet to catch the gullible.

1.4.3   Share scams

Share scams come in various forms, but have the objective of persuading you to purchase shares which are usually of dubious value, and may be traded on overseas stock exchanges. In reality, there is likely to be a very limited or non-existent market in the shares.

Some scams start with a telephone call from an individual who is likely to be very persistent, and who will want to convince you to buy a holding of shares which the caller will claim are expected to increase in value dramatically, probably over the next few days. He will be keen to persuade you to act swiftly in order to get the full benefit. You will probably be asked to make payment, perhaps with a debit card or to arrange a transfer of money, but you are likely to find that the shares do not exist, or are valueless.

Other scams often involve unsolicited emails which will highlight the attractions of a particular share and once again suggest that you buy the share quickly in order to benefit from an expected vast increase in price. These shares may be genuine, traded shares, and because you are not asked to send money to the person who sent the email, you may feel that the sender has little to gain. In reality, it may be that the sender has bought a holding of these shares, at a low price, and then by sending emails to other potential investors, creates demand for the share. This in turn increases the price, at which point the email sender will sell his holding at a profit. For other investors, the increase in the value of these shares is an illusion because it has been created artificially and the share price will fall again once the temporary buying pressure has ceased.

Those who bought the shares at a price which was part way through the rise will therefore face a considerable loss.

Many people, even experienced investors, have been tempted by share scams of these types, and by other similar scams. They sound tempting, but of course should be avoided.

1.4.4 Role of the Financial Services Authority

The Financial Services Authority (FSA) regulates financial services within the UK. Part of their role is to protect consumers and to reduce financial crime, which includes scams. This is a difficult task, because in most cases, the originators of the scams described in this section are resident overseas, generally in areas where there is little or no regulation locally.

However, the FSA does publish details on its website (www.FSA.gov.uk) of the latest scams which it has become aware of. It is useful to have a look at the details on their website because it will give you an insight into the type of scams which are being currently operated and their potential consequences.

2   Savings and Investment

2.1   Why save?

Through your life, you will receive money (or assets) from many different sources. This might be in the form of income from employment or perhaps from your own business, gifts from others or inheritances on their death, or from the State in the form of one or more of the various benefits available. You may also already have some capital behind you, which you can draw on when you need to.

In this chapter, we look at savings and investment. By savings, we mean putting money aside from the income you receive in order to build up capital. Investment is about the way in which the capital which you already have is handled. Many considerations are common to both of course, and the division between the two is not absolute.

Many people would like to be less reliant on the income they receive month by month or week by week. Some of the things we need money for would be difficult to meet simply from income, for example, it might be necessary to save for a period to pay for an exotic holiday.

Also, few people want to work for the whole of their lives. Instead, they want to stop working at some point and enjoy what will hopefully be a long and active retirement. (There are people who say they want to carry on working until they drop, and this could be true in some cases. But for many, it may simply be that they have no realistic alternative.) The pension arrangements discussed in Chapter 8 are specifically designed for this need, though other forms of savings can also help to build up money for retirement.

Sometimes, people suffer unexpected setbacks. For example, for those who are employed, there is always the possibility that they will lose their job, often through no fault of their own. For those who are in business themselves, it could that the business will fail. Although there may be some benefits available from the State in these circumstances, they are not particularly generous and certainly would not support the sort of lifestyle most of us would like to have.

The only way to become less reliant on income is to build up an alternative source of money. This is why it is so important to save from income to build up a nest egg which can be drawn on later, when needed.

2.2 Now or later?

The problem with trying to save from income is that there are always competing priorities. However much income we have, we tend to feel that we would like a little more (or perhaps a lot more). Indeed, as you read this, you may be thinking that, at the moment, your income is not enough to cover the spending needs you have day by day. You might conclude that the idea of saving appeals in principle, but finding some money to put away on a regular basis would still be difficult.

This is a question of balance. Some of your income will be spent on necessities, such your rent or mortgage payments, on food, clothing, heating and so on. But you almost certainly have some 'discretionary income', in other words, income that you can decide what to do with. It is from this discretionary income that any savings must come.

2.2.1 Striking the balance

The more you save, the more capital you will build up for the future, but it would be wrong to suggest that you should save all of your discretionary income. There would be nothing left to spend on anything but necessities, and life would then be very dull indeed.

But it is sensible to try to strike a balance between spending on the things you want to have and do now, and saving for the future. After all, the savings you make are not lost – they will provide for the things you want to have and do in the future.

It can still be hard to save from your existing income. A good way of starting is to make use of any increases that arise, for example, if your salary rises. Before you get used to the higher level of income, and absorb the increase into your normal spending pattern, you could decide to save a part of the increase. You would still have more to spend, but you would also know that you were building up money for the future.

2.2.2 The sooner the better

When you are young, it is easy to feel that you have plenty of time ahead of you to save, and that it is not necessary to start straight away. Certainly, if you have been used to having only a relatively small amount of money to spend, while you have been at school or university for example, it feels good to have more financial freedom when you first start to bring in a salary on a regular basis.

So, what is the point of starting early?

The straightforward answer is that the earlier you start saving, the easier it is to build up a sizeable amount of capital. The interest or growth that is achieved on the amount you save adds to the capital and itself starts to grow.

To illustrate the power of this 'compounding' effect, we will look at an example of someone who saves £50 per month for a number of years. Assuming the savings are kept up, the table which follows shows how the capital (i.e. savings plus interest) builds up at four-yearly intervals, and compares it to the amount saved. The figures assume that interest or growth at 6% per year is achieved.

Number of years	Total amount saved	Total capital built up
4	£2,400	£2,656
8	£4,800	£5,883
12	£7,200	£9,807
16	£9,600	£14,576
20	£10,800	£20,373

Initially the interest or growth adds only a little to the amount saved, but it becomes increasingly important as the capital builds up. In the twentieth year for example, the amount of new savings made would be £600 (as in every year), but the investment growth would be greater, in fact around £950.

Of course, these figures are just an illustration (and do not, for example, make any allowance for taxation. Nor does the table demonstrate the effects of inflation). In practice, you are unlikely to want to save the same amount each month for 20 years without taking any money out, and the rate of interest or growth will vary from time to time too. We discuss investment returns in more detail later in this chapter.

Another reason to start saving early is that the future is unknown; the only certainty is that your circumstances and needs will change. You might be very successful and enjoy a substantial increase in earnings, in which case you will find it easier to save in the future. On the other hand, you might have need of capital to draw on much earlier than you expect, for example, if you lose your job, or, more positively, because you start a family, and have to deal with all the associated costs.

2.3   Savings objectives

Savings objectives are as varied as savers themselves. Some savers will have a definite objective in mind, while others will be vague. Some save for the relatively short term, but others are aiming to build up capital over a long period. You must decide what your reason for saving is, but some examples, which may be relevant to you, are briefly discussed below.

2.3.1   Short term

You may have plans, or expectations in the short term, which will require saving. Some of these have already been mentioned, for example, saving to pay for next year's holiday. Other objectives might be to buy a new piece of furniture, or a car. Short term objectives tend to be definite (otherwise it would not be certain that the period involved would be short) and the date the savings will be needed is also usually either known, or at least known approximately.

Some short term objectives are less motivating than those mentioned so far. For example, you may know that you have an income tax liability to meet in the future. If you are employed, income tax is deducted by your employer and paid to HM Revenue & Customs (HMRC), but if you work for yourself on a self-employed basis, you will need to pay tax to HMRC yourself, usually every six months. The basis of payments is described in section 7.1, and other situations where you might have to pay tax direct are also discussed in Chapter 7.

2.3.2   Medium term

There is no precise boundary between the short and medium term, but for our purposes, by medium term we mean a period of, say, two years or more, but less than ten years.

Your medium term ambitions may be less clear, but you might expect over this period to have to cope with change which is likely to bring costs which will require capital. For example, you might aim to move from rented accommodation to a flat or house that you own. You might expect to get married, or be planning to start a family. Timing is likely to be less certain than in the case of short term objectives, and the amount you will need to build up may also be uncertain.

2.3.3   Long term

Long term objectives also usually focus on life changes, for example, having the option to retire and stop working without reducing living standards. Although these plans are inevitably uncertain in timing, and the amount required is difficult to estimate, we have seen that the earlier you start saving, the easier it is.

2.3.4   Deciding your savings objectives

A first stage in saving is to identify your own savings objectives. The ideas just discussed may help you, but only you can decide what it is that you want to do and therefore what you need to save for. Only you know your starting point too, and this will have a major effect on what your objectives should be.

Divide your objectives between the short, medium and long term. Once you have done this, you will need to consider your priorities, in the light of the amount you want to save and can afford to save.

2.3.5   Effect on savings options

The timescale over which you intend to save for something will influence the choices you make. We will consider some of these choices in the rest of this Chapter. In general terms, the shorter the term over which you save, the more important is security because you want to be sure that the amount required is available when needed. In the longer term, you can afford to risk fluctuations in value along the way, if the ultimate return is potentially greater. However, this is a complex and personal issue, which needs consideration in detail.

2.3.6 The effect of inflation

One factor which is always important in thinking about savings and investment is the effect of inflation. Generally, prices increase over time and as a result, if you simply leave your money in, say, a current account at the bank, earning no interest, its purchasing power will fall.

Inflation has been relatively low, and quite stable, for some years now. However, in the past, this has not always been the case. The Retail Prices Index (RPI) measures the movement in the prices of a selection of goods and services over time and is the most widely used measure of inflation (although a number of others also exist). The index is published monthly, but, as a sample, the table below shows the figures for January each year from 1987 (when the index was set at 100) to 2007, together with the annual rate of inflation each year.

Month	RPI	Inflation rate		Month	RPI	Inflation rate
Jan 1987	100.0			Jan 1998	159.5	3.3%
Jan 1988	103.3	3.3%		Jan 1999	163.4	2.4%
Jan 1989	111.0	7.5%		Jan 2000	166.6	2.0%
Jan 1990	119.5	7.7%		Jan 2001	171.1	2.7%
Jan 1991	130.2	9.0%		Jan 2002	173.3	1.3%
Jan 1992	135.6	4.1%		Jan 2003	178.4	2.9%
Jan 1993	137.9	1.7%		Jan 2004	183.1	2.6%
Jan 1994	141.3	2.5%		Jan 2005	188.9	3.2%
Jan 1995	146.0	3.3%		Jan 2006	193.4	2.4%
Jan 1996	150.2	2.9%		Jan 2007	201.6	3.9%
Jan 1997	154.4	2.8%				

Source: Office for National Statistics

As the table shows, the annual rate of inflation was as high as 9.0% in the year to January 1991. Although it seems hard to believe now, the annual rate was over 25% at times in the mid-1970s. This may seem a long time ago – over 30 years – but for an individual in his mid 20s now, retirement, for which savings will need to be accumulated, is likely to be more than 30 years away.

Interest rates and investment returns generally tend to be higher in times of high inflation, but it is inevitably harder for investments to maintain their value. To estimate the effect of inflation on money, there is a simple rule known as the rule of 72. The rule gives an approximation of the time it takes for money to halve in value at any given inflation rate. To find the period, you simply divide 72 by the inflation rate.

For example, if inflation was running at 4% per year, the value of money (i.e. its buying power) would halve in about 72/4 = 18 years. If it was running at 6%, the period would be 12 years and at 9% (the highest inflation figure from the table above) it would be 8 years.

(Although the rule of 72 is an approximation, the results are surprisingly accurate. The rule suggests that after 18 years at 4% inflation, £1,000 would have fallen in terms of its buying power to £500. A more precise calculation gives £494 to the nearest £. After 12 years at 6% inflation, the buying power would be £497, and after 8 years at 9% inflation it would be £502.)

The following table illustrates how the buying power of £1,000 falls over 20 years at a range of different inflation rates.

End of Year	2%	4%	6%	8%	10%
1	£980	£962	£943	£926	£909
2	£961	£925	£890	£857	£826
3	£942	£889	£840	£794	£751
4	£924	£855	£792	£735	£683
5	£906	£822	£747	£681	£621
6	£888	£790	£705	£630	£564
7	£871	£760	£665	£583	£513
8	£853	£731	£627	£540	£467
9	£837	£703	£592	£500	£424

10	£820	£676	£558	£463	£386
11	£804	£650	£527	£429	£350
12	£788	£625	£497	£397	£319
13	£773	£601	£469	£368	£290
14	£758	£577	£442	£340	£263
15	£743	£555	£417	£315	£239
16	£728	£534	£394	£292	£218
17	£714	£513	£371	£270	£198
18	£700	£494	£350	£250	£180
19	£686	£475	£331	£232	£164
20	£673	£456	£312	£215	£149

When investing money for the long term, you will want to try to achieve a return in excess of inflation. Otherwise you might as well spend the money now, because you can buy more now than you will be able to later. Your investment decisions should always keep this in mind, and you should review your decisions if the rate of inflation changes to any great extent. As you can see from the table above, the effect of higher inflation is dramatic.

Also, if you look ahead to the way in which you expect you savings to grow, the accumulated amount that you will build up in the future can look impressive. You should always adjust the figure to allow for the effect of inflation, and thus its real buying power.

2.4 Lump sum investment

Although so far, we have discussed saving on a regular basis, you may be lucky enough to have a lump sum to invest, or to receive a lump sum in the future. This might come from an inheritance for example, or something like a lottery win.

Many of the considerations involved are the same as for regular savings. You need to consider your objectives in the same way and will need to consider the asset classes in which you intend to invest.

It can be daunting to make the decision to invest in assets which can go down in value, and you may be concerned that you might buy some assets and then immediately see their value fall substantially. With regular savings, this is not so great a concern, because your initial commitment is less, and if values fall, your next investment will buy assets at the reduced price. You may therefore see a gain if values later recover.

Some people favour splitting a lump sum into smaller amounts, and investing them gradually, which in part duplicates the profile of regular saving. However the trade-off for this is that you will only benefit from growth on a proportion of the total lump sum initially, and therefore could lose out if values go up rather than down.

In general, you should only invest in assets whose value can fall if you are in a position to leave that money invested for a reasonably long period. You should therefore be more concerned with long term investment return rather than short term. What ultimately matters is the difference between the price at which you invest and the price at which you sell, and fluctuations along the way are unimportant. Such fluctuations can be a worry of course and advice from investment professionals is always worth considering. We discuss this further in Section 2.16. This advice will help you understand the potential for gain and for loss, whichever decisions you ultimately make.

2.5   Asset classes

One of the most fundamental decisions which is needed in relation to savings and investment is the choice of the asset class(es) to use. The main asset classes are:
- Cash deposit
- Fixed interest securities
- Equities
- Property

We will describe each of the main asset classes and then consider their advantages and disadvantages.

The choice of asset classes is a major factor governing the degree of risk the individual is taking, and the potential return he hopes to receive. It is usually a good idea to decide on the split of your investments between the asset classes before choosing individual investments within each class.

2.6 Cash deposit

Most people are familiar with the idea of cash deposits. These can take the form of money invested in building society or bank accounts, as discussed in Chapter 1, but there are other forms, including products offered by National Savings & Investments, which are government-backed.

Cash deposits are regarded as very secure, because the monetary amount invested will not generally fall, unless the bank, building society etc fails (assuming the depositor does not withdraw money of course).

However, some accounts do carry charges – for example, increasing numbers of current accounts which may charge a monthly charge plus handling charges for transactions such as paying cheques or receiving deposits. In recent years, most current accounts have been free of charges, but this looks set to change over the next year or two.

Some accounts pay interest on money deposited, and there is a wide range of interest rates in the market place. For sizeable deposits, it can be very useful to shop around to get the best rate, but for smaller amounts, the difference may not make the time spent in comparing accounts worthwhile. Many current accounts may either pay no interest or pay interest at a very low rate anyway.

Cash deposits are also usually accessible, though some accounts require notice of withdrawals, or either limit or prohibit withdrawals during a set period, in return for a better interest rate than would otherwise be on offer.

The various types of deposit account were considered in detail above in Chapter 1.

The advantages of security and accessibility need to be balanced against the disadvantage that the return on cash deposits is generally relatively low. Indeed, often, particularly over relatively long periods of time, the interest paid may not keep pace with the effect of inflation.

2.7   Fixed interest securities

This is a less familiar asset class to most people and includes gilts (also known as gilt-edged securities) issued by the government and corporate bonds, which are similar in nature, but issued by companies. Some building societies also issue similar securities known as PIBS (Permanent Income Bearing Shares).

Fixed interest securities are a way in which the issuer – whether that is the government, a company or a building society – can raise money from investors. They represent a loan from the investor to the issuer.

These securities essentially provide the investor with a stream of regular income payments, which are usually fixed in monetary terms, so investors who hold them know exactly how much income they will receive each year. This can be very attractive for those who are investing for income, and find this certainty appealing. Fixed interest securities are therefore popular with many elderly investors, perhaps seeking to supplement a pension income, though this is by no means the only group which holds them.

Most fixed interest securities have a fixed life, and they are redeemed by the issuer at the end of that life. Some are 'undated' – in other words they continue to produce income at the fixed level indefinitely. A brief description of the most common types is given in the next section.

Many of these securities are bought and sold on the Stock Exchange, and prices are determined by market forces. The investor cannot require the issuer to redeem the securities before they reach redemption date, so if he wants to convert his investment into money early (encash it), his only option is to sell it on the market. There is therefore an opportunity to make a capital gain as well as having received income, but there is also the possibility of a loss.

2.7.1 Types of fixed interest securities

The main types of fixed interest securities are as follows:

- **Traditional gilts:** These are issued by the government and pay a fixed income from issue until a known redemption date. Some gilts are redeemed within a known period, of perhaps two years, with the government deciding exactly when they should be redeemed. Traditional gilts are released to the market at, or very close to, their 'nominal value' and can be bought and held in any quantity. The income is expressed as a fixed percentage (known as the coupon) of the nominal value of the gilt, and income is paid in half-yearly instalments. On redemption, the nominal value is repaid to the holder by the government.

- **Index-linked gilts:** These function in a similar way to traditional gilts except that both the income and the eventual redemption value are linked to inflation as measured by increases in the Retail Price Index (RPI).

- **Undated gilts:** These were issued by government many years ago in most cases, and the income paid to investors is usually relatively low. The government has the right to redeem them at any time, but if it did so and wanted to replace the borrowing, it would need to pay a higher rate of interest on a new gilt issue. It is therefore unlikely to do so.

- **Corporate bonds:** These are issued by companies and generally have the same structure as a traditional gilt. They can also be traded on the Stock Exchange. However, corporate bonds involve greater risk than gilts, because gilts are government-backed and payments are therefore entirely reliable. If the company which issued a corporate bond fails, both income payments and the redemption value may not be made or may not be made in full. The credit standing of the issuer is important therefore in the same way as with any other type of borrowing.

- **Debentures:** These are similar to bonds, but are secured against a particular asset of the company (for example, a property), or sometimes a range of assets. These provide a further degree of security because, if the company fails, its obligations to debenture holders can be met or partially met by the sale of the asset(s) against which they are secured.

- **Building Society PIBS:** These are issued by building societies, and are similar in nature to undated gilts, because they have no redemption date.

2.7.2 Influences on price

There are a number of factors which influence the price at which fixed interest securities trade. Some of the main influences are discussed in this section.

An important factor is the level of interest rates in the economy. This is bound to affect what an investor would be prepared to pay to buy into a particular security, and what an investor who already holds it would be prepared to accept in order to sell it. Deals are carried out through the dealing processes of the market rather than investor to investor, but the effect of the market is to find a price at which there are both willing buyers and willing sellers. The price must therefore be acceptable to both.

A large part of what the fixed interest security provides is a stream of income at a known level, and the market price must be reasonable relative to alternatives, for example placing money on deposit. If interest rates generally are high, relatively little money would need to be placed on deposit to generate a similar amount of income. It follows from this that generally, the higher interest rates are, the lower the price of these securities will be; similarly, low interest rates tend to imply high prices for fixed interest securities.

Sometimes, investors believe that if there is a general expectation that interest rates are about to fall, there is easy money to be made by investing in fixed interest securities and waiting for the price to increase as the expected fall in interest rates occurs. However, life is rarely as simple as this. The market makes allowance for expected future movements in rates – this is part of the effect of the market finding a price which is acceptable to both buyers and sellers.

The allowance for future change which is built into the price will not be quite as much as the total price movement which the change in interest rates will produce, so there is still some potential gain for the investor.

However, the remaining margin, in effect, allows for the risk that the expected movement does not in fact occur.

Another factor is the remaining term of the security. If it is short, the price is likely to be close to the redemption value. Interest rates have less influence as redemption date gets closer, because the redemption value becomes more and more important and the income stream becomes less important.

Undated securities on the other hand are most sensitive to changes in interest rates, because the income will continue indefinitely and there is no certainty of redemption.

The other main influence on price is the standing of the issuer, because this affects the risk the investment carries. This was briefly discussed earlier in this section. In general, an investment which carries a relatively high risk needs to provide investors with a greater potential return to compensate for that risk.

For example, suppose we are comparing £100 nominal of a gilt with a similar holding of a corporate bond issued by a particular company. We will assume that the income which is promised to investors is the same in both cases, and we will also assume that the redemption date, when investors expect to receive the nominal value of £100, is the same.

The gilt is guaranteed by the government, and it is hard to imagine circumstances in which a payment of income or the redemption value would not be paid.

For the corporate bond, however, payment is dependent on the company continuing to be able to meet its obligations. Corporate bonds are generally issued by large and sound companies, but their future prosperity is not guaranteed and from time to time, large companies do fail.[2]

An investor would, therefore, pay less for a corporate bond than he would for a gilt promising the same income and redemption value. If the

---

[2] Countries can also default on their financial obligations, but this is, thankfully, even rarer than the collapse of a blue chip company.

price was the same, a rational investor would always choose the gilt, so the market will settle on a lower price for the corporate bond.

The extent of the difference in price will reflect the credit standing of the issuer (there are measures available from credit rating organisations which allow investors to consider this). The difference will be greatest for companies regarded as representing the greatest credit risk.

2.7.3 Buying fixed interest securities

You can buy fixed interest securities through a stockbroker. Various services are available at a range of prices (this is discussed further in Section 2.8.4 below).

It is also possible to buy gilts through a service established by the Treasury's own Debt Management Office – details are available on their website at www.dmo.gov.uk. This has the advantage of low costs, but there is no advice available, and dealings take place by post.

2.7.4 Advantages and disadvantages

The main advantage of fixed interest securities is the fixed income they provide. The certainty of income is important for those who are wholly or largely reliant on income from investments, as distinct from earned income. These investors are likely to hold the securities for long periods, often through to redemption, so the amount of capital they will receive is also known in most cases.

An important disadvantage for these investors is that the income is usually fixed in monetary terms, so inflation will affect its purchasing power. (An exception is the index-linked gilt, which is linked to the RPI.)

Also, in the case of securities with a redemption date, although the expected amount and timing of the redemption value is known, it cannot be certain how this can be reinvested at that point. For example, if the investor's need is still for income, the amount of income that he will receive by reinvesting the redemption value will depend on investment conditions at the time.

It is also important to understand that although the redemption value is known, if the security is sold on the market before redemption, the amount realised can be more or less than the redemption value.

Some investors buy and sell fixed interest securities in order to try to generate capital gains, perhaps by accurately predicting interest rate movements. These investors must take into account the potential for losses as well as gains, in addition to which, they must meet the dealing costs involved.

Overall, returns from investing in fixed interest securities in the long term tend to be greater than from investing in cash deposit. However, generally, returns have tended to be less in the long term than could have been achieved from investing in equities or property.

2.8 Equities

Equities are shares in companies – each share is a share in the ownership of a particular company. Shares in many public companies are traded on the Stock Exchange and the share price fluctuates with the fortunes of the company concerned, as well as in response to more general economic issues.

The companies whose shares are traded on the Stock Exchange are large companies, often household names. They must meet various requirements including making a great deal of information available to investors. Shares traded on the Stock Exchange are often referred to as quoted companies – their share price is quoted on the Stock Exchange.

The Alternative Investment Market (AIM) is a market on which shares in smaller, often newer and expanding companies are traded. The requirements on companies are less (though still significant) and many companies first join AIM and then a few years later, progress to the full Stock Exchange. These may be referred to as AIM quoted, or sometimes as unquoted shares.

The unquoted category of shares extends beyond AIM, however, and includes private companies. These are usually small companies, sometimes set up by one or two individuals who work for the company and own all or most of the shares. Shares in private companies cannot be promoted as investments to the general public and are not investments in the usual sense. They are not therefore considered further here.

2.8.1 Returns for investors

Shareholders hope to benefit from their shareholding in two ways – in the form of income and in the form of a capital gain when they sell their shares, hopefully at a higher price than they paid when they bought them.

Generally, the company will pass on part of its profit to shareholders in the form of an income payment, known as a dividend. This will not usually be the whole of the profit the company has made because part will be retained in the business in order to allow it to grow. The growth of the business will eventually (all being well) be reflected in growth in the share price.

Most companies declare two dividends each year, the first an interim dividend, based on the company's position part way through its trading year, and a further final dividend, declared once the full year's profits are known. A few companies pay dividends at different frequencies, for example, quarterly.

If profits are growing, dividends will usually increase, unless there is a particular reason for holding back money within the company, perhaps to pay for anticipated future costs. If profits are reducing, dividends may fall, or even cease entirely, at least for a temporary period. If, however, the company believes the downturn in profits is temporary – perhaps the result of a one-off event – the level of dividend may be maintained or even increased slightly. If the amount paid out exceeds profits in the relevant trading year, it must be paid for from accumulated profits carried forward from earlier years.

The price at which shares trade on the Stock Exchange reflects the market's view of the likely future profitability of the business. The better the company does, in general, the greater the positive impact on the share price. However, there is a degree of 'sentiment' involved, in the sense of how the market rates future prospects. Sometimes, although a company's profits may be poor at present, the market's view may be that management is running the business well and is taking the right decisions to bring future success. This is likely to result in a higher share price than would be the case if the view was that the company was likely to continue to decline into the future.

Analysing what is a fair price for a share is a complex business therefore and a lot of research is involved. Professional investment managers will aim, in part, to do this and if they are right, they may guide their investors to acquire shares which the market as a whole has undervalued.

2.8.2   Share perks

Some companies give their shareholders specific perks, for example, a discount on goods or services bought from the company. These can provide a useful bonus for shareholders.

However, you should be careful to consider their value before being influenced to buy the shares concerned. There are various points to consider:

- Is there a qualification, such as a minimum number of shares, or a minimum holding period, before you qualify? If so, does that fit in with your investment plans?
- Is the perk of real value to you – for example, would you have bought the discounted item at full price if you did not own the shares?
- Above all, are the shares a good investment? If they are not, the value of the perk may not compensate for the poor overall return you achieve?

Remember that the market determines a price which is acceptable to buyers and sellers. The value of the perks, if substantial, will have been factored into the share price.

2.8.3   Influences on price

As already discussed, the performance of a company, and the market's view of potential future performance, will affect the share price. As an investor, you hope that growth will lead to increased dividends, but also to an increased share price.

In part, this reflects how well the management of the company does its job. Fashion can also play a part, making the products of a particular business or sector much sought after in one period, but then much less so in another.

However, economic conditions also have an impact as do other external factors. For example, an increase in interest rates is likely to have a negative effect (which may mean a reduction in share price, or a slowing in the growth of the share price). This reflects a number of aspects, including the fact that the increase in interest rates makes other investments such as cash deposits relatively more attractive.

Also, increased interest rates affect the cost of any borrowing the business has (most businesses depend, at least to an extent, on borrowing). This therefore is likely to reduce profitability.

Inflation is likely to affect costs and this in turn will also affect profitability. The extent to which a company can adjust its own prices may not fully compensate for the increased costs in some cases. Earnings inflation will affect businesses with a large workforce very substantially, but may have less impact on other businesses with smaller workforces.

Currency exchange rates will also affect businesses which either buy from or sell to other countries. Movements in currencies can be substantial and difficult to predict, and this can therefore be a significant area of risk.

Other events may also have a massive effect on the market and on share prices. Immediately following the terrorist attack in the USA on 11 September 2001, markets across the world were affected badly, with the value of many shares on the UK market losing 25% in value in a day, with further losses the next day.

This is not an exhaustive list of all the possible influences on price, but clearly some of these factors are specific to the company concerned – in particular, the effect of decisions made by management. Some may affect a whole sector, for example fashion and what is currently 'in'. Others affect businesses in all areas, for example, interest rates and inflation.

Factors which affect investment values are risks to the investor, and we return to the subject of risk later in this Chapter.

2.8.4 Buying shares

You can buy shares through a stockbroker. Investors who regularly buy and sell shares may have their own stockbroker already. Otherwise you can do some research yourself through the internet and/or through investment orientated magazines.

You may have friends or relatives who invest in shares, and their views and recommendations are likely to be useful too.

There are various services available from stockbrokers (though not all stockbrokers provide all services). The main types are:

- **Dealing service:** you place an order with the stockbroker to buy or sell shares (or fixed interest securities), and he carries out your instructions, but offers no advice or comment on whether the deal is wise in his view. This is often known as an execution only service, because the stockbroker only executes your instructions and does not advise.

- **Advisory service:** the stockbroker contacts you with suggestions based on his view of the market and his knowledge of your investment objectives, but you decide whether and when to deal, and whether or not to follow his advice.

- **Discretionary service:** you agree your objectives and any constraints with the stockbroker, who then runs your portfolio on your behalf, making decisions to buy or sell as he believes appropriate, and reporting back to you at agreed intervals.

The cost of the various services varies considerably from stockbroker to stockbroker, and of course a discretionary service is likely to be considerably more expensive than a dealing service, because you are using the stockbroker's expertise.

Execution only dealing services are now available through the internet and costs have come down substantially in recent years. This can be an easy way to deal in shares. However, remember that if you do not seek advice, you will be entirely responsible for your investment decisions. Few individual investors have the expertise to successfully choose individual shares in which to invest.

2.8.5 Investing via funds

Because of the difficulties for most investors in choosing individual shares, using a specialist investment manager has an appeal. However, costs can be high and are often out of the reach of relatively small investors.

For this reason, there are many funds available which allow small investors to share in the performance of a large portfolio. In effect, many small investors are pooling their resources to create the fund, and the costs of management, dealing and so on are shared. We discuss these funds (commonly known as collective investments) in Chapter 3.

2.8.6 Preference shares

Most shares which are traded on the Stock Exchange are 'ordinary' shares, and these are the shares which have been described so far.

Some companies issue other classes of share, the most common of which is the preference share. This type of share provides an income which is generally fixed in monetary terms, and usually is redeemed at the end of a known life, for a known redemption value. In many ways these shares resemble corporate bonds as discussed earlier in this chapter. They have similar advantages and disadvantages for the investor.

They are known as preference shares because the dividend income due to holders must be paid in preference to paying dividends to ordinary shareholders – in other words, ordinary shareholders cannot be paid any dividend unless preference shareholders have been paid in full. However, if the company does not make sufficient profit, it can pass (i.e. not pay) the dividend to all shareholders, both preference and ordinary.

This would not create a debt, whereas if the company failed to make a payment of interest under a corporate bond, it would owe the amount not paid to the bondholder. Preference shares are therefore a little less secure than corporate bonds.

If the company fails, and its assets are used to pay debts, with any balance distributed to shareholders, preference shareholders will also rank before ordinary shareholders and are therefore more likely to receive the full expected redemption value.

2.8.7   Advantages and disadvantages

Investing in equities provides the opportunity to share in the growth of businesses. Historically, this type of investment has done better over long periods than investment in cash deposit or fixed interest securities, and has offered a better chance of returns in excess of inflation.

However, share prices fluctuate in the short term, often dramatically and unpredictably. Investors cannot therefore rely on getting a good price on a particular day. Costs, such as the difference between buying and selling prices of shares and stockbroker fees, also erode returns in the short term, so investors should only invest in equities if they are prepared to leave the investment in place for a reasonable period (at least five years and preferably longer).

Also, investing heavily in a few companies exposes the investor to the risk that one or more of those particular companies may not do well, and any decline in the share price could have a large effect on the overall portfolio. Investors need to diversify their holdings to avoid this effect, either through a larger number of direct holdings, or through a collective investment.

It remains the case that there is the possibility of companies failing and there being little or nothing to return to investors. The risk of loss is real therefore.

Equity investment can generally be expected to produce an income through dividends, and this should also increase as the profits of the companies whose shares are held grow. However, the level of income can fluctuate, and could stop entirely from some shares if profits fall. This may create problems if investors are reliant on the income.

2.9   Property

Property is a popular investment, partly because it is tangible in a way that something like a share is not. We live in flats or houses, and most adults either own their home or aspire to do so at some stage in their lives.

Property prices are often in the news too, and there is often comment as to the rate at which prices are increasing. This sometimes makes it seem as if they will always do so, and that investment in property is very secure – 'as safe as houses' in fact.

Although there has been good growth over the years in house prices, it is important to understand that there have also been periods when house prices have stood still, or declined. It is likely that there will be similar periods in the future too.

We will consider various types of property investment in this section, starting with one of the most common – buying your own home.

2.9.1 The owner occupier

Many people have seen substantial increases in the value of the property they live in over a period of years. Often people move into larger and more expensive properties as time goes on, partly perhaps as their need for space increases with the arrival of children, but also to reflect growing prosperity as their income increases.

As the value of the property grows, so people feel wealthier and more secure. In some ways, the increase is illusory, because the value is tied up in the property and cannot easily be accessed. Each time they move into a more expensive property, most or all of the increase in value is usually ploughed into the new property. However, many people now plan to trade down (i.e. move into a smaller and cheaper property) at some stage in their life and this would liberate some of the capital for other purposes. This may coincide with children leaving home and becoming independent, or may be intended to happen at the point of retirement, so that the capital can provide some of the financial resource necessary for a comfortable old age.

All of this is perfectly reasonable, though as already mentioned, it would be wrong to assume that property prices will always increase, so there remains a need not to rely solely on property as an investment.

If you do not own a property at the moment, you may be considering trying to buy one to live in. You may have to borrow heavily to do so – for most people, the mortgage loan they take out to buy their property is the largest debt they ever incur. We discuss mortgages in Chapter 5.

MONEY

Having a loan means making repayments and these can be a substantial drain on income. However, the alternative for most people is to pay rent to someone else who owns the property. You have the right to live in the property in return, but will not benefit in any way from any increase in the property value. Mortgage repayments on the other hand give you both.

In addition, rental payments generally increase periodically, and continue to do so indefinitely. Mortgage repayments may go up or down as interest rates change, but the loan on which they are based either reduces or remains the same (assuming you do not choose to borrow more money), so the repayments should not keep on increasing year after year.

Living in your home is a benefit in itself, and having somewhere to live is a necessity, so you should not consider your home in the same way as other investments. For example, if you have some money on deposit with a bank, you can withdraw all or part of it to spend. You cannot do this so easily with your home. Certainly you could sell it, but you would then still need somewhere to live, and solving this problem would bring other costs.

2.9.2 Tenure

Residential property may be held on a number of different ownership bases. This is known as the tenure of the property.

Freehold tenure means that the property is owned outright and is the highest form of tenure. It is not limited by time.

Leasehold tenure is essentially a right to live in the property (and should be distinguished from a normal "tenancy" agreement where a person lives in a property in exchange for the payment of regular rent), but, in the case of leasehold tenure, there is a freeholder to whom ownership of the property will revert at the end of the lease. In the meantime, a ground rent, which is generally small (it will be far less than the rent for a normal rented property) is payable to the freeholder.

Leases are issued for long periods, often 99 years, though in the past, 999 year leases were not unknown. If there is a long period remaining until the end of the lease, the value of a leasehold will not be much less than the value of an equivalent freehold property. However, if there is only a short term remaining, the value may be considerably less.

Changes to the in recent years have increased the rights of leaseholders to demand an extension to the lease or buy the freehold. This has reduced the disadvantage of leaseholds. However, lenders are often reluctant to lend on the security of short leases, and this in itself reduces demand and therefore value.

Leasehold tenure often applies to flats, with the freeholder retaining ownership of shared areas such as hallways and stairs. There may also be a head leaseholder (leasing the whole property from the freeholder) with subleases for individual flats. The head lease and sublease are likely to have restrictions on the use of the property which you need to be aware of. There may, for example, be an express prohibition on further subletting (see 2.9.3 below).

A new form of tenure – commonhold – was introduced in 2004 and is now increasingly being applied to flats. Here the freehold is in effect shared between the flat owners and a Commonhold Association is set up to control and maintain the shared areas. No ground rent is payable, and there is no limitation by time. This basis is therefore likely to be seen as more attractive to many potential property purchasers.

2.9.3 Buy to let

In recent years, many people have looked to buy property purely as an investment, which they intend to let to other people. This is generally called 'buy to let' property and will usually be in addition to their owning their own home.

Much of the popularity of buy to let property has sprung from positive experience of growth in the value of the individual's own home, but the issues are a little different. In most cases a loan will be raised to buy the property and the intention will be that the rental income generated will cover all or most of the loan repayments, leaving the investor with the eventual capital gain on selling the property.

This can work well, but the arithmetic needs to be thorough. For example, the initial level of rent expected may cover the loan repayments, but the investor would need to be able to deal with any increases resulting from interest rates. Allowance must also be made for the costs of running the property, including routine maintenance, but also the need for occasional repair work which could arise from something unexpected, such as damage to the roof. Insurance costs must also be met, and if a letting agent is used, this will also increase costs.

A further potential problem is the potential for 'void periods' to occur. These are periods when the property remains empty for a time after one tenant has left and before a new one moves in, and there is no rental income. Loan repayments must still be met, and maintenance costs etc continue to arise of course.

Worse, there could be a tenant who remains in the property, but is unable or unwilling to pay the rent which is due. The investor would have legal remedies available to obtain vacant possession of the property and to claim the rent due. However, it can be time consuming and expensive to pursue these and cashflow problems can result in the meantime.

These points should not necessarily put you off considering buy to let property, but as with any investment, it is important to understand the good and bad points. The need to consider cashflow and available resources also means that buy to let is most likely to be suitable as an investment after you have built up other, more liquid, resources.

2.9.4 Commercial property
So far, we have discussed residential property. Commercial property, which means property such as shops, offices and factories, is a very different market and is less familiar to investors generally. Most people, particularly those in the early stages of thinking about investment, will find that commercial property requires too great an investment to be a realistic possibility, and we therefore do not consider it in any detail here.

2.9.5 Factors affecting residential property prices
As already discussed, property prices do not simply go up and up. There are various factors which have an influence.

Because most people buy their property with a loan, interest rates are a major factor. Increases in interest rates tend to reduce demand for property, and this is likely to slow the rate of growth in property prices. If high interest rates persist, or if the increase is large, the effect could be to reduce prices.

Interest rates have increased through the latter part of 2006 and the early part of 2007, but are still at low levels compared with recent history. Mortgage interest rates are currently around 5% - 6%, but in the late 1980s, for example, rates of 15% were not uncommon.

Location is a vital factor affecting particular properties too. A location considered good now may become unfashionable over quite a short period, and this can have a negative effect on prices. Other currently undesirable areas could become popular, which would lead to increases in prices. These changes can be difficult to predict and some homeowners will be fortunate, but others may be less so.

The property's condition is important too. This will generally be in the control of the owner, and it is important to keep repairs in hand. However, property can sometimes be affected by events beyond the owner's control, such as storms, floods, fire or subsidence of land. It is important to have adequate insurance for these matters (though insurance against flooding or subsidence may be hard to obtain in areas prone to these problems).

Tenure – freehold, leasehold or commonhold – will also affect price, and this was discussed earlier in this section.

2.9.6 Buying property

Property is generally sold through estate agents, and this is where potential buyers will probably first look. Alternatives are becoming available however, particularly via the internet.

The main function of property in most cases is to live in, so the nature of the property relative to the buyer's need for space, location etc will be more critical than investment related aspects.

A further issue will be the suitability of the property from a lender's point of view if a loan is required to assist the purchase. This is discussed in detail in Chapter 5.

Buying a property is a major commitment for most of us, and expert advice is usually needed. A solicitor or a licensed conveyancer will usually be involved therefore and is a wise precaution. The house-buying process is also discussed in Chapter 5.

2.9.7 Advantages and disadvantages

Ownership of property is enormously appealing to many people and the advantages of ownership as against renting as a tenant have already been discussed. However, if property prices fall, the property owner will be faced with a loss, while the tenant will not. (On the other hand, the tenant will have been regularly paying rent for no financial return.)

Buy to let property can be a rewarding investment, provided that all aspects are considered. However, it is worth saying that the size of most property investments is very large, and investors should generally try to avoid having too much of their total investment portfolio in one type of asset. Otherwise, a fall in the value of that type of asset could have disastrous consequences. This underlines the importance of deciding the mix of asset classes before choosing individual investments.

Although the size of the investment required is one of the major potential disadvantages, it is worth mentioning at this point that as with equities, there are funds available that allow individual investors to share in a large, professionally managed property portfolio.

With direct investment in individual properties, the tangible nature of the asset is an advantage, though this in turn means that maintenance and insurance costs arise, which is not the case with most other investments.

Overall, returns on property investment have been good in the long term, and like equities, property offers a good opportunity to more than keep pace with inflation, provided the potential for a loss is appreciated.

2.10 Risk and reward

From our discussion of asset classes, it should be clear that there is always a balance to be struck in choosing investments. In general terms, the greater the potential reward that you seek, the greater the risk you will need to take. Different people have different attitudes toward risk, and we look at this shortly. However first, we should consider what risk is.

This is not as straightforward a question as it might seem. Although many people perceive investment risk only as the risk that they might lose some of their capital, there are really a number of different types of risk. The main ones are:

- **Capital risk:** This is the risk that the money you invest might reduce in amount, because of a fall in the value of whatever you invest in. For example, share prices rise and fall, so an investment in shares carries a capital risk.

- **Inflation risk:** Investors generally want to at least see the value of their investments keeping pace with inflation, and ideally outperforming it. Although deposit interest may be more than inflation at times, historically it has often been less, so there is an inflation risk. Assets such as equities and properties are most likely to outperform inflation, but few investments guarantee to do so.

- **Interest rate risk:** Changes in interest rates affect investments in various ways. If you have money on deposit, the interest rate you earn is usually variable, so there is a risk that future interest rates will be lower (and the potential for them to be higher too). Even accounts which pay a fixed rate of interest will only do so for a limited period and then the money must be invested elsewhere, probably at a different interest rate. The capital value of some assets is affected by interest rates, for example, the value of fixed interest securities (see Section 2.7) tends to fall if interest rates rise and vice versa.

- **Shortfall risk:** Most investors have some idea (even if it is quite vague) of the return they hope to obtain from an investment. In some cases, there is a specific target, for example where the individual is saving for a particular thing, such as a holiday, a house deposit or a wedding. The shortfall risk is the risk that expectations are not met. Some investments offer a guaranteed return, in which case there should be little or no shortfall risk (though conditions may apply, so care is needed in considering this). However, guaranteed returns are usually relatively low, so you might want to accept a higher level of shortfall risk in order to have the opportunity of a better potential return.

- **Volatility risk:** Many investments, including fixed interest securities, equities and properties fluctuate in value from time to time (even from moment to moment in the case of equities). Volatility is a mathematical measure of the extent of that fluctuation, with high volatility meaning wide and frequent fluctuations in value. Volatility risk is the risk of such fluctuations occurring – the danger is in the possibility that values will have dipped at the time you want to encash your investment.

- **Opportunity risk:** Investing money in one place includes the decision not to invest that same money somewhere else. If a different investment selection would have produced a higher return, you have been disadvantaged, though you should be wary of judging your decisions too harshly with the benefit of hindsight. It is much easier to identify last year's best performing investment than next year's!

The possibility of losing money may still be uppermost in many people's minds, but these other risks also need to be considered.

There is no investment which is entirely risk free if the full range of risks is considered. You may think of an investment in a bank deposit account as being risk free, but although you know that if you invest £100, you will get at least £100 back, the deposit is certainly exposed to inflation risk. In addition, there is opportunity risk, because, certainly over the long term, other investments such as equities are very likely to outperform deposit interest. You might not have lost anything, but you may not have done as well as you would have done if you had invested elsewhere.

If you save money or invest, you must therefore accept risks in some forms. What is important is to understand the risks that you are taking, their relationship to the potential rewards involved and how these fit in with your own attitudes, objectives and timescales.

2.11 Acceptance of risk

There is much said about the attitude to risk of individuals. Some individuals may be categorised as being cautious, some adventurous, and so on. However, perhaps it is better to talk about an individual's ability to accept risk in the context of particular objectives.

For example, if you are putting aside money to pay an income tax liability due in a few months' time, you need to be sure that you will have the right amount available at the time it is needed. HM Revenue & Customs will not allow any leeway just because it is not a good time to encash an investment! The level of return you achieve over the investment period is less important than not losing any of the money, so you would invest cautiously, perhaps in a deposit account.

On the other hand, if you are saving money from income to build up capital over a period of years, you will probably be less concerned if the value of your savings fluctuates, provided you get a good return over the years. You might then be prepared to accept more risk to have access to greater potential returns.

The ability to accept of risk therefore has something to do with the individual and his attitudes, but also is affected by a number of other issues.

2.11.1 Personal attitude

Undoubtedly, some people are more adventurous in their outlook than others, and this is true in investment as in anything else. For some people, the risk of losing any of their capital is completely unacceptable, so only an investment in deposit, or something with a similar level of guarantee is acceptable. These individuals must accept that if they adopt this approach, the returns they receive will be modest.

Others are far more adventurous, and expect to achieve high levels of return. They are prepared to accept risk, including volatility risk and capital risk, in order to benefit from good long term performance. It is very important that they do not allow optimism to completely overrule other considerations. Risk is real and can result in adverse events. No one, however optimistic, is immune from this.

For example, with an investment in a well-chosen portfolio of shares, growth prospects may be good, but there is a risk that values will fall and that the value of some may fall to nothing if they are shares in a company that eventually fails. Not everyone therefore will reap the rewards of the potential growth.

Most people should fall between these two extremes and will seek a balance between risk and reward across their portfolio.

2.11.2 Timescale

The period of time available for investment is also an important factor. It is likely that you will have some long term financial objectives, and some short term ones. As already discussed, it is usually unwise to take any substantial degree of risk if the timescale is short, because the higher potential return over the short term is not sufficient to justify the risk of loss. Over a longer period, risk is likely to be more acceptable, because the effect of the higher potential return is greater.

Historically too, investments such as equities have performed well over the long term, but have fluctuated in the short term. If the investment is retained for a long period, the return achieved when it is sold may still be good, even if at the time of sale, values have dipped below higher recent levels.

2.11.3 Certainty of objective

The degree of certainty attaching to an objective can vary. You might know that you have to repay a loan of a precise amount at a precise future time, for example. This requires more certainty as regards investment than if the objective is less well-defined – for example, saving money which will eventually be used as a deposit for a house purchase, but with no fixed timescale in mind, nor a precise amount.

Volatility risk might be unacceptable in aiming for a precise objective, particularly if the timescale is limited. Even if the timescale is long, a change in investment strategy may be appropriate as the remaining investment period shortens, to limit any further volatility risk.

2.11.4 Other resources

The extent to which you have access to other financial resources also influences your ability to accept risk. For example, suppose you have substantial savings in a building society account, and have now received a lump sum – perhaps as a bonus at work – and you are thinking of investing this for the future. You have no definite plans for its use, either in terms of time of purpose. You might decide to invest in equities, accept the capital risk, the volatility and so on in the hope of good returns in the long term. This could be a very sensible approach.

If unexpected events arise, for example, your car breaks down and needs to be replaced, you may need money quickly. If share values are low, it might not be a good time to sell your holdings – you might prefer to wait and hope that their values recover. The fact that you have money in a building society account means that you can draw on that, and leave your share investments in place.

If on the other hand, you had no other investments apart from the shares, you might have to sell them, even if the timing was not ideal. The potential impact of the risk of investing in shares is greater in this situation therefore. The risk of making the investment in the first place is therefore much less likely to be acceptable. Instead, it might be a good idea to build up an emergency fund as a cushion against future events, before considering higher risk investment.

2.11.5 Other people's money

There are various situations where you may find yourself investing money for others. The most common is probably parents investing money for their children. This might be money gifted by others, such as godparents, grandparents etc, or could be money saved by the parents themselves for the benefit of their children.

The government also provides some savings through the Child Trust Fund arrangements in some cases.

Different emotions come into play in this situation. There is a tendency to avoid risk when investing on behalf of others, probably because it might feel worse to lose someone else's money than to lose your own. In reality, the same considerations should apply as for any other investment decisions.

When investing for young children, the timescale is long, and the importance of achieving a good level of return is great. Short term volatility is not usually a concern, because the investment is intended to build capital for later life, and will not be drawn on. Equity investment might be appropriate therefore.

However, deposit investment is often used, in order to avoid any possibility of loss. The risks here are inflation risk and opportunity risk and often a far better result would be achieved with other investment choices.

2.11.6 Past experience

Those who have personal experience of investment in the past will often be greatly influenced by it. Someone who invested heavily just before a stock market crash, for example, may be wary about investing in the market again.

We have already said that investing in assets such as shares should be considered long term. However, if you invest a significant sum of money and see its value fall sharply in a short period, there is a natural desire to cut your losses, sell your holdings and invest in something more secure. This crystallises the loss and in effect makes it permanent.

Ideally you should stick to your original objective, and leave the money invested, because history shows that the market is likely to recover. This takes nerve, and there are no guarantees that recovery will occur and no certainty of how long it will take. The most courageous will go a step further and invest more money while prices are low, and these investors stand to make the most from any recovery that occurs.

What this highlights is that investors need to understand the risks involved in their investment choices as well as the potential rewards. They need to adopt an overall strategy which is in line with their objectives, so they can, for example, choose to remain invested through temporary market downturns. They also need to diversify between different asset classes so that they are never wholly dependent on the performance of one asset class.

2.12 Past, present and future

Past experience shows that deposit-based investment carries the lowest level of risk, but has offered limited returns.

Fixed interest securities have provided better returns, but with some risk, with capital values fluctuating.

Equities and property have performed best over long periods, though price fluctuations are greater than they have been for fixed interest securities.

None of this past experience offers any guarantees for the future however. Nevertheless, we have discussed the fact that the operation of the marketplace sets prices for investments that provide both buyers and sellers with acceptable terms at any particular time. In order for an investor to consider an investment which carries risk, the price must be such that the potential return is greater than with an investment with lower risk.

The likelihood is then that assets such as equities and property will continue to outperform deposits and fixed interest securities over the long term. The problem is that downturns are not predictable in their timing or their length.

It seems to be part of human nature that if share prices are currently doing well, we expect this to continue indefinitely – investors are often more inclined to invest in a rising market, so some will be adversely affected when the market starts to go down again. These fluctuations are part of the natural operation of the market.

You should learn from the past, evaluate the present, but be prepared for the future to bring the unexpected.

2.13 Reviewing your portfolio

You should always keep your portfolio under review. You will have taken your initial investment decisions carefully, but investment conditions change, as do your own objectives and timescales. Your portfolio always needs to keep up with these changes.

2.13.1 Gains and losses

If you have invested in shares (or related funds) you may have done very well over a period, or you may have been disappointed. One of the hardest lessons for investors to learn is to take profits and cut losses.

If you invested in the shares of a particular company, and that company has been highly successful, the share price may have increased a lot more than other shares you own. It is easy to regard this as a 'star holding' and you may want to keep it in the portfolio. However, these shares now represent a larger proportion of your portfolio than they did before, simply because their value has gone up faster than other holdings. You are therefore more exposed to the risk that their value could fall sharply too.

There is no guarantee that strong performance in the past will lead to more strong performance in the future. Gains are only paper gains until you encash, so after a period of strong performance, you might consider selling your holding, or perhaps just part of it, to lock in the gain you have made.

If you have shares which have fallen in value, investors are often reluctant to sell them and crystallise the loss. In a way, this reluctance perhaps reflects the admission of a mistake. However, although the share price might recover, it is wise to review disappointing holdings and consider if there is a more attractive investment opportunity available. Certainly there needs to be a good reason for a belief that there will be a recovery and therefore it is worth retaining the holding.

2.13.2 Taxation

There may also be taxation implications to reviewing the portfolio. Gains on the sale of assets such as shares and property are potentially subject to capital gains tax (CGT). The operation of this tax is covered elsewhere, but it should be taken into account in considering any encashment.

For example, sometimes a delay into a new tax year can be attractive so that a new annual exemption becomes available. At other times, encashing an asset at a loss may be useful in order to set the loss against an otherwise taxable gain on another sale.

2.13.3 Costs

There are costs involved in buying and selling some assets, notably in the case of shares and property (including related funds) and also in buying and selling fixed interest securities. If your portfolio is only slightly out of line with what you believe to be ideal, it may not be worth incurring costs in order to correct it.

2.14 Borrowing

Borrowing can affect investment decisions in two main ways. First, is it worth borrowing in order to invest? Second, if you already have some cash, but also some borrowing, should you invest the cash or use it to repay all or part of the borrowing?

2.14.1 Borrowing to invest

From a pure investment point of view, it is not usually advisable to borrow to invest, because the return on the investment (after allowing for any tax liability) needs to exceed the amount that you pay in interest. However, as is often the case, there are exceptions to the rule.

Probably the most obvious is when you buy a house or a flat to live in. Most people need to raise a mortgage to do so, and this will be a substantial amount in most cases. The property you buy is certainly an investment, but is also your home, so you are getting much more than the opportunity to make a profit. This alone may justify the borrowing, because if you did not borrow, you would probably end up paying rent, with no possibility of any capital growth.

There may also be a case for borrowing to buy an investment property, because the interest may be financed from the rent received. From a tax point of view, you can usually offset interest from otherwise taxable rent in this situation too. Even so, as discussed earlier in this Chapter, taking on a loan in this situation needs careful consideration.

In most other cases, the return from your investment will be taxable, but you cannot offset interest against it. This means the pressure on the investment to perform is very great. It is this which makes borrowing to invest unattractive for most people in most situations.

2.14.2 Repaying borrowing

In the same way, if you have a lump sum to invest, it will often be a good idea to consider repaying all or part of any borrowing you may have. You will save interest by doing so, and reduce your future outgoings. If you are wise, you may choose to save all or part of this reduction to build up your capital again.

In this situation, with a lump sum at your disposal, it is tempting to go on a spending spree, or to invest, in the hope of increasing the capital substantially. These are the decisions we all face from time to time, and there is no universally right answer. You should certainly consider spending at least some of the money – but make this a positive decision that you can afford to spend a certain amount, and know what you want to achieve with the rest.

It can also be a good idea to make sure you have enough emergency money to call on, in case the unexpected happens. Then think carefully about any investment you might make, taking a rational view of the risk as well as the potential gain.

2.15 Tax efficiency

It is important that the investments you make are as tax efficient as possible, in other words that you pay as little tax as necessary on your investments, and make use of any available tax reliefs as far as possible. In the next chapter, we consider some investment products, many of which have tax advantages.

However, you should make your basic judgements first, for example about the asset classes which would be most suitable and the timescales involved. You should then aim to try to invest to fulfil these decisions, with as many tax advantages as possible.

It is a mistake to put tax efficiency first. For example, there are a number of ways of investing money on deposit with tax free interest. However, it might be better to invest some of your money in a different asset class with a greater potential return, even if this is taxable. It is not the tax status, but the return after tax which is important, so a gain of 10% before tax, which perhaps equates to 6% after tax, is better than a return of 5% tax free.

2.16 Do I need advice?

This book is intended to introduce you to handling money from various points of view. You have probably already realised that it is a complicated subject, and mistakes can be costly.

As with anything complicated, advice is often useful. It can help you understand fully the options available to you, and can help you find the best terms available.

2.16.1 How do I find an adviser?

There are many ways to find an adviser. Whichever you decide on, do not feel that you must select the first one you find. You need someone you feel understands you, and that you feel you can relate to and trust. This may mean meeting two or three, and seeing what each offers, before you make a decision.

A good starting point is to ask other people – perhaps your parents, other relatives or friends – who they go to for financial advice. If they have a trusted adviser, he or she might also be right for you. Bear in mind that different people have different needs though, so meet the adviser and see if you find them as good as the person who recommended them does.

You could choose an adviser through the website of one of the professional bodies for financial advisers. The websites below all have a search facility which allows you to select according to the area you live in and what sort of advice you are looking for.

The Personal Finance Society: www.thepfs.org
The Association of Independent Financial Advisers:
www.unbiased.co.uk
The Institute of Financial Planning: www.financialplanning.org.uk

2.16.2 Does my adviser need to be independent?

The most important things about a financial adviser are that they understand you, that they can communicate with you effectively, and they act in your best interests.

Independent advisers can choose products from across the market place as a whole, rather than being 'tied'. Tied advisers can only recommend or advise on products from the one provider they work for, while 'multi-tied' advisers can use a limited number of providers.

Independent advisers are not restricted in this way, and should therefore offer a better range of products.

2.16.3 Are advisers regulated?

All financial advisers are authorised and regulated by the Financial Services Authority (FSA). You can check whether any particular firm is authorised through the FSA website at www.fsa.gov.uk and there you will also find a lot of helpful advice aimed at the public.

One of the effects of regulation is that advisers will give you information (called an Initial Disclosure Document or IDD) explaining the services which they provide and whether or not they are independent.

You will also receive full details of any investments that are recommended to you, with a full explanation of why they are thought to be suitable for you, and what risks are involved. Remember that you are not under any obligation to accept the recommendations made to you and indeed you should be very sure that you understand what is being recommended before you proceed.

Many products have a cancellation period, during which you can change your mind about an investment without the provider taking any charges (though in some cases you will have to bear any loss resulting from a fall in investment values). This does not apply to all investments, so you should ask about this when considering the recommendations which have been made.

2.16.4 Do I have to pay for advice?

All advisers need to be rewarded for the advice they give, but there are different approaches to this. Some advisers charge fees, usually a fixed amount for each hour they spend dealing with your case. You will therefore have to pay the fees direct to your adviser (or his firm). The level of fees varies from firm to firm, so you should compare the fees charged by the different advisers you contact.

Some simply take a fee from the product provider for the business they write (this is called 'commission'). This has the advantage that you do not have to pay the fees direct, but the cost to the product provider will inevitably be reflected in the charges they build into the product concerned. Also, these advisers will not be paid at all if you decide against their recommendation and do not take up a product. In some cases this could affect their advice – they might not recommend that you take no action, for example. However, choosing your adviser carefully should ensure that they always act in your best interests.

Where a commission is payable to your adviser, or his firm, the amount must always be disclosed to you.

Some firms offer a choice of different combinations of fees and commissions, but your adviser will explain these to you. Independent advisers must always give you the choice of paying fees rather than having the adviser rely on commission.

2.16.5 What if I have a complaint?

All firms offering advice must have a written complaints procedure and must give you the details of this if you ask.

Generally, you should put your complaint in writing and the firm will give you a written response. If they were in the wrong, they may offer you some form of redress. However, remember that they cannot be held responsible if investment values fall rather than rise, provided they explained that this was a possibility and provided that the investment was suitable for you taking into account your attitude to risk, objectives and so on.

If you are not content with the firm's response, you can take your complaint to the Financial Ombudsman Service (FOS), which is an independent body. You will be given contact details for the FOS by the firm, as part of their standard complaints procedure, but you can also get further information from the FOS website at www.financial-ombudsman.org.uk.

3 Investment products

3.1 Introduction

There is a huge range of investment products available to UK investors from a wide range of institutions. It is impossible within a book such as this to cover all these products, however we aim to discuss the main products which are likely to be of interest to a relatively inexperienced investor.

The details here will give you an idea of the possibilities which are available, but if you are uncertain what to do, or if you have a substantial amount of money to invest, you should seriously consider getting the advice of an investment professional as discussed in Chapter 2.

3.2 Deposits

Deposit accounts were discussed in Chapter 1, and we will not repeat the details here. It is however important that everyone needs to have some money available which is readily accessible if necessary for emergency needs. It is always worthwhile making provision for the unexpected, whether this is a repair to where you live, a replacement for your car, or having the ability to take up an unexpected opportunity such as a spur of the moment holiday trip. Deposit accounts are ideal for this, and you have the certainty that the amount you deposit will not reduce.

Deposit investment always forms the basis of a portfolio, and provides an element of low risk investment, albeit at the cost of a relatively low level of potential return. More exciting and potentially lucrative investments such as shares and related funds can reduce in value as well as increase, and therefore it is wise to be in a position where if you wish to withdraw money from your investment portfolio you have a choice of asset classes. If your holdings in equities, for example, have done well, you may choose to withdraw money from there, but if market values are low, you may instead choose to make your withdrawal from your deposit holdings.

Remember that some deposit accounts require notice of withdrawal, or alternatively impose a penalty, generally in the form of a loss of interest, so it is likely to be a good idea to have at least some money in an account which offers instant and unrestricted access.

3.3   National Savings and Investments

There is a range of essentially deposit-based products available from National Savings and Investments (NS&I). These products are government-backed and all offer a guarantee that there will be no loss of capital on any investment from its range.

Some products offer tax free interest, but generally, these are best suited to those who pay higher rate tax. Otherwise, the interest rate can generally be bettered by investment in a taxable account, and allowing for the tax payable.

Many people are attracted to NS&I Premium Bonds. You do not receive interest on your investment, but instead, what would have been the interest on all the money invested in Premium Bonds is used to award prizes to the holders of Premium Bonds whose numbers come up in a monthly random draw.

The highest prize is £1 million (two £1 million prizes are presently awarded every month), and there are many smaller prizes, so some investors will be fortunate. However, if your numbers are not drawn, you will receive no interest at all. The outcome is something of a gamble therefore, but without any risk of losing your investment. Remember that if you do not win a prize in the draw, inflation will gradually erode the buying power of the money invested.

The full range of NS&I products is explained on their website at www.nsandi.com and it is certainly worth looking at the range and comparing them with what is on offer from banks and building societies.

There is an NS&I ISA product, which is often very competitive for example. ISAs are discussed in the next section.

3.4   Individual Savings Accounts

Individual Savings Accounts (ISAs) are straightforward investment arrangements which offer considerable tax advantages. They will therefore often be the first type of investment which individuals should consider.

3.4.1 Investment Components

There are two investment 'components' which can be included in ISAs. These are the cash component, which allows investments in cash deposit accounts and similar investments, and the stocks and shares component, in which can be held equities, fixed interest securities and collective funds investing in these areas. Under current rules, all money which is invested into an ISA must be allocated to either the cash component or the stocks and shares component, and cannot subsequently be transferred from one component to another. It is however planned that from 6 April 2008, it will be permitted to transfer money from the cash component to the stocks and shares component, but not the other way around.

3.4.2 Mini- and maxi-ISAs

Some ISAs are what are known as mini-ISAs, which only have one of the two investment components. Alternatively, you can invest in a maxi-ISA, which must have a stocks and shares component, but can also have a cash component, included within the same account. As we see below, the investment limitations on mini- and maxi-ISAs differ, so this is an important distinction.

An investor can either invest in one maxi-ISA in the current tax year, or can invest in a cash mini-ISA and/or a stocks and shares mini-ISA, but it is not possible to invest in both a mini- and a maxi-ISA in the same tax year. It is also not permitted to invest in more than one cash mini-ISA in one tax year, nor to invest in more than one stocks and shares mini-ISA.

Changes are also planned in this are from 6 April 2008, and it is intended that the distinction between mini- and maxi-ISAS will disappear.

3.4.3 Investment Limits

If you invest in mini-ISAs, you can invest up to £3,000 per year into a cash mini-ISA, and up to £4,000 per year into a stocks and shares mini-ISA.

If you invest in a maxi-ISA, you can invest in total up to £7,000 per tax year, and of this, up to £3,000 can be invested in the cash component.

MONEY

The complications of these limits perhaps indicate why the government has chosen to remove the differentiation between mini- and maxi-ISAs from April 2008.

Note that the maxi-ISA route currently allows you to invest anything up to £7,000 in stocks and shares, whereas if you choose the mini-ISA route, only £4,000 can be invested in the stocks and shares mini-ISA. Those who wish to maximise their stocks and shares investment through ISAs are therefore likely to choose the maxi-ISA route.

3.4.4 Tax Advantages

The tax advantages of ISAs are that:

- There is no income tax liability on income received on investments within the ISA, although dividend tax credits cannot be reclaimed; and
- Capital gains made on the disposal of assets held within the ISA are exempt from capital gains tax.

Any type of investment which provides the investor with tax advantages is also likely to have limitations on the amount which can be invested, and these limits in terms of ISAs have been described above.

The effect of these tax advantages is initially small for many investors, particularly if they are basic rate taxpayers who do not currently utilise their capital gains tax annual exemption. To the extent that they invest in shares through their ISA, income is received in much the same way as it would be received by an individual, and the tax credit which would discharge the basic rate tax liability of the individual is not reclaimable by the ISA and therefore there is no tax advantage.

The exemption from capital gains may also seem to have no practical effect if the individual has few other investments and therefore any gains which might be made would fall within the annual exemption anyway.

The impact is likely to build in the longer term, however, as the amount of investment held within the ISA grows, and indeed the individual's wealth and possibly income increases too. There is no time limitation on the tax shelter provided by the ISA, so assets held within the ISA will continue to enjoy the same tax advantages even if the individual becomes a higher rate taxpayer and/or has a substantial investment portfolio which could expose gains to capital gains tax if they had been held personally.

These comments assume that the law governing ISAs and their tax advantages remains essentially unchanged, and this is never certain. However, in 2006, the current government stated that it regarded ISA as being at the root of its policy of encouraging individuals to build their savings, and they anticipated that the tax advantages would remain in place.

3.4.5 Using ISAs

As well as there being no limit on how long ISAs can remain in force and enjoy their tax advantages, there is also no minimum term. This means that a cash ISA can be used in much the same way as an ordinary bank or building society deposit account to house a cash investment which can be added to or drawn from time to time. Remember that the maximum that can be invested in any tax year is currently £3,000, and this limit cannot be exceeded, even if money is subsequently withdrawn. For example, if you deposit £2,000 in September 2007, then later withdraw £500, you can still only invest a further £1,000 during the 2007/08 tax year.

Some banks and building societies offer ISAs which are designed to allow investments and withdrawals to be made at will (subject to the normal limits) and the fact that the interest is not taxable makes these accounts attractive. Not all cash mini-ISAs will allow further investments, and some limit withdrawals, so if you wish to use a cash mini-ISA in this way, you will need to check that the terms of the account allow the flexibility you require.

The cash component can also be used for longer term deposit investment, as part of your emergency fund, and again the tax free nature of the interest will be attractive.

Investing in the stocks and shares component provides the investor with the opportunity for growth with no potential liability to capital gains tax and generally, as with all investments in shares, fixed interest securities, property or related funds, this should be regarded as a relatively long term investment. Because of the possibility of the value of these investments going down as well as up, you should only commit money to this form of investment if you are confident that you can leave it invested for a minimum period of at least five years, and preferably longer. There is nothing to stop you withdrawing the money earlier if performance has been good, but if it has not been good, and you still wish to withdraw it, it is likely that you will face a loss.

Although investment limits apply each year to the amount which you can put into an ISA, and (at the moment) your choices are limited regarding mini- and maxi-ISAs, each tax year allows you to invest a further amount, and to make new choices. For example, you might choose to invest in an ISA with one provider this year, but choose another provider next year, so you build some diversification into your overall portfolio.

3.4.6   Changes in 2008

The government has announced a number of changes which will be made to ISAs from 6 April 2008. As already mentioned, this will mean that the current distinction between mini- and maxi-ISAs will disappear. There will also be a small increase to the total amount which can be invested to £7,200 per tax year. Of this it will be possible to invest £3,600 in the cash component. (The terminology will also alter so this will generally be referred to as a cash account.)

One of the problem areas with ISAs to date has been the prohibition on transferring money from cash to stocks and shares, but this will be lifted from 2008. However it is not proposed that it will be allowed to transfer money the other way, from stocks and shares to cash. This means that, if you build up a substantial amount in the stocks and shares account, but then start to feel that the value of your equity investments might fall, you cannot simply encash and move your money to the cash component.

3.5   Unit trusts and collective funds

3.5.1   Background

One of the easiest ways to invest in equities is through a collective fund. There are a number of different types including unit trusts and Open-Ended Investment Companies (OEICs). The differences between them are not of major importance for our purposes and in this section we use the term 'unit trusts' to cover them all.

The idea is to group together the investments of large numbers of usually relatively small investors into a single fund, which is then professionally managed, with all those investors sharing in the return achieved in proportion to their investment.

There are a number of advantages including:

- the cost of the management of the fund is shared between all the investors and is proportionately much less than if each investor wanted his investments managed individually;
- dealing costs when assets are bought and sold are proportionately less because of the size of the deals undertaken; and
- the investment portfolio is diversified across a large number of holdings (usually more than 100 in the case of a unit trust investing in equities).

The diversification point is particularly important. A small investor who invests directly in shares must choose either to invest in a small number of holdings or to spread his money very thinly across a large number of holdings. Neither approach is ideal. Investing in only a small number of holdings exposes the investor to the risk that the companies chosen perform poorly, perhaps because of poor management, or because of fierce competition. The return may therefore be out of line with the market as a whole.

Spreading money across many holdings reduces the risk of being unlucky and choosing relatively poorly performing companies. However, costs escalate quickly, because each buying or selling transaction (or 'deal') will attract fees, which invariably include a monetary minimum. These fees will therefore be proportionately greater for a large number of small transactions than would be the case with a relatively small number of large transactions.

The collective approach of unit trusts and other similar collective funds avoids these problems by allowing investors to share in a diversified portfolio at reasonable cost.

3.5.2 The range
There is a wide range of unit trusts, and they can be useful almost whatever your needs as regards asset mix.

Most invest in equities, but there are many variations on this theme. Some invest only in the larger companies listed and traded on the London Stock Exchange. Others concentrate on shares in smaller companies (which generally offer potentially greater returns, but carry higher risk), or on particular sectors of the market, such as technology shares.

Many unit trusts focus on overseas markets, for example Europe, North America or Japan. These funds offer good diversification in case the UK market performs poorly, but in many cases, there is a currency risk involved as well as a stock market risk. Good gains in the stockmarket could be offset by a fall in the value of the currency in which the shares are priced, though it is also true that appreciation in the currency can add substantially to gains achieved.

There are also unit trusts which invest in fixed interest securities or in property, and some which invest in the money markets and therefore provide an alternative to deposit investment. Some unit trusts are 'managed funds', in other words they invest in a range of assets and sectors, chosen by the manager to try to achieve defined objectives. Some unit trusts are 'tracker funds' which aim to produce performance in line with the market, as measured by a suitable index, or sometimes a range of indices. There are various indices, of which perhaps the best known in the UK is the FTSE 100 index, which reflects the performance of the shares of the 100 largest companies whose shares are traded on the London Stock Exchange. A managed fund generally tries to outperform the market as a whole, using the skills of the manager(s) and extensive research facilities, but this can be costly. A tracker fund simply aims to match the index, which is a more straightforward process and these funds usually have lower charges as a result.

3.5.3 Choosing a unit trust

There are many unit trusts and similar funds available, offered by a wide range of investment houses. The task of choosing which are most appropriate for your needs is demanding. You may want to seek advice from a professional as discussed in Chapter 2, which also discusses how to choose an adviser. He or she should be familiar with the range available and will aim to collect enough information from you to be able to recommend those best suited to your needs and objectives.

You could decide to investigate the market yourself. There are various magazines available which give information, and the Investment Management Association (IMA) has a wide range of statistics and other details on its website at www.investmentfunds.org.uk.

However, the amount of information may convince you that it is worth seeking advice. There are over 2,000 funds covered on the IMA website, split between 30 sectors.

It is never possible to be sure that one fund will outperform another in the future. Past performance information (which is published in various magazines) is useful, but is not by any means certain to be repeated in the future, particularly if the fund manager moves on to another organisation (which happens frequently).

Other factors to consider include volatility, which measures how much unit values fluctuate and is therefore a good indicator of risk. Size is important, because a fund which has performed well whilst small and growing may not be so impressive when it becomes large and therefore more difficult to manoeuvre.

Investment objectives are important too, because they determine how the fund will invest and the objectives need to be aligned to your needs. In addition, the charges, which vary between different investment trusts, should represent good value for what is provided.

3.5.4 Ethical investment

Some unit trusts are invested according to a published set of ethical criteria. If you have feel that you should avoid investing in certain areas, such as armaments production, alcoholic beverage manufacture or distribution, animal experimentation and so on, these ethical funds are worth investigating.

There are many funds to choose from, and each has different criteria for investment. The approaches adopted include:

- Negative criteria, where certain investments are excluded, such as shares in armament manufacturers;

- Positive criteria, where the manager tries to identify investments with certain attributes, for example shares in companies with particularly good environmental policies; and
- Engagement, where the manager aims to influence the policies of companies in which the fund is invested towards, for example, lessening their environmental impact.

You can identify ethical funds through the Investment Management Association (IMA) website at www.investmentfunds.org.uk. You can then research the precise criteria adopted by each fund on the websites of the investment houses concerned.

3.6 Savings

Most of the investments identified within this chapter are available not only to those with a lump sum to invest, but also those who want to save regularly.

For example, most ISAs can accept regular monthly contributions, usually by direct debit. Similar arrangements are available for investment in NS&I Premium Bonds.

Unit trusts generally offer a Regular Savings Plan, under which you pay a fixed amount by direct debit and this is invested in units when received by the manager. It is surprising how quickly these arrangements can build into quite sizeable sums.

Although you initially agree to pay a fixed amount each month, these arrangements usually allow you to increase or decrease the amount (generally subject to a minimum acceptable level of contribution) at any time. You can also usually top-up the contribution with a lump sum if you wish, though again there will usually be a minimum size set by the product provider. You must bear in mind also that some products (in particular ISAs) have a maximum permitted contribution level, and this cannot be exceeded.

It is also possible to stop contributing at any time and you can then choose to withdraw your savings if you wish. Alternatively, in most cases, provided you have built up a reasonable amount in savings, you can leave your money invested to continue growing. In this case, you will also usually be able to restart contributions at a later date.

3.7 Life insurance policies

Life insurance policies (in particular, endowment policies) can also be used for saving, with contributions payable monthly or annually (and sometimes at other frequencies such as quarterly if you wish).

These arrangements are discussed in Chapter 4. It is worth pointing out however that generally there is less flexibility in terms of being able to vary contributions, or to start and stop contributing with life insurance policies, because of the tax rules which apply.

3.8 Pension arrangements

Pension arrangements are discussed in Chapter 8, but are also essentially a means of saving. They offer considerable tax advantages, but you cannot usually gain access to your benefits until you reach the age of 55 (50 is the minimum age until April 2010).

4 Insurance products

Almost everyone makes use of insurance products during their lifetime and in this chapter, we discuss the main types of insurance available.

These can be broken down into two major categories: personal insurances and property insurances. The idea behind all insurance arrangements is that small premiums are paid by a large number of people, to enable substantial benefits to be paid out to the comparatively small number who are affected by the event or circumstances insured against.

4.1 Personal insurances

Personal insurances usually protect either the person who takes out the insurance or his family and dependants. The types of insurance which fall into this category include life insurance, and various other forms of insurance which provide benefits in the case of illness, injury or certain forms of unemployment.

4.2 Life insurance

Life insurance policies provide a payment if the person whose life is insured dies. In some cases, the policy lasts only for a specific period (the term) and pays out only on death during that period. In other cases, the policy will stay in force for as long as premiums are paid and so can cover death whenever it occurs. These policies are usually described as 'whole of life' policies.

Sometimes the term life assurance is used instead of life insurance. Historically, insurance was used where the policy had a specified term so it might or might not pay out, depending on whether death occurred during that term. Assurance was used where the policy was on a whole of life basis and so would pay out, whenever death occurred. These days however, the terms are used interchangeably.

Although life insurance policies can be used as a means of saving, and we discuss this later in this chapter, their main use is as a form of financial protection.

4.2.1 Do I need life insurance?

Life insurance can be used in various ways. If you have dependants who rely on your income, life insurance can be used to protect them by providing either a lump sum or an income benefit if you die. If you have a spouse or partner who is not working, perhaps because they are at home looking after a young child, or because they are still studying, they may be reliant on your income to provide for their everyday needs.

One point to remember is that someone may need financial protection even if not fully dependant on your income. For example, if a couple are living together, but both working and generating an income, neither seems dependent on the other, but each is interdependent with the other in the sense that they rely on both incomes to provide for their needs. If one dies, the other will need to adjust their way of life, perhaps having to move to cheaper accommodation unless there is some other financial resource such as the proceeds of life insurance.

Sometimes in the case of a couple, one partner is working full-time, producing all or most of the income, whilst the other is either not working or working only part-time, whilst caring for a young child. It is easy to see the need to insure the life of the main earner, but it is also important to insure the other partner. If they were to die, the job of caring for the child must either be taken on by the survivor, with a resulting erosion of earning power, or child-minding costs must be met which can require considerable financial resource. In either case, the proceeds of a life insurance policy would be extremely valuable.

If you have a loan outstanding (whether a large amount such as a mortgage used to buy a house, or a small amount borrowed, for example, to pay for a holiday), life insurance is useful to provide for its repayment on death.

It can also be used to provide what amounts to a legacy for children, godchildren, and so on.

Each individual needs to consider their own position and to reflect on the question 'What happens if I die in the near future?' It is the answer to this question, and in particular, consideration of whether financial needs will result, which reveals whether life insurance is necessary.

4.2.2   How much do I need?

If there would be financial needs arising on your death, you will need to think about quantifying these needs.

It is useful to consider specifically:

- Immediate income needs to carry on meeting normal expenditure (food, rent etc) and bills (gas, electricity, telephone etc);
- Immediate capital needs to repay outstanding loans (including credit cards) and to meet the cost of funeral expenses; and
- Longer term needs, for example to meet the education costs of children.

If you already have some arrangements in place, you should take these into account, but you should still be conscious of any shortfall. If you are employed, you may be covered by a life insurance scheme provided by your employer, and if so, you should take the level of cover under the scheme into account. Remember that if you change jobs, the cover is likely to end, however, and you would then need to review your arrangements.

There is no shortcut to making these calculations, which you should do carefully and realistically. You should then consider the type(s) of cover you need, and we discuss later in this chapter the various policies available. Some of these policies provide regular payments which can substitute for income, whilst others provide a lump sum.

Even if the need is for income, this can be provided by means of investing a lump sum, and this is often the most flexible approach to take. (You would need to be realistic about the income which can be taken from a lump sum without eroding it too quickly. It would be unwise to anticipate that your dependants would invest the money in a very adventurous way, which could prove to be dangerous if markets move the wrong way. Instead, assume a realistic interest rate from a deposit account, after allowing for tax – currently perhaps 3.5% or 4% per year would probably be reasonable.)

You may find that the cover you need is much greater than you might have thought, and you might not be able to afford to provide it in full. Whatever you decide to do must be affordable. However, it is better to provide some protection than none at all, and you can generally take out further cover later if your income increases.

4.2.3   What about State benefits?

The State benefits payable on death are only available if you are married, have a registered civil partner, or have dependent children. They are generally modest, with a maximum lump sum benefit of £2,000.

An income benefit is payable to a surviving spouse or registered civil partner for up to 12 months if they are over 45. If there are dependent children, the benefit is usually payable until the youngest child reaches 16 or sometimes up to age 20. The amount of the income benefit is generally well under £100 per week.

Other benefits such as Income Support may be available on a means-tested basis. You can get full details of State benefits from the DWP (Department for Work and Pensions) website at www.dwp.gov.uk, but the structures are complex, and are subject to change by the government.

In general, it is sensible not to rely heavily on State benefits if you have dependants. The benefits available are unlikely to provide the level of protection you would wish and making provision personally gives you greater control and certainty.

4.2.4   Term insurance

The simplest type of life insurance is term insurance (or term assurance). You fix the period for which the policy will run (the term) and the policy pays out if you die during the term. It is a very simple and very effective way of dealing with your life insurance needs.

You do need to be aware that the policy does not pay out anything if you do not die during the term. It has no cash-in value if you decide to stop the policy part way through the term, and has no maturity value when the term ends. The cover simply lapses. This is why the premiums to the policy are relatively cheap.

Deciding the term is not always easy. You estimate how long the protection is needed, for example, if you are protecting a young family, this might be the period before they become financially independent.

However, as any parent of young adult children will testify, this may be longer than you expect.

For a slightly higher premium, you can have options included which allow you to renew the policy at the end of the term, or to convert it to a whole of life policy (see below). These options allow this to be done even if your health has deteriorated, and so can be very valuable in creating certainty that the cover will be there when needed. You will pay a higher premium when the policy is renewed or converted, because you will be older then, and generally, premiums are greater at older ages because the risk of death occurring in any particular period increases.

It is also possible to include options to increase the cover, usually either at a fixed rate or in line with an index (generally the Retail Prices Index). The premiums will increase as cover increases, but irrespective of changes in health in most cases. These increase options are helpful, because most people's need for cover increases over the years, particularly as income goes up. You should still review your cover from time to time, but automatic increases take some of the pressure off doing this every year, unless of course your circumstances change.

Specifically designed policies are available alongside some types of mortgages and are designed to pay out a reducing amount, which should be broadly in line with the reducing balance of the mortgage as you gradually pay it off. These are discussed in Chapter 5.

Most term insurance policies pay out a lump sum on death. An exception is the Family Income Benefit policy, which provides an income from the time of death for the remainder of the term. This is a low cost but very effective form of cover, particularly to protect young families.

4.2.5 Whole of life insurance

A whole of life policy remains in force as long as you keep up premiums, and so will pay out on your death whenever that occurs. These are particularly useful if you need to provide protection for an indefinite period, for example for a spouse or partner who relies on your income. They are also useful to provide for the inheritance tax liability which can arise on death.

Premiums may be fixed throughout life, in which case they will be substantially higher than term insurance premiums initially. If you provide cover through a series of term insurance policies, each of which you renew at the end of the term, the term insurance premiums will increase each time you renew and will eventually overtake the fixed whole of life insurance premiums. However, the initial premium level under the whole of life insurance policy may not be easily affordable.

Because of this, many whole of life policies now do not aim to maintain a constant premium. Instead they have reviewable premiums, which start low, but are reviewed every few years, to take into account increasing age. This means that the progression of premiums will be similar to that under a series of term insurance policies.

The whole of life insurance premiums will still usually be a little higher, because there is an element of investment under these policies. This means that if you cancel the policy, there is likely to be a surrender value payable if the policy has been in force for a reasonable period. However, this is usually not great and these policies should not be seen as savings vehicles.

Whole of life policies may include a range of options, including increase options, much like those discussed above in the case of term insurance policies. Some include special event increase options, which allow increases in specific circumstances, such as the birth of a child.

4.2.6 Endowment policies

Endowment policies are a combination of protection and savings. They have a fixed term, and pay out on death during the term, or on survival to the end of the term.

There are various different approaches to the savings element, but most policies invest part of each premium in one or more underlying funds, and so build up value within the policy which will be paid out at maturity. The rest of the premium is used by the insurance company to pay its own costs and to provide the insurance element payable on death during the term.

At one time, these policies were very popular and were encouraged by government as an effective means of saving. Until the mid-80s, some tax relief was available on premiums, but this is no longer the case with new policies, and they are therefore less attractive. Also, the arrival of ISAs (see Chapter 3), which are more tax advantaged has meant that endowments are no longer suitable for most people as an initial savings arrangement.

Endowments do still have a place, particularly for higher rate taxpayers who have used their ISA allowances and have also used pension saving to the extent they wish to. However, they should generally only be taken out with careful consideration and usually professional advice.

This is because they have a number of disadvantages. These include the fact that usually, they have a minimum term of ten years. Also most endowment policies require regular, usually constant, premiums with no ability to reduce or miss them. These constraints are the result of the taxation rules that apply to these policies.

Endowments can be surrendered before the end of the term, but surrender values are often quite poor. As a result, they are likely only to be a suitable choice for those who can be reasonably certain that they want to keep the policy going throughout the term selected at outset.

For those seeking to provide life insurance as a protection for others, term insurance or perhaps whole of life insurance will usually be a better choice.

4.2.7 Joint life policies

Policies can be established on the life of one person, which is probably the most common basis. The policy then pays out on that person's death.

However, policies can also be established on the joint lives of two, or occasionally more, people. This is often the case for policies taken out by married couples, civil partners or others living together.

A joint life policy for a couple may be arranged to pay out on the first death i.e. if either of the two people dies. This is appropriate, for example, if the policy protects a mortgage, and the requirement is that this be repaid if either dies.

A second death policy (sometimes called a last survivor policy) pays out when both have died and is considerably cheaper than a first death policy. This is because the death benefit is never paid earlier than would be the case under a first death policy and is often paid many years later, after many more premiums have been paid.

Whole of life policies on a second death basis are often used by married couples or registered civil partners to pay the inheritance tax due on death. If the survivor inherits the major part of the deceased's estate on the first death, there will be no tax at that time, but the liability will arise on the second death (subject to the usual exemptions etc).

4.2.8 Medical underwriting

If you apply for a life insurance policy, you will be asked to complete a medical questionnaire as part of your application. Some questionnaires are lengthy, but most ask just a few fairly basic questions about your health. The questionnaire is then submitted to the insurance company for 'medical underwriting'. This is a process where your answers to the questions are considered, and the insurance company underwriter decides whether to accept the application (often called the proposal) for life insurance.

If the amount of cover is not very large and the answers to the questions reveal no particular medical problems, the insurance company will probably accept the application on its standard terms. Otherwise, it may ask for a more detailed questionnaire, may request a medical examination, may impose special terms, or in extreme cases, may reject the proposal entirely.

The insurance company has a wealth of experience of dealing with medical questionnaires and assessing the effect on the risk it is taking on. It would not be fair to other policyholders if it accepted on standard terms an application from someone who knew they were terminally ill. The policy would pay out and the cost would be reflected in the premiums the company would need to charge others.

The insurance company does not require people to be in perfect health to accept them on standard terms, just that they are in normal health. If the person concerned has a medical condition which increases the risk of a claim, there are various types of special terms which may be offered. The most common is simply to offer cover but for a higher premium that usual.

In some cases, there will instead be what is known as a 'debt' imposed against the policy, which means that on death during an initial period, part of the sum assured will not be paid. The 'debt' i.e. the reduction in the amount paid out is usually imposed on a decreasing basis over a known period, and this is useful to the insurer if the person to be insured is recovering from an illness and will only represent an increased risk for a limited period.

As well as medical conditions, this underwriting process takes account of hobbies and work activities. Some insurance companies will decline to provide cover, or impose special terms, for those in hazardous jobs (for example, those involving handling explosives) or those who undertake extreme hobbies (for example, hang-gliding). In some cases, death arising from a specific activity might be excluded from risk so that the policy would not pay out if death resulted from a related cause.

4.2.9 Non-disclosure

If an individual is aware that he has a medical condition which would probably result in the insurance company rejecting his application for cover, or imposing special terms, he may be tempted simply not to disclose the relevant information. This would be most unwise.

The law governing insurance policies requires the person applying for cover to do so with the 'utmost good faith'. In other words, they must disclose everything they believe to be relevant. If they do not, the insurer may be able to reject a claim (even if it does not arise directly from the matter which has not been disclosed). This can mean that the cover is not in place when most needed – at the time of a claim.

4.2.10 Financial underwriting

Larger policies may also be subject to financial underwriting by the insurance company. This process is designed to ensure that the cover being applied for is reasonable in relation to the individual's needs and resources. The point here is that there have sometimes been attempts to defraud insurance companies by faking deaths and claiming on policies.

Such attempts are thought more likely to occur if the cover being applied for is unusually large.

It is also important for the insurance company to be certain that there is insurable interest if the policy is on a life of another basis i.e. the person applying for the policy is not the person whose life is being insured. Insurable interest exists if a loss would arise to an individual on the death of another.

For example, if someone lends you money to start a business, they might be concerned that they might not be repaid if anything happened to you. They would have an insurable interest in your life up to the amount of the debt. They could therefore take out a life insurance policy on you to repay the debt if you were to die. (You would have to agree to this because it would be your medical and personal details that the insurer would require to consider the application.)

Financial underwriting would ensure that the cover being applied for is no more than the insurable interest.

The existence of insurable interest is a legal requirement for establishing a valid insurance policy. It must exist at outset of the policy, though if it ceases later the policy can be maintained and would remain valid. You are regarded as having an unlimited insurable interest in your own life and that of a legally married spouse or registered civil partner (but not any other person, even if you are living together). An insurer can still reject an application if it believes the cover requested is excessive however.

4.3   Other personal insurances

There are many other available types of personal insurance in addition to life insurance, and some of the main ones are discussed here. It is a good idea to seek professional advice in relation to the most important types of cover in your own personal circumstances. All the types of cover discussed can be useful, but inevitably, you probably cannot afford them all, so prioritisation will be necessary.

4.3.1 Income Protection Insurance (IPI)

If you are unable to work for a prolonged period because of illness or injury, the financial consequences can be serious. You may receive some benefits from the State, but usually, these will be much less than you were previously earning. Your choices are limited if you have no insurance cover. You will probably need to either reduce your living standards or become dependent on someone else – neither of which is a palatable option.

Although most people consider life insurance, far fewer seem to consider the consequences of long term incapacity. Not only does your ability to earn an income reduce or fall away entirely, but your living expenses continue and often increase.

Some employers provide cover and if you are employed, you need to check what is provided, but often the cover is not complete and may only provide payments for a relatively short period.

Income Protection Insurance or IPI (sometimes also called Permanent Health Insurance or PHI) is designed to deal with this situation. Essentially it provides an agreed level of income in these circumstances, until recovery, or until an agreed date (usually your 60th or 65th birthday) if you remain incapacitated. Benefits also cease on death.

Benefits start to be paid after an agreed period following the onset of incapacity. This is generally called the deferred period. The longer the deferred period is, the cheaper the cover, because fewer claims will be paid and the payment period will be shorter. You need to consider how long you could met your financial needs if your income reduced dramatically or ceased in these circumstances in order to decide on what would be a reasonable deferred period for you.

To qualify for benefits, you need to meet the requirements of the definition of incapacity as set out in the policy document. You should consider this carefully. Some definitions are very tight, and require a very high degree of incapacity to qualify. For example, an 'any work' definition of incapacity requires that you be unable to undertake any paid work as a result of your incapacity.

Other definitions are less tight, for example requiring only that you be unable to undertake any work for which you are reasonably suited on the basis of your education, experience and training, and this definition is more easily met. A policy with an 'any work' definition of incapacity is likely to be cheaper than one with a less tight definition, but it is harder to claim, so you should not choose an IPI policy purely on price.

If you are incapacitated and benefits are paid, they will cease if you recover and return to work, but you will be covered if you are incapacitated again in the future. Also, if you are only able to go back to work in a reduced capacity, perhaps part time, or at a lower level of responsibility, and as a result your earnings are less than before you were incapacitated, many policies pay a proportionate benefit.

If you remain incapacitated, your benefits will cease at the agreed age, which is usually tied to your expected retirement age. You should therefore ensure that the IPI benefits are sufficient to maintain your pension contributions during your incapacity. Otherwise the reduction in income at retirement age is likely to be very difficult to accept.

Premiums under IPI policies are sometimes fixed and sometimes are subject to review in the light of the claims experience of the insurer. You should be very clear which applies under your policy, as well as understanding all its other terms and conditions before you enter into it.

As with all insurance policies, there may be exclusions – in other words, causes of incapacity which may be excluded as a cause of incapacity which can result in a claim. If you are incapacitated as a result of one of the excluded causes, the policy may pay out nothing, or may simply refund premiums.

Exclusions vary from policy to policy, but some of the most common are:
- self-inflicted injury;
- taking drugs other than on prescription;
- participation in a criminal act;
- AIDS and HIV related conditions;
- participation in dangerous sports; and

- pregnancy (although complications arising from pregnancy may be covered).

You should check the exclusions under your policy carefully.

4.3.2 Accident, Sickness and Unemployment cover

Accident, Sickness and Unemployment (ASU) policies offer cover if you are unable to work as a result of an accident, sickness or if you are unemployed as a result of compulsory redundancy. (Note that although the word 'unemployment' is included in the name of this type of insurance, voluntary redundancy and dismissal as a result of gross misconduct are generally excluded from cover.)

Cover is cheaper than under IPI policies as described above, but is also less extensive. In particular, income benefits are limited to payments for a maximum period, usually of one or two years, though policy conditions vary. However, policies generally pay modest lump sum benefits on death, or loss of limbs or eyes.

This type of cover can be useful, particularly if you cannot afford IPI cover, but its limitations need to be recognised.

Personal Accident and Sickness policies are similar in nature, but generally do not cover unemployment.

4.3.3 Payment Protection Insurance

If you have credit card debts, or other borrowings, you may take out Payment Protection Insurance alongside, in order to provide for repayments if you are incapacitated. Although this cover is potentially useful, it is limited to the repayment amounts and usually pays out only for a limited period.

Some insurances of this type are expensive and before you enter into such an arrangement, you should carefully consider alternatives, such as an IPI policy.

4.3.4 Critical Illness Cover

Critical Illness Cover pays a lump sum on diagnosis of various specified conditions. The range of conditions covered varies from policy to policy, but generally included are:

- heart attack;
- coronary artery bypass surgery;
- stroke;
- most forms of cancer;
- kidney failure; and
- major organ transplant.

Multiple sclerosis and motor neurone disease are also often covered, as is total and permanent disablement.

The policy pays out on diagnosis of one of the defined range of conditions. There is often a clause which requires survival for a certain period (generally only a few days) after onset, because the policy is not intended to be a life insurance policy paying out on death.

This cover is however sometimes added as a rider (i.e. an additional benefit) under life insurance policies, in which case it amounts to an accelerated payment of the death benefit, and no survival clause is necessary. Cover as a rider is cheaper than under a freestanding policy, but you should be aware that if the policy pays out because of a critical illness, it will then lapse and there will be no further benefit on death.

Critical illness cover may be taken out for a variety of purposes. For example, it is often taken out alongside a mortgage, to repay the loan in the event of the borrower suffering from one of the conditions covered. This would remove the financial pressure of continuing to service the loan.

The benefit could also be used to pay for modifications to the home, for example, if stair ramps or stair lifts are needed as a result of a stroke. Alternatively, the benefit could be used to pay for specialist treatment not available under the National Health Service.

The benefit is in lump sum form, and does not serve to replace income in the way that an IPI policy does. The cover should not be seen as an alternative to IPI therefore, but rather as an additional form of cover for particular purposes. Also, IPI only pays out on incapacity, but does not limit the conditions which cause that incapacity other than through a small number of exclusions. Critical illness cover deals with the effects of a relatively small number of conditions, but does not require that the individual be incapacitated in order to claim. If an individual has both types of cover, there will be situations covered by IPI but where the critical illness policy will not pay out, and vice versa.

4.3.5 Private Medical Insurance

Although in the UK we are proud of our National Health Service (NHS), it is true that sometimes, the availability of care through private medical facilities is an important alternative. Treatment for certain conditions under the NHS can involve lengthy waiting periods, which may be difficult to accept, but the condition may be capable of being treated more quickly in the private sector.

The importance of being able to fund private treatment will be greater for some people than others. Some will not want to be treated privately in any circumstances, because of their political beliefs, for example. Others, often in particular the self-employed and those running small companies, need treatment as quickly as possible in order to continue to earn a living. Each person must assess his own needs carefully.

Private Medical Insurance (PMI) provides insurance cover to meet the cost of private medical treatment, which can be substantial.

Various levels of cover are available, at different levels of premium. Some policies only cover conditions where NHS treatment is subject to a long waiting list for example. Limiting cover in this way reduces premiums compared to an all-embracing policy covering all conditions.

Other policies apply an excess (an amount of each claim which must be met by the insured before the policy pays out) while others limit total payouts, or the hospitals in which treatment can be obtained. As with most sorts of insurance, individuals must decide what balance between premiums and cover suits their needs best – the more extensive the cover, the more costly the premiums will be.

PMI policies are generally renewable each year, and premiums usually increase each year. This is partly because the cost of treatment and therefore the potential cost of claims is ever-increasing, but also because the likelihood of a claim being made increases as the individual gets older.

4.3.6 Underwriting

As with life insurance, personal protection policies are subject to medical underwriting and also financial underwriting. Benefit limits also apply under IPI policies in particular, where cover cannot generally exceed 60-65% of pre-incapacity earnings. If cover was greater than this, there would be little real incentive to return to work.

4.4 Property insurance

As well as protecting ourselves and our dependants against the financial consequences of death, illness or injury, we also need to consider the protection of our property. Various types of insurance are available.

4.4.1 Contents insurance

Contents insurance is relevant whether you own your home or rent it. This provides protection against damage to or loss of your personal possessions. There is a wide range of cover available, and once again, the more comprehensive the cover, the greater the premium, though it is worthwhile shopping around or taking professional advice in order to find the best overall package.

This insurance will cover events such as a fire which damages your possessions, or theft, though there will often be conditions – for example, the theft cover might be invalidated if you go out and leave your door unlocked, or a window open. Valuable possessions such as jewellery and electronic items (which are often high value but very portable) may need to be specifically declared and a higher premium paid. This is always likely to be true if you want cover against loss or damage outside your own home. There will also usually be a limitation on the extent to which money (i.e. coins, banknotes etc) is covered.

Accidental damage is not normally covered unless you request it and pay an additional premium.

Most policies include an 'excess'. This is an amount of each claim which you must pay yourself and is a means by which insurance companies keep premiums down by reducing the number of very small claims they deal with and the amount they pay. For example, if there is an excess of £200 and the loss for which you are claiming is £1,000, the insurer will only pay out £800 (assuming the claim is accepted).

You may have to prove the loss for which you are claiming, so it is a good idea to keep receipts for your valuable items. This proves both ownership and value and this can be helpful in the event of a claim.

Some policies are arranged on a 'new for old' basis, which means that the insurer will cover the replacement cost of the item concerned rather than make an allowance for wear and tear, which would have reduced its second hand value. You need to check this and all the other details of the cover offered before taking out the policy.

These policies are renewable each year and premiums may change. It is worth shopping around each year, or at least every few years, to see what is available. You may also be able to secure a lower premium by, for example, improving the security of your home with better locks or a burglar alarm.

4.4.2 Buildings insurance

If you own your own home, you should insure the building itself. If you have bought your home with a mortgage, this type of insurance will usually be a condition of the mortgage. If you own your home on a leasehold basis (the various types of property tenure are discussed in Chapter 2), the insurance will usually be arranged by the freeholder, but you will have to meet the cost.

Sometimes, if you rent your home, you will be required to pay the cost of insuring it, although in most cases, it will be the owner of the property who arranges the insurance.

Buildings insurance covers a range of 'standard perils' which generally include:

- fire and smoke damage;
- lightning, explosion and earthquake;
- storm and flooding;
- subsidence, landslip and heave (subsidence is downward movement of land and heave is upward movement);

- impact by cars or other vehicles, falling trees or poles, aerials and satellite dishes;
- damage caused by theft or an attempt at theft;
- vandalism and riot;
- escape of water as a result of burst pipes; and
- escape of oil

Accidental damage to basins, toilet fittings and so on can usually be included for an additional premium.

As with contents insurance, there will usually be an excess applied to claims, and the greater the excess is, the lower the premium will be as a result.

The amount you insure your property for should cover the cost of rebuilding it (after clearing the site) in the event of its destruction through, for example, a serious fire. This amount may be more or less than the market value of the property (market value is influenced to a greater extent than the rebuilding cost by the location). If you buy the property with a mortgage, the lender will usually stipulate the cover required.

Most policies increase the level of cover each year in line with an index reflecting changes in rebuilding costs, and the premium will therefore also increase, but you should still review the cover yourself from time to time to ensure that it is adequate.

4.4.3 Average
You should not be tempted to underinsure your property. If you do, the insurer will usually be able to apply the principle of 'average' to all claims, not just those relating to substantial losses. The best way to explain the principle is by means of an example.

Suppose you own a property, and the rebuilding cost is £200,000. This should be the level of cover you choose under your buildings insurance policy, but in order to save money on premiums, you decide only to insure it for £150,000. If the property is completely destroyed, you would only be paid £150,000 and would have to find the rest of the cost yourself.

Now suppose there was a smaller claim for damage, say as a result of a fallen tree, and the cost of repair was £1,000. The principle of average allows the insurer to reduce the amount it will pay in the same proportion as the under-insurance. As you had only insured for 75% of the appropriate amount, they would pay only 75% of the claim i.e. £750 rather than £1,000.

At first sight this might seem unfair, because the claim is well below the cover level, but you will only have been paying 75% of the premium level you should have been paying. Note also that if there is an excess, it will be deducted as the final stage of the calculation, so in the example above, if there was an excess of £200, the insurance company would only pay out £550.

You can seek professional advice on buildings insurance, or your mortgage lender may also offer help. You can also research different companies on the internet. If you need to decide the level of cover yourself, most of these companies provide guidance on calculating the cover level required based on factors such as the number of rooms and the style of your home.

4.4.4 Motor insurance

Motor insurance is a legal requirement if you own or drive a car on public roads. The minimum cover you are required to have essentially provides for your potential liability to pay damages to others in respect of personal injury to them or damage to their property.

This cover is clearly very limited, and is often referred to as Road Traffic Act cover only. Most people take out more extensive cover which will fall into one of the following categories:

- Third party
- Third party, fire and theft
- Comprehensive

Third party only cover is slightly more extensive than Road Traffic Act cover, and, for example, usually covers the insured if he is driving a car other than the one to which the insurance relates. It also covers the liability of passengers in the car if they are held to be responsible for causing an accident. There may also be cover for legal costs incurred in defending a claim for damages against the person insured.

Third party, fire and theft cover goes further and provides some cover for the insured's own vehicle (there is no cover for repairs to or loss of the insured's own vehicle under Road Traffic Act only or Third party cover). The cover is limited however to damage caused by fire (including lightning and explosion), theft or an attempt at theft (including if the vehicle is not found after it has been stolen).

Comprehensive cover is the most extensive, and includes provision for accidental damage to the insured's vehicle, and malicious damage. It does not however include costs arising from normal wear and tear, nor repairs to or replacement of tyres. There may be cover for serious injury to the insured, and for loss of or damage to personal effects, though this cover is not usually great. (It is not a good idea to leave valuable items in your car, even if locked in the boot or out of sight.)

Premiums are greater for more extensive cover, so once again, in deciding what cover you need, you must balance the extent of protection against cost. Premiums will also be affected by other issues such as the length of time you have been driving, your past claims record and any driving offences, including speeding. You are required to declare driving offences at outset and at renewal and they may result in an increased premium.

You can build up a 'no claims discount' over time if you make no claims under your policy and this is very valuable. Many insurers allow you to protect this for a small extra premium, and this means that if you subsequently have a small number of claims, you do not lose the discount.

The market for car insurance is very competitive, but the precise terms vary considerably. You can shop around on the internet, or use a professional intermediary, but always make sure you understand exactly what cover you have. Some policies provide a replacement vehicle if yours is damaged in an accident and needs repair, for example, whilst others do not.

4.4.5 Loss adjusters

Straightforward claims are settled by the insurer, direct with the insured person, but sometimes a loss adjuster is appointed by the insurer at their expense. They will obtain further details of the loss from you and will aim to agree a basis for settling the claim. His role is primarily to protect the interests of the insurer.

5   Buying a home

5.1   Introduction

Buying a home is a complicated process and is one of the largest commitments most of us make. Their home is a major asset for most people, and often they borrow a substantial sum by way of a mortgage to pay for it, so they must make arrangements to meet the related outgoings.

This chapter provides a brief introduction to the process of buying your home, but cannot deal with all the details. This is an area where you should seek advice, for example from a solicitor who will be involved to protect your interests. The size of the transaction is such that a mistake could have long term consequences.

Note that Scottish law varies in a number of respects and is not specifically covered here.

5.2   Property ownership

Property takes many forms. You might initially buy a flat, or a small house, perhaps with the intention of moving on as your income and resources increase, to a larger and more valuable property. Property has proved a profitable investment over recent years, but values can reduce, particularly during times of high or increasing interest rates. You should therefore not rely on prices continuing to increase – the main purpose of the home is to live in.

Residential property may be held on a number of different ownership bases – freehold, leasehold or commonhold. This is known as the tenure of the property, and was discussed in Chapter 2.

Some properties have conditions attaching to them, for example restrictive covenants (which limit what you can do, by for example, prohibiting trading from the premises) or positive covenants (requiring certain action such as maintenance of fencing). These covenants will have been imposed by a previous owner, often the original owner of the land when it was first sold for residential development, and they 'run with the land', in other words they bind future owners as the property is sold on.

'Easements' sometimes apply and these generally provide access across the land as a right of way. These also run with the land.

There are also legal requirements, for example, the need to obtain planning permission from the local authority in the case of substantial changes to the property, such as building an extension. Some property is subject to particularly stringent control, perhaps because it falls into a conservation area or is a listed property (i.e. one of historical interest). There may be implications affecting repair and maintenance costs in these cases, for example, a requirement only to use certain materials.

Part of the role of the solicitor or licensed conveyancer (discussed below) is to identify any such restrictions when he investigates ownership of the property. (Although a property sale does not necessarily require a solicitor to act, a mortgage lender will usually require it, and the advice of a good solicitor can be invaluable.)

You should ensure that you fully understand the nature of the ownership of any property you consider buying. Your solicitor is best placed to advise you on this.

5.2.1 Joint ownership

Property is often owned on a joint basis, usually by a couple who are living together. Joint ownership can be as joint tenants or as tenants in common and the distinction is important. ('Tenants' here is nothing to do with a rental tenancy, but refers more generally to the holding of the property.)

The different between the two arises on the death of one of the joint owners. If the ownership is as joint tenants, the share of the deceased passes automatically to the survivor, without passing through the estate, or being subject to the deceased's will or the laws of intestacy (these are discussed in Chapter 6).

If ownership is as tenants in common, the deceased's share falls into his estate and passes on under the terms of his will or the laws of intestacy as appropriate.

Ownership as joint tenants ('joint tenancy') is often appropriate for married couples, registered civil partners and other relationships which are intended to be long term, and where each would wish the other to inherit ownership in this way. Ownership as tenants in common ('tenancy in common') is appropriate if the property is owned by otherwise unconnected individuals. An example would be where two young professionals buy a property jointly, to share. On the death of one, his share would be expected to pass to his heirs through his estate, rather than to the other tenant in common.

Tenancy in common also has uses in planning to minimise inheritance tax liability, though this is generally applicable to older individuals, and is beyond the scope of this book.

Note that in either case, the deceased's share in the ownership of the property forms part of his estate for inheritance tax purposes on death (though if it passes to a spouse or registered civil partner, its value will usually be exempt from any tax liability).

5.3 The process
5.3.1 Finding a home
Your choice of home is for you to decide. The price of properties varies substantially of course, and is influenced greatly by location and by fashion. You need to take into account the cost of running your new home – larger properties generally result in higher bills for gas, electricity and council tax for example – as well as the cost related to your mortgage.

Estate agents offer many properties for sale and it is a good idea to visit a number of agents for details of properties within your price range and which meet your requirements, for example, in relation to size.

You should know in advance how much you can afford to offer for a property. This is partly a matter of knowing how much you can pay from your own resources, but also how much you can borrow. You should approach mortgage lenders early in the process to find out how much they will lend you on what terms.

The agents will usually invite you to be put on their mailing list so they can send you details of further properties which come onto the market. Estate agents will offer you advice and will answer your questions.

Remember however that they act as agents for the seller, not the buyer. (The estate agent is also paid by the seller, not the buyer.)

You can also search for properties for sale in the area(s) you are interested in via the internet and this is becoming increasingly common, with sites such as www.primelocation.com providing useful local information as well as searchable databases of properties.

Location will be important not just in terms of how attractive the area is, but also its convenience in terms of travelling to work, to the shops and to other places you commonly go. Public transport may be important if you use this extensively and parking may also be important if you have a car.

It is often a good idea to visit an area you might want to move to at different times of day. For example, the road you are considering might be a busy short cut during rush hour, or could be close to a club, with a noisy clientele leaving in the late evening. You will often only find these things out by actually being there.

Take advice from others who know the area and know you. This might include friends and relatives, for example, as well as professionals such as estate agents and your solicitor. In the end however, you must make up your own mind.

5.3.2 Deciding to buy

When you decide you want to buy a property, you will make an offer for it, and you may need to negotiate with the seller until a price is agreed. If there is an estate agent involved, he will act as intermediary and in general, he is obliged to pass on offers to the seller. He may also be able to guide you as to what might be an acceptable offer.

The offer you make will need to be confirmed and this will generally be done by your solicitor, usually in a letter to the seller's solicitor. The offer is generally made 'subject to contract' which means that it is not binding on either party until a formal contract is exchanged. This must be stated clearly however.

This arrangement has advantages, because you will need to go through a number of further stages before you can commit to the property fully. However, you should be aware that the seller could accept someone else's offer instead of yours at any time before contracts are exchanged. This is one of the reasons why property transactions can be extremely stressful.

Once the price is agreed, and the offer confirmed, your solicitor will start work to check the title to the property – in other words, the ownership. This ensures that the person selling you the property is the legal owner and therefore has the right to sell. This is done primarily by checking the details at the Land Registry.

The solicitor will also check other matters, for example whether the property is listed (and therefore subject to restrictions on what can be done with it) or in a conservation area. He will check for covenants and easements as discussed earlier, and will also check for any planning permissions relevant to the property, and local development schemes, such as plans to build a new road close to the property.

At the same time, if you will need a mortgage to buy the property, you will approach the lender you intend to use in order to obtain a formal offer. (You should already have had discussions to determine how much you can borrow.) The lender will appoint a valuer to view the property and value it for mortgage purposes (usually, you will be liable for the cost of this, but the valuer's responsibility is nevertheless only to the lender, not to you).

The valuer's job is very specific. He advises the lender whether the property is suitable as security for the loan you want, and usually he will also fix the value for insurance purposes. He may identify any significant faults in the property, if they affect the valuation as security, but if he misses anything, you have no recourse against him.

Because of this, it is a good idea to appoint a surveyor to examine the property on your behalf. You can instruct him to carry out a full structural survey, which is very detailed, but most surveyors offer a Homebuyer's Report which is a little less detailed, and therefore less expensive, but should pick up major faults. You can find a surveyor through their professional body (the Royal Institution of Chartered Surveyors or RICS), from the internet, or from a recommendation from family, friends or the estate agent. It is a good idea to talk to a number of surveyors to compare costs and the service provided.

The lender may be content as a result of the valuation, but in some cases will only be prepared to offer a smaller loan that you had applied for. You then need to consider whether the purchase is still viable (or negotiate a lower price). Sometimes the valuer will have seen a problem, perhaps requiring a more detailed or specialist survey, and the lender will only consider offering a mortgage if you pay for this further survey.

Sometimes the lender will impose a retention – an amount of the loan which will be held back until after some repairs are completed. You would then need to fund that part of the purchase price from other sources until you take ownership and then have the work done. In less serious cases, the lender may require an undertaking that you will complete some repairs, but will not hold any part of the loan back.

If serious problems are revealed by the lender's valuer or your own survey, you may need to reconsider the purchase. Buildings insurance will not cover faults in existence at the time of purchase and correcting major subsidence, for example, can be extremely expensive.

5.3.3 Higher lending charge
You should take into account the fact that some lenders make a higher lending charge if the mortgage you require is more than a certain percentage of the value of the property. This is a charge which compensates the lender for the higher risk involved for them. (If the loan is a high proportion of the value, and you default on payments, it is more likely that the value which could be realised from the property will fall short of what you owe.)

5.3.4 Exchange and completion
Once you are satisfied, and the lender has confirmed the mortgage offer, contracts can be exchanged. You sign a copy of the contract which commits you to buy the property, and the seller signs one committing him to sell. The contracts are exchanged by the solicitors, and then the contract is binding on both sides.

Completion, when the ownership of the property is conveyed to you as purchaser, is usually set for about four weeks after exchange, though this is a matter to be agreed between buyer and seller.

5.3.5   Home Information Packs

Home Information Packs (HIPs) including Energy Performance Certificates are being phased in from 1 August 2007. From then HIPs will be required for the sale of properties with four or more bedrooms. The requirement will extend to smaller properties at a later date (yet to be announced at the time this book went to press). The aim is to reduce delay and uncertainty in the process of buying and selling.

The Home Information Pack comprises compulsory documents:
- Home Information Pack Index
- Energy Performance Certificate
- Sale statement
- Standard searches, and
- Evidence of title

For leasehold there are further requirements, such as:
- A copy of the lease
- Any regulations or rules that apply to the property that aren't mentioned in the lease and any proposed amendments
- Statements or summaries of service charges covering the previous 36 months.

For commonhold additional required information includes:
- An official copy of the individual register and title plan for the common parts.
- An official copy of the commonhold community statement.

Then additional information may be included such as the Home Condition Report.

There are a number of temporary measures in place to get the scheme working as quickly as possible. It is advisable to check the website before starting the process of buying or selling a home:
http://www.homeinformationpacks.gov.uk/

MONEY

5.3.6   Stamp Duty Land Tax

The buyer of a property is liable for Stamp Duty Land Tax on completion of the purchase, assuming that the price paid exceeds the threshold which is currently £125,000.[3]

The solicitor acting for you will arrange for payment of the tax to HM Revenue & Customs (HMRC) on your behalf, but you will need to ensure that he has sufficient money available to do so.

The rate at which SDLT is levied depends on the purchase price according to the following table:

Purchase price	SDLT rate
up to £125,000	0%
over £125,000 up to £250,000	1%
over £250,000 up to £500,000	3%
over £500,000	4%

The rate of SDLT is determined by the purchase price, but is applied to the whole of the price, so there are jumps in the amount of liability where a new rate starts to apply. For example, if you buy a property for £125,000, the SDLT is nil, but if you pay £126,000, the SDLT is 1% of £126,000 = £1,260.

Similarly, if you buy a property for £250,000, the SDLT is 1% of £250,000 = £2,500. However, if the purchase price is £251,000, the SDLT is 3% of £251,000 = £7,530.

This affects house prices to an extent, and it would be unusual for a buyer to pay just over £250,000 for a property for example.

In some cases, there may be moveable items such as carpets and curtains included with the property, and these can be made part of a separate contract. Paying £250,000 for the property and a separate £1,000 for carpets and curtains would mean that the SDLT was based only on £250,000. The split must be reasonable however, so for example, paying

---

[3] If the property in question is situated in areas deemed by the Government to be disadvantaged the nil rate band is £150,000 rather than £125,000. The nil-rate band for non-residential property is £150,000, and disadvantaged areas relief does not apply.

£125,000 for the property and £126,000 for the carpets and curtains is unlikely to be acceptable.

Note also that only moveables can be treated in this way, not fixtures such as fitted wardrobes or kitchen units, which are regarded as being part of the property itself and cannot be separated.

5.4 Costs involved

One of the most important considerations when deciding to buy a house is to take account of all the costs likely to be involved. These could include:

- Solicitor's fees
- Mortgage fees
- Higher lending charge
- Removal costs
- Stamp duty land tax
- Purchase of new carpets and curtains
- Purchase of new furniture etc
- Mortgage repayment costs
- Council tax and water rates
- Utilities (gas, electricity etc)
- Buildings insurance premium
- Cost of redecorating new property
- Increased travel costs

The list is not exhaustive but gives an idea of the range of costs which could be involved, both directly in relation to the purchase and on an ongoing basis. You should list the costs you expect to have in your own circumstances, and ensure they are budgeted for.

5.5 Mortgages

As we have previously noted, buying a property is expensive and the vast majority of people require a loan – known as a mortgage – to do so. The word 'mortgage' is generally used to simply describe the loan, but strictly means the giving of a property as security for the loan.

Mortgages should not be taken on lightly. If you default on the mortgage by missing repayments, the lender can obtain a court order to take possession of the property and sell it to discharge the debt. Although you would be entitled to any excess of the proceeds over the amount owed (including interest and charges), often the amount realised is less than you might hope, because it is a forced sale. You may therefore suffer a substantial capital loss.

In addition a default on a mortgage is damaging to your credit standing and may make it difficult to raise loans in the future.

There are many things to consider in relation to mortgages, and we cover the main issues in this section.

5.5.1 Interest rate options

Interest will be charged on your mortgage, but there are a range of different possibilities. Some of the main ones are:

- **Variable rate:** The lender sets the rate according to market conditions, and can then vary it as those conditions change. This used to be the normal offering from lenders, but increasingly, special 'deals' have come to dominate the marketplace. Although the lender has discretion over the rate, the market is competitive, and it is unlikely that the lender could sustain an uncompetitive rate for long.

- **Fixed rate:** The interest rate is fixed for an initial period, which might be two, three or four years. This gives you certainty, because the monthly repayments are known precisely for that period, which will help with budgeting. If interest rates in the marketplace increase, the fixed rate will not, so there is a real saving. On the other hand, if interest rates fall, the fixed rate will not, so you may end up paying more than if you had accepted a variable rate. (Generally there would be an early repayment charge if you repaid the mortgage during the fixed rate period, and sometimes during a longer period, so you cannot simply switch to a new lender if interest rates fall.) After the fixed rate period, the lender will usually charge its standard variable rate.

- **Discounted rate:** This is akin to a special offer for new mortgages and it means that the rate is below the lender's standard variable rate for an initial period, often of one or two years. This gives a clear saving, but does not limit the potential for the interest rate to fluctuate as the variable rate changes. An early repayment charge would usually apply, at least during the discounted rate period, and often for longer.

- **Capped rate:** With a capped rate mortgage, the interest rate is the lender's standard variable rate, but subject to a maximum, set at outset, for an initial period. You benefit if interest rates fall, but the extent of any increase is limited, to help budgeting. Again, there is likely to be an early repayment charge.

- **Tracker:** The interest rate on a tracker mortgage is not set by the lender, but tracks a chosen market rate, usually the Bank of England base rate. It will usually exceed base rate by a fixed margin. This removes discretion from the lender and ensures that the interest rate is always in line with market rates.

The mortgage market is very competitive, and innovations are occurring all the time, so the list above does not cover all possible variations. The point is that you will have choices and should shop around for the best type of arrangement for you. For example, think carefully about whether you need a fixed or capped rate. If you are stretching your finances to meet your mortgage repayments, it could be difficult to cope with any increase in the interest rate during the first year or two, until your income increases.

There are specialist mortgage advisers who can help you decide and point out the best terms available on the market place. They will also guide you on how much you can borrow. Alternatively you can survey the market yourself using magazines and/or the internet.

5.5.2 Flexible mortgages

Flexible mortgages are a growing section of the market. In principle, they allow you to increase or reduce payments, within agreed limits, as your financial position and needs alter.

This can be useful and means that if you have a period of high expenditure, you may be able to reduce your payments, but if you have a salary increase, you can pay more, and reduce your long term interest costs considerably.

Some accounts are allied to a current or savings account and offset the credit balance from the amount of the mortgage on which interest is charged. This in effect is equivalent to earning interest on your credit balance at the rate charged on your mortgage. If you maintain repayments ignoring the interest reduction, you will repay your loan early and will save a substantial amount of interest too.

These mortgages are certainly attractive in today's market, but you need to compare the overall package with what is available elsewhere, in particular taking into account the interest rate charged, and the extent to which you are likely to have a credit balance in any related current or savings account.

5.5.3 Islamic mortgages

Islamic law prohibits the payment or charging of interest and as a result, a conventional mortgage would be unacceptable. However, there are specifically designed mortgages (referred to as Islamic or Sharia mortgages) which avoid interest payments.

There are two main methods. With the Ijari method, the property is purchased by the institution offering the arrangement and is then gradually purchased by the buyer from the institution by monthly payments made up of capital and rent. At the end of the term of the arrangement, the property passes to the buyer.

The Murabaha method is an alternative, under which the institution buys the property, but then immediately sells it to the buyer for a higher price, which is then paid off by monthly instalments.

Neither of these methods involves interest payments and so they do not contravene Islamic law, though the payment profile is not dissimilar to that under a conventional mortgage.

5.5.4 Repayment or interest only?

As well as interest, you will need eventually to repay the capital borrowed. This can be done either through a capital and interest repayment mortgage, or an interest only mortgage with an investment product (or products) running alongside to build up the capital repayment.

With a capital and interest repayment mortgage, each monthly payment consists partly of interest, partly of capital, so the loan is gradually repaid through the term. The payments are designed to stay the same unless interest rates change. Initially therefore, they consist mostly of interest, with only a small amount of capital repayment. As the term progresses, and the capital outstanding reduces, so the interest is less and the speed of repayment of capital becomes faster.

The advantage of this route is that the amount you owe reduces month by month, and as long as you keep up your repayments, the loan is certain to be repaid by the end of the term. There is therefore no risk that there will be anything outstanding at the end of the term.

If you choose the interest only route, the amount you pay to the lender each month is less, but it does not include any capital repayment. You need to build up capital to repay the loan, so you should establish an investment product (or products) alongside and also contribute to that. The idea is to build up sufficient over the mortgage term to repay the loan.

Here there is a risk that the amount you build up will not be sufficient to repay, particularly if investment returns are less than you hoped and expected. However, there is also a possibility that if investment returns are good, you will reach your target early and be able to repay the loan before the end of the term. Alternatively, you could build up a surplus which will be available to you at the end of the term.

Some lenders have in the past insisted that you should use a particular investment product, for example an endowment policy, but this is now relatively unusual. Most lenders allow you to make the decision yourself (though you may benefit by taking professional advice). Endowment policies are not particularly tax efficient for most people, and a better choice might be an ISA. (These investment products are explained in Chapter 3.)

In general, you should be aware that using the interest only basis really amounts to borrowing to invest, because you are choosing to invest money rather than pay off part of your borrowing. The return you achieve from investment must exceed the interest you pay if you are to gain from this therefore, and this puts a lot of pressure on investment performance. This was discussed in Chapter 2.

The interest only approach therefore carries a higher risk than the capital and interest repayment approach.

5.6 Protection alongside a mortgage

In Chapter 4, we discussed the range of personal protection products which you may consider as a means of protecting yourself and your dependants from the financial consequences of events such as death or incapacity.

A mortgage will need to be repaid whatever happens, so you should consider carefully the protection requirements that result.

5.6.1 Life insurance

Life insurance is usually taken out alongside the mortgage, so that the loan can be repaid on your death. If you have a spouse or partner living in the property, or a young family, this is particularly important. A mortgage protection policy is a particular type of term insurance policy designed for this purpose. It has a cover level which decreases, broadly in the same way as the amount outstanding under a capital and interest repayment mortgage. The term would be the same as the mortgage term.

If your mortgage is on an interest only basis, it is better to take out an ordinary term insurance policy with a constant death benefit equal to the amount of the loan. This ensures the mortgage can be repaid on death, whatever the value of the investment you have so far built up. (Endowment policies build in life insurance equal to the amount of the loan, and in this case, no additional life insurance is necessary.)

In the case of a joint mortgage, which you might take out with a spouse or partner, the protection should also cover both people, and should usually be arranged to pay out on the first death.

5.6.2 Other protection

It is also useful to protect your mortgage repayments with an Income Protection Insurance (IPI) arrangement, which would ensure your income is replaced to an extent if you are incapacitated and unable to work. You should choose a level of cover which will allow you to meet your mortgage repayments as well as your other regular outgoings.

A Mortgage Repayment Protection Policy is an alternative. This is a type of ASU policy (see Chapter 4), linked directly to your mortgage repayments and it will provide for them if you are incapacitated through injury or accident, or are made compulsorily redundant. However, the benefits will only last for a limited period, usually of one or two years. The cover is cheaper than but less extensive than IPI in the case of incapacity, though the coverage of compulsory redundancy can be useful.

Critical Illness Cover is often taken alongside a mortgage, so the debt can be repaid if you are unfortunate and suffer from one of the conditions covered. This can remove a financial worry at a very important time.

Many people stretch their cashflow when they buy a property, and it may be difficult to afford all the protection that you might wish to have. However, even if this is the case, as time passes, and all being well, your income increases, you should consider adding to your protection as you can afford to do so.

6 Other money matters

6.1 Effect of change

There are few certainties in life, but perhaps one is that things will change. Our own circumstances change over time, financially, in terms of our family and other commitments and in relation to health, to mention just a few aspects.

The decisions you make about financial matters should always be kept under review, and adjustments made as necessary. For example, when you first start work, and perhaps have few commitments to others, you can afford to spend most of your disposable income, and save just a little. Protection needs may be a low priority.

As you take on more commitments, perhaps a mortgage and a family, your need for protection increases, and you may have little left to save.

These are generalisations of course, and everyone has a different path through life. The point then is to make sure that you do not just let your financial affairs drift, but instead that you are active in reviewing them.

6.2 Coming into money

Many people will inherit money and/or other assets at some stage in their lives, perhaps on the death of their parents. This can provide a major boost to your financial position, but it does require that you handle the situation wisely. If you have a substantial inheritance, it is almost certain to be a good idea to seek professional advice, and we discussed in Chapter 2 the ways in which you might select an adviser.

Much the same is true if you are fortunate enough to win a large amount of money on the lottery or from other gambling activity. There is no tax to pay, but using the money wisely will allow it to change your life in the long term, rather than simply finance a short-lived spending spree.

6.3 Internet auction sites

Internet auction sites are popular these days, and some people use them as a means of increasing their income by selling articles through them. If activity is occasional, this should not present a problem, but if it is regular, it could constitute trading, with the result that an income tax liability could result.

Trading is not defined in a water-tight way in law, and there have been many court cases on the subject. HMRC have published some useful guidance on the subject, which is available on their website at www.hmrc.gov.uk/guidance/selling/index.htm. If you do buy and sell articles regularly, you would be well advised to read this guidance and take note.

Some aspects of activity tend to indicate trading, and the main ones are:

- **Profit-seeking motive:** for example, you regularly buy items with the intention of selling them at a profit
- **Number of transactions:** trading is more likely if there is a large number of transactions, or a repeated pattern of events
- **Nature of goods:** if the goods are only really useful as something to sell, rather than producing income, or having a 'pride in possession' aspect, as might be the case with a work of art, this may indicate a likelihood of trading
- **Changes to goods:** if items are purchased, then improved and sold at a profit, this may constitute trading
- **Source of finance:** borrowing to buy goods which are then sold is likely to indicate trading
- **Interval:** if goods are bought and then quickly sold again, this is more likely to constitute trading than if there is a lengthy gap

Trading generally requires the purchase of goods and their resale, whereas selling something you have inherited, but do not want, is unlikely to be regarded as trading.

This is not a straightforward issue, but HMRC can levy penalties as well as collecting back tax liabilities and interest if trading activity takes place but is not declared. If you think you could be affected, you should seek professional advice.

Trading at car boot sales gives rise to similar issues.

6.4 Charitable giving

Although most of this book is about building up financial resources, you may also want to make charitable donations to help others who are less fortunate than you. There are tax advantages available which can increase the amount charities receive without costing you any more.

When you make a donation, if you complete a Gift Aid declaration, the charity will be able to reclaim basic rate tax on the gift from HMRC. The effect is to increase the value of your gift by about 28%. If you are a higher rate taxpayer, you will also receive higher rate tax relief yourself.

Most charities can supply the declaration forms, and there are also similar arrangements in operation through payroll at many employers. You can then make your donations direct from your pay.

It is necessary that you pay sufficient tax to cover the amount reclaimed by the charity, otherwise HMRC will ask you to repay the amount of the relief. If you are a low-paid worker, you should check this carefully.

6.5 Employment benefits

If you are employed, your employer may provide you with various benefits as well as paying you a salary. If this is a flexible package (where you pick from a menu of benefits), you need to decide what the priority order should be.

You will need to check with the Human Resources department of your employer exactly what is provided, but the benefits might include:

- Pension benefits
- Life insurance
- Income protection on incapacity
- Share schemes and share option schemes (where you buy, or are given, shares or options to buy shares in your employer company at a favourable price and, in some cases, with tax advantages)
- Private Medical Insurance
- Interest-free loans to buy a travel season ticket or a bicycle.

You may find that your employer provides other benefits as well as or instead of some of these, and it is important to know exactly what is on offer. Some employers simply pay a salary, with little or nothing by way of additional benefits. In comparing jobs however, you should take account of the value of the benefits as well as the salary.

6.6 State benefits

The range of State benefits is wide, and full coverage is beyond the scope of this book. However, benefits are provided in a range of circumstances including:

- Incapacity
- Unemployment
- Bereavement

There are also benefits available to help the lower paid, and those with dependent children.

Some benefits are dependent on your having paid (or been credited with) a minimum number of National Insurance contributions. Some are means-tested and only available to those with limited income and savings.

Initially, the best source of information on State benefits is the DWP website at www.dwp.gov.uk. If you then feel you may qualify, you should contact the relevant local office – there are different offices for different benefit types. The DWP website contains a search facility which will help you identify the appropriate office. This facility is at http://www.dwp.gov.uk/localoffice.

6.7 Do I need a will?

A will comes into effect on the death of the person who made it, and gives instructions as to how his assets should be distributed. If you want to have control over this, then you should make a will, particularly if your assets are substantial.

You should also keep your will under review, so that it reflects your current wishes and your current assets.

There are also some events which affect an existing will. In particular, marriage or entering into a registered civil partnership generally invalidates a will made before the marriage or partnership (unless it specifically states that it is to be effective afterwards). It is reasonable to suppose that your intentions would be affected by the event, so you should make a new will.

If you get divorced, or your registered civil partnership is dissolved, this makes any bequest in the will to your former spouse or partner invalid, but otherwise the will is unaffected. The presumption is that the financial settlement would have made any necessary provision for the spouse or partner so any further provision in the will is superfluous. Again however, it is wise to make a new will.

6.7.1   Making a will

You can buy a 'will kit' from most stationery shops, intended to allow you to draw up a will yourself, and this will include instructions on the legal requirements. The will must be in writing and your signature must be witnessed by two people (who cannot then benefit from the will).

Alternatively, you could ask a solicitor to draw up your will. This will be more expensive, but can be a wise decision, because the solicitor may be able to offer advice on your intentions. He should also avoid mistakes, which are easy to make if you draw up your own will.

6.7.2   Intestacy

If you die without leaving a valid will, you are said to have died 'intestate'. The law then requires that your estate be distributed in a particular manner, depending on who survives you. The most common situations are summarised in the table on the next page.

Survived by	Distribution of estate
Spouse or registered civil partner and children	Spouse or partner takes the personal effects and the first £125,000 of the estate. The children take half of any residue in equal shares The spouse or partner has a life interest* in the other half until death, when the capital passes to the children in equal shares.
Children only	Children take everything
Spouse or registered civil partner, no children, but surviving parents or siblings (or their children)	Spouse or partner takes the personal effects, the first £200,000 of the estate and half of any residue. The other half of the residue is taken by the surviving parent(s) or if none, the siblings or their children
Spouse or registered civil partner, but no children, no surviving parents and no siblings nor children of siblings	Spouse or partner takes everything
* a life interest means being entitled to the income generated, but not to any of the capital	

The rules of intestacy are not unreasonable, but equally, they are unlikely to be precisely what you would like to happen in many cases. It is therefore usually wise to make a will.

One point to note in particular is that there is no provision for a partner other than a legally married spouse or registered civil partner. If you have such a partner, it is therefore particularly important that you make a will.

7   Tax

What is income tax?
How is it calculated?
Other forms of tax
    VAT
    Capital gains tax
    Inheritance tax
    Stamp duty
What are National Insurance Contributions?
Termination Payments
Personal service companies
How does your tax code work?

Benjamin Franklin once famously observed that "in this world nothing can be said to be certain except death and taxes". Alas, this is true, and we therefore need to consider tax and related matters.[4]

7.1   Income Tax

As an employee resident in the UK, you will pay income tax on your earned income above the minimum tax threshold applicable to you, otherwise known as your personal income tax allowance. (Details of the various income tax allowances for the tax year 2007/2008 are set out on the next page). Income tax is paid to Her Majesty's Revenue and Customs (commonly as abbreviated to "HMRC" (as in this book), and also known as "the Tax Office"). Personal allowances are determined each year by the Chancellor of the Exchequer and announced in the Budget and as a general rule, they rise each year in line with inflation. Effectively, no income tax is payable in respect of the element of your income below the personal allowance threshold (but you should note the points we make below in relation to National Insurance contributions before celebrating too vigorously). We should add that in the past, there was an extra

---

[4] This not being a book dealing with theological issues, we do not feel able to comment on death. Although we do discuss death benefits in the chapter describing pension schemes.

allowance available for married couples; this however, no longer exists for people aged under 70.

Annual income is determined by reference to the tax year, which runs from 6 April to the following 5 April. Income includes all earnings from employment, including basic pay, bonuses, and so on. It will also include any earnings attributable to work carried out on a self-employed basis (for example, as a self-employed contractor or consultant) and "unearned" income (for example, interest received on bank or building society accounts, dividends from investments in shares and so on). Certain payments which you may receive will however, be exempt from income tax; for example, any payment you may receive from a tax exempt investment such as an Individual Savings Account (ISA) and any premium bond wins - we discuss such tax exempt investments in Chapter 3.

The rate of tax you pay will depend upon the amount of your (taxable) income in the relevant tax year, and different rates apply to different "slices" of your taxable income. For the tax year 2007/2008, the rates of income tax applicable to a person's taxable income (i.e. income above the personal allowance) are as follows:

	Tax Rate
Starting rate on taxable income up to £2,230	10%
Basic rate on taxable income from £2,230 to £34,600	22%
Higher rate on taxable income from £34,600	40%

If you qualify for a standard single person's tax allowance of £5,225 (for the tax year 2007/2008), you can therefore earn £39,825 (£34,600 plus £5,225) before paying tax at the higher rate. These tax bands are generally (but not inevitably) raised each year, but often at a rate which is lower than the rise in average salaries. This process is an example of what is known as "fiscal drag" (which has been labelled a "stealth tax") and means that, over time, a growing number of people are finding themselves treated as higher rate tax payers (thus increasing the amount of tax collected by the Government). However, in his March 2007 Budget, the Chancellor announced that changes would be made to the way in which the tax band limits were calculated, including an above-inflation increase in 2009/10. He also announced the prospective abolition of the 10% starting rate of earned income tax (but not in respect of savings income or capital gains) and the reduction of the basic income tax rate from 22% to 20% with effect from April 2008. Consequently, the lowest income tax rate for tax year 2008/2009 in respect of earned income will be 20%.

Income tax due on your earned income will be deducted directly from your gross salary by your employer under what is known as the PAYE (Pay As You Earn) system. If you have other sources of income from which tax has not been automatically deducted, for example, under the PAYE system, you should declare this income by means of a tax return e.g. rental income from property or investment income. HMRC should automatically send you a self-assessment tax return form; however, if they do not do so, you are obliged to obtain one and submit it yourself.

Tax returns are available online:
http://www.hmrc.gov.uk/sa/forms/content.htm
or from your tax office, and must be filed before specific deadlines. Specifically, paper returns must be filed by 31 October immediately following the relevant tax year (so that for the tax year 2007/2008, paper returns must be filed by no later than 31 October 2008). Alternatively, it is possible for returns to be submitted online, in which case the relevant deadline is 31 January (i.e. so that for the tax year 2007/2008, the deadline is 31 January 2009). If you submit a paper return by the 31 October deadline, HMRC will calculate your tax liability for you (indeed, this happens automatically when a tax return is filed online).

In addition, any taxable unearned income you receive in the form of "onshore" bank or building society interest (by which we mean interest paid by a bank or building society situated in the UK) will be subject to tax at the rate of 20%, which will automatically be deducted "at source" (i.e. by the relevant bank or building society). If you are a higher rate tax payer you will be subject to an additional tax charge upon your taxable unearned income (which should be declared in your self-assessment tax return) so that the effective tax rate imposed on your unearned income is

40%. Conversely, if your total income (from all sources) in any tax year is below your personal allowance threshold for that year, you should be able to arrange to receive your interest gross (i.e. without the deduction of any tax). If you fall within this category, and wish to claim your interest on a gross basis, you should contact your bank or building society, which should be able to provide you with the relevant form which you will be required to complete and submit to the bank or building society. Similarly, if your income is above your personal allowance threshold but only subject to the 10% starting rate, you should be entitled to a tax rebate and again your bank or building society (or your local tax office) should be able to provide you with the relevant form.

Any claims in respect of any relevant tax year must be brought within five years after 31 January immediately following the end of the tax year. So, for example, if you wish to reclaim tax deducted in respect of the 2006/2007 tax year, your claim must be brought before 31 January 2013.

If you receive dividend income from UK companies, that income will be subject to a deduction known as a "tax credit". The tax credit will be equal to one-ninth of the gross value of the dividend. If you are not a higher rate tax payer, the tax credit will satisfy your liability to income tax in relation to the dividend (i.e. you will have nothing more to pay). However, if you are a higher rate tax payer, you will be subject to a further income tax liability in relation to the dividend, effectively equal to 25% of the amount of the dividend payment you actually received. This additional liability should be declared in your self-assessment tax return.

7.2 Other Forms of Tax

Income tax is not, unfortunately, the only kind of tax you may encounter. Other forms of tax (or "duty") include:

7.2.1 Value Added Tax

Value Added Tax (VAT) is a tax on consumer expenditure involving the acquisition of goods and services, and consequently it is virtually impossible to avoid paying it (legally) if you live and work in the UK. Broadly speaking, VAT is collected by the seller from the buyer of relevant goods and services when they are purchased. The seller in turn passes the VAT proceeds to HMRC. At present, the standard rate of VAT in the UK is 17.5%, although reduced rates apply to certain items, for example, domestic fuel and power supplies which are subject to VAT at the reduced rate of 5%, and books which are supplied at a VAT rate of 0%.

Some goods and services are exempt from VAT, such as the provision of certain medical and educational services, and some activities of registered charities.

7.2.2 Capital Gains Tax

A capital gain is essentially the profit that can be made by purchasing an asset at one price and subsequently selling it at another (higher) price. Similarly, a capital loss is the financial loss incurred when an asset is sold for a price that is lower than the original purchase price.

Individuals are liable to capital gains tax ("CGT") on any capital gains they make (above a CGT annual exempt amount), after allowing for any capital losses they may have incurred, in each tax year. The basic calculation is sale price less original cost equals net capital gain. Each individual has a CGT annual exempt amount and if an individual's gains (net of losses) in any tax year do not exceed the annual exempt amount, no CGT will be due in relation to that tax year. For the tax year 2007/2008, the annual exempt amount is £9,200.

CGT is payable at the individual's marginal rate for income tax purposes. In other words, a higher rate tax payer will pay CGT at the rate of 40% of any net gain. An individual with total (taxable) income and capital gains not exceeding £34,600 (as shown in the table above) will pay CGT at the rate of 20%, whilst if (taxable) income and gains do not exceed £2,230, the applicable CGT rate will be 10%.

In addition to the annual exempt amount, a further relief known as taper relief may be available. Taper relief reduces the proportion of any gain which will be subjected to a CGT charge, depending on how long the individual has owned the asset giving rise to the gain. There are two rates of taper relief, one applying to "business assets" (for example, certain types of shares) and another to "non-business assets" (essentially assets which do not qualify as business assets, such as a weekend cottage which is not your main residence, but which is not used for commercial letting). If business assets have been held for one year, the amount of gain which is taxable is reduced by 50%. If the assets have been held for two or more years, the gain is reduced by 75% (so in effect, if you are a higher rate tax payer and you are disposing of an asset which you have owned for two years or more, the applicable CGT rate in respect of any (taxable) gain you realise will be 10% rather than 40%).

The rate of taper relief available in respect of non-business assets is considerably less generous, and reductions only begin to apply if the assets have been held for at least three years.

No CGT liability arises upon the transfer of assets between spouses or civil partners and there is an exemption for any gain which arises on the sale of your main residence.[5]

7.2.3 Inheritance Tax

Subject to certain exceptions, inheritance tax ("IHT") is payable on an individual's estate when that individual dies, and on "lifetime gifts", to the extent that the (aggregate) value of the estate and gift(s) exceeds the IHT "nil rate band". The nil rate band for the tax year 2007/2008 is £300,000; this is scheduled to rise to £350,000 by 2010.

IHT will not however arise if the transfer of the estate or gift is an "exempt transfer" (i.e. made to a spouse, civil partner or charity).

If any IHT charge arises in respect of a deceased individual's estate, the relevant rate will be 40% of the value of the estate in excess of the nil rate band. The rate applying to lifetime gifts (in excess of the nil rate band) is 20%; however, no IHT charge will arise on a simple gift made between individuals if the person making the gift survives for seven years from the date of the gift. For this reason, such gifts are known as "potentially exempt transfers" or "PETs". If the individual makes the gift but does not

---

[5] In addition, there are other "specified" reliefs which may be available, for example, in relation to investments involving the Enterprise Investment Scheme and Venture Capital Trusts. This, however, is a complex area, and specialised advice should always be sought in relation to such matters. Consequently we do not consider these reliefs further in this book.

survive for at least three years, the value of the gift will be added to the value of the estate for IHT purposes. If however, the individual survives for more than three years (but less than seven), and if IHT is payable in respect of the gift, it will effectively be levied at a reduced rate in respect of the gift (depending on how long the individual survives after making the gift).

7.2.4 Stamp Taxes

Today, the most significant stamp taxes are payable in respect of transfers of property and shares. We have already discussed stamp duty in relation to property in Chapter 5 (see section 5.3.6). So far as share transfers are concerned, stamp duty applies to (paper) share transfers at the rate of 0.5% of the total amount of the consideration paid (which may differ from the market value). Stamp Duty Reserve Tax (SDRT), also at the rate of 0.5%, applies to electronic share transfers under the CREST system.

7.3 National Insurance Contributions

We now turn to the issue of National Insurance ("NI") contributions. Though NI contributions are not officially a tax, contribution rates are determined by the Government, and the payment of NI contributions is mandatory (if your salary exceeds the minimum known as the "primary threshold") and they are automatically deducted from an employee's (gross) salary (just like income tax). If you qualify as an NI contributor, those contributions have to be paid, and (as we explain in the section on pensions), your NI contributions history is vital in determining your entitlement to a state pension, as well as other social security benefits.

The first question to ask is: who pays NI contributions? The answer is that you will pay NI contributions if you are an employee or self-employed, (with earnings above the primary threshold) and aged 16 or over but have not reached your state pension age. You will have (or should have) a National Insurance number allocated to you when you reach the age of 16 if you were resident in Great Britain at that time. This acts as the reference number for your NI contribution history. If you do not have an NI number (but are entitled to one), you can apply for one at your local Jobcentre Plus or social security office.

There are various "classes" of NI contributions.

Class 1 contributions are paid by all employees whose earnings are above the lower earnings limit ("LEL") and are paid in respect of income between the LEL and the upper earnings limit ("UEL"). The LEL is set a little lower than the primary threshold. If your salary is below the primary threshold (but above the LEL) you will not in fact be required to pay Class 1 contributions (but will be treated as having done so for the purposes of your NI contributions history). If your salary exceeds the UEL, you will also pay 1% on your earnings in excess of the UEL.

Your employer will also pay NI contributions in respect of your earnings (and it should be noted that there is no UEL in respect of employer NI contributions).

If you are self-employed you will pay Class 2 NI contributions, which are flat rate contributions.

If you are not obliged to pay compulsory NI contributions (for example, because your earnings are low), you may pay Class 3 voluntary NI contributions to improve your contributions history (although before doing so, you should consider consulting an Independent Financial Adviser (IFA) or your local Citizens Advice Bureau).

Class 4 contributions are a further form of (flat rate) NI contributions, which are paid by the self-employed on profits between two thresholds known as the "lower profit limit" and the "upper profit limit".

Details of the various NI contribution rates, primary threshold, LEL, UEL, lower profit limit and upper profit limit for 2007/2008 are set out below:

National insurance contributions

£ per week (unless stated)	2007-08
Lower earnings limit, primary Class 1	£87
Upper earnings limit, primary Class 1	£670
Primary threshold	£100
Employees' primary Class 1 rate between primary threshold and upper earnings limit	11%
Employees' primary Class 1 rate above upper earnings limit	1%

Class 2 rate (per week)	£2.20
Class 2 small earnings exception	£4,635 per year
Class 3 rate (per week)	£7.80
Class 4 lower profits limit	£5,225 per year
Class 4 upper profits limit	£34,840 per year
Class 4 rate between lower profits limit and upper profits limit	8%
Class 4 rate above upper profits limit	1%

7.4 Personal Service Companies

Sometimes, people who would otherwise be employees establish what are known as personal service companies in an attempt to minimise the tax and NI contribution costs of employment. This was, for example, quite common in the IT sector; rather than the individual being employed by the relevant "employer", the individual's personal service company would enter into a consultancy (or similar) arrangement with the "employer" who would in fact be a client of the personal service company rather than a "true employer". Since the consultancy arrangement was not an employment relationship, the client's employment costs were reduced and the individual, operating via his own personal service company, had the added advantage of limited legal liability.

Inevitably, such approaches attracted the interest of HMRC, who were concerned about the tax and NI contributions being lost as a result of the exploitation of this "loophole". HMRC therefore took steps to stop the more excessive uses of this approach by introducing a new tax regime (known as "IR35", named after the press release which announced the changes). Essentially, if HMRC believe that notwithstanding the use of a personal service company, the reality is that the individual is in fact an employee of the client to whom the services are provided, HMRC can effectively require the personal service company to pay the tax and NI contributions which would have been payable assuming the individual was an employee of the client.

Whether or not this will apply in any particular circumstances will depend very much upon the relevant facts, for example, whether the personal service company provides services to more than one (independent) "client". As this is a complex area, should you consider establishing a personal service company (and of course, you may never do so) we would always recommend that before doing so, you seek appropriate legal and accounting advice.

7.5   Taxation of termination payments

When your employment with an employer comes to an end, you may be entitled to one or more types of "termination payment", depending upon the exact circumstances of your departure from employment. Identifying the type of termination payment to which you are entitled is important, not least because not all termination payments are taxed in the same way by HMRC.

The basic rule is that all payments which can be classified as "earnings" attributable to the work you carried out for your employer as an employee will be treated as being liable to income tax and NI contributions. Furthermore, any payment you may receive from your employer in return for a variation of the terms of your employment contract (for example, the introduction of restrictive covenants to apply for a fixed period of time following the termination of your employment) will also be treated as being liable to tax and NI.

The situation becomes more complicated when we consider payments intended to compensate an employee for the loss of his job (for example, a payment in compensation for unfair dismissal). Here, the general rule is that the first £30,000 of any compensation payments is tax free (and furthermore not subject to NI contributions). Similarly, payments made on redundancy are also capable of benefiting from the "£30,000 exemption" (as it is commonly known), although HMRC may well require evidence that the redundancy to which the payment relates is indeed a genuine redundancy and consequently, when dealing with redundancy payments, it is (in our view) always advisable to obtain appropriate employment law advice at (or preferably before) the termination date.

Payments "in lieu of notice" – or "PILONs" – can pose particular difficulties. A PILON is a payment given to an employee upon the termination of his employment in compensation for not being given the appropriate notice by his employer (see section 10.1.3 sub-heading "Notice") and is intended to compensate the employee for the salary and other benefits he would have received had the employer been willing and/or able to employ him throughout the requisite notice period.

HMRC's current approach to the tax treatment of PILONs is that if the employment contract permits the employer to make a PILON, any PILON made will be subject to income tax and NI contributions. If the contract does not provide for PILONs to be made, and the employer pays a lump sum on termination of employment, HMRC take the view that if it is the employer's usual practice to make such payments, the payment derives from the employment relationship and is thus taxable as earnings (rather than as a compensation payment which would be eligible for the £30,000 exemption). This view is controversial and it is therefore essential that specialist employment law and tax advice is obtained when a PILON is going to be made at the end of an employment.

PILONs should be distinguished from "garden leave" lump sum payments. The term "garden leave" refers to a situation where an employee remains employed for the duration of his notice period (and thus remains bound by all the obligations imposed upon him as a result of being an employee) but is not actually required to work. In such circumstances, the employer will sometimes make a lump sum payment to the employee, the lump sum representing advance payment of the salary (and other benefits) the employee would otherwise earn whist working out his notice. As you would expect, garden leave payments will be subject to income tax and NI contributions in the same way as the salary and other benefits they replace.

Lastly, your employer may provide you with an "ex gratia" payment when your employment comes to an end. Genuine ex gratia payments[6]

---

[6] In other words, the payment by the employer must genuinely be voluntary and not connected to the employee's employment. Ex gratia payments upon

will benefit from the £30,000 exemption referred to above. Unsurprisingly, HMRC often require considerable evidence to support the proposition that the payment is indeed ex gratia in nature. Furthermore, if an employer has regularly been in the habit of making ex gratia payments to departing employees, so that employees develop an "expectation" that such payments will be made if their employments are terminated, a contractual right to such payments may arise by reason of "custom and practice". If this occurs, the payment will be treated as earnings for tax and NI purposes, notwithstanding the fact that the payment is described as being ex gratia in nature.

7.6 Tax forms and tax codes
7.6.1 P45 and P46

When you move from one employer to another you will be provided with a P45 form by your old employer and asked to supply it to the new employer. This is a certificate which contains the information the employer needs to deduct the correct amount of income tax and national insurance contributions from your salary. It shows:

- your previous PAYE reference;
- your NI number;
- your names;
- the date you left your last position;
- whether you are repaying a student loan;
- your tax code;
- pay received in the tax year to date; and
- tax paid in that period.

If you are starting your first job, or have lost your P45, you will be asked by your new employer to complete a P46 form. This will enable your employer to set your tax code.

---

termination are indeed paid by employers from time to time, although the authors feel obliged to point out that they themselves have sadly never benefited from such "employer largesse".

7.6.2 P60

This is a certificate which your employer must provide you with at the end of each tax year. It is a summary of your earnings, income tax, NI contributions, statutory payments (maternity, paternity or adoption payments), student load deductions and tax credits.

Keep your P60 in a safe place. You will need to refer to it if you are asked to complete a tax return or if you make a claim for tax credits.

7.6.3 P11(D)

The P11(D) is a statement of taxable benefits you have received from your employer in the tax year, which will be taken account of by your employer (and reflected in your tax code) for the next tax year. If you complete your own tax return, the amount shown needs to be declared on the return form.

It is worth taking time to check that your employer is attributing the correct level of benefits to you. You do not want to pay tax on a gym membership or company car if you do not, in fact, receive that benefit.

7.6.4 Tax code

A tax code is usually made up of one letter and several numbers, for example: 503L or K497.

If your tax code is a number followed by a letter, the number (multiplied by ten) indicates the total amount of income you can earn in a year before paying tax. The letter shows how the number should be adjusted following any changes to allowances announced in the Budget.

Common tax code suffix letters and what they mean

- L indicates that you are eligible for the basic personal allowance;
- P is used if you are aged 65 to 74 and eligible for the full personal allowance;
- V is used if you are aged 65 to 74, eligible for the full personal allowance and the full married couple's allowance (for those born before 6 April 1935 and aged under 75) and estimated to be liable at the basic rate of tax;
- Y is used if you are aged 75 or over and eligible for the full personal allowance; and

- T indicates that your tax allowances are being reviewed by HMRC.

Other tax codes

If your tax code has two letters but no number, or is the letter 'D' followed by a zero, it normally indicates that you have two or more sources of income and that all of your allowances have been applied to the tax code and income from your main job:[7]

- BR is used when all your income is taxed at the basic rate ;
- D0 is used when all your income is taxed at the higher rate of tax; and
- NT is used when no tax is to be taken from your income or pension

Tax code prefix K

K is used when your untaxed income in the previous year exceeded the tax allowance.

K code example

K497 means:

- your untaxed income was £4,970 greater than your tax-free allowances;
- as a result, £4,970 must be added to your total taxable income to ensure the right amount of tax is collected.

---

[7] If you have two jobs, it is likely that all of your second income will be taxed at the basic or higher rate, depending on how much you earn. This is because all of your allowances will have been used against the income from your main job.

8 Pensions

Why are pensions important?
What is a pension scheme and how do they work?
What are the tax advantages?
What about the State Pension Scheme?

There seem to be a few basic principles concerning pensions which apply to just about everybody when they start work for the first time. These are:

- All the experts will tell you that you should start contributing to a pension as soon as possible.
- Despite this, you may well not do so (at least not for the first few years).
- When you do eventually start contributing, you probably won't be saving enough to fund a pension which will be adequate for your likely needs when you actually retire.

In addition, to these three basic principles, the last few years have seen the emergence of a fourth principle:

- Unless you are very, very lucky, no matter how good your ultimate job is, it is increasingly unlikely that you will be able to take "early retirement" (at, say, some time between 55 and 60). On the contrary, it is increasingly probable that most people now aged between 20 and 30 will have to continue working (in one form or another - not necessarily in the same career that they started) until they reach their state pension age (currently age 65 for people within this age bracket but this is likely to change over the next few years, as we discuss below) or even later.

The reasons for these apparently depressing statements are easy to understand.

First of all, it is obvious that you will need some sort of pension in due course eventually. What else are you (and your family) going to live on in your old age? And the sooner you start saving for your pension, the longer the period of time you will have to build up your pension.

The reality is that many people do not begin to contribute towards their pensions as soon as they start earning money - some do not start for several years (and some sadly never think of saving anything at all, until it is too late for them to make any meaningful contributions. Such people are running the very real risk of living in poverty in the last years of their lives). There are, of course often good reasons why many people delay starting to contribute to their pensions. Many people today start work burdened with debt, often in the form of student loans, credit card debts and so on. (We discuss debt, and what you can do about it in Chapter 1). This simply wasn't a common occurrence twenty or thirty years ago, and it is quite understandable that many people at the start of their working lives feel they should give a higher priority to paying off their existing debts than contributing to a pension scheme.

Also, it's a fact of life that people who are earning a salary for the first time want to go out and enjoy themselves whenever they can, now that they have a good job, often in ways which might almost be guaranteed to dispose of a fair percentage of their incomes. Given that this is what each of the authors (and indeed our esteemed publisher) did, it is difficult to argue against this. However, the more you can keep this phase to a minimum (at least as regards the expenditure aspects), the sooner you will hopefully be in a position to start saving for your retirement.

As regards the third principle, again the reality is that most people underestimate how expensive pensions can be; that is, how large a capital sum you need to accumulate to pay for a pension of a particular size. There are several reasons for this, not least that the cost of providing a pension seems to be continuously revised upwards, in part due to rising life expectancy (generally perceived as being a good thing, of course, but expensive for anyone seeking to save for a good pension).

The fourth principle is easy to understand once you recognise the financial effects of spending increased periods of time in higher education or otherwise delaying entry into the workforce (for example, by spending a year travelling overseas before starting work). If a person delays their entry into the workforce (all other things being equal) they will have a shorter working life over which to accumulate a pension fund. Taking early retirement exacerbates this problem, since it shortens still further a person's probable working life, whilst at the same time, it increases the period of retirement during which a person will be relying upon their pension to provide them with the necessities of life. Increasing life expectancies extend the likely period of retirement even further. This process has been under way for years - certainly since the concept of early retirement became popular in the 1980s when many companies used early retirement as a method of reducing the size of their workforces without entering into large scale (and unpopular) redundancy exercises. Now however, life expectancies and the cost of pensions have increased so dramatically that it seems that not only is early retirement likely to become increasingly rare, but retirement ages themselves will have to rise. Indeed, this necessity has already been widely recognised, in (for example) the Report of the Pensions Commission chaired by Lord Turner which was released in 2005, and the Government's subsequent proposals which envisage state pension ages rising (in stages), ultimately to age 68 by 2046.

For all these reasons, pensions and retirement savings generally are important and (to be blunt) the sooner this is recognised and the sooner you can begin to save for your retirement, the better.

8.1   What is a pension scheme?

In the last section, we gave a brief explanation as to why it is important to start saving for a pension as soon as you reasonably can and why you should save as much as you can. In this section, we provide a brief description of the different types of pension schemes you may encounter, and some of their advantages and disadvantages. However, before we get into the detail, it's worth emphasising that a pension scheme (of whatever type) is really just a savings vehicle - a tax advantaged one to be sure - but just a savings vehicle. This means that you should consider your pension scheme in the light of other savings vehicles, for example ISAs, unit trusts, high interest deposit accounts and perhaps (in due course) even more "exotic" investments such as buy-to-let properties etc. In other words, there is more than one way (and not just one right way) to save. Indeed you will probably find yourself saving by a variety of routes and this may well be a good thing (though we would urge you to check your financial position periodically with an independent (fee-based) financial adviser). For present purposes, however, we are going to focus solely on those arrangements which are generally recognised as "proper" pension schemes operating in the private sector; i.e., occupational pension schemes, personal pension schemes and stakeholder pension schemes. We will also briefly describe the state pension system, and possible changes which may be made to it over the next few years.

There are various different ways of classifying pension schemes. One way of doing so is to ask whether they are occupational pension schemes or personal pension schemes (or stakeholder pension schemes). An occupational pension scheme can be described as a scheme set up by an employer (or group of employers) for the benefit of employees. It will be established under a trust and thus have a board of trustees (or alternatively a board of directors of a trustee company) who are (principally) legally responsible for the operation of the trust, in accordance with the trust deeds governing the trust (although it is usual for the trust documentation to grant powers (and responsibilities) to the sponsoring employer(s) as well as the trustees). Such schemes can have many members (who will be beneficiaries of the trust).

In contrast, personal pension schemes (and stakeholder pension schemes) are essentially "one man arrangements", each such arrangement being an arrangement between the member and the "provider" of the personal (or stakeholder) pension scheme, typically an insurance company or similar organisation. Employers play no role in the actual administration of such arrangements (but can pay "employer contributions" to such arrangements if this is agreed). You may sometimes hear the term "group personal pension scheme" or "GPP" used, particularly by employers who have chosen to make use of such pension arrangements in order to make pension provision for their employees. A GPP in fact has no legal reality as such, it is merely a collection of individual personal pension schemes, (in much the same way as a herd of horses is simply a collection of individual horses), generally all provided by the same provider, and sometimes "branded" as the employer's pension scheme.

Another way of classifying pension schemes is by considering their benefit structures, that is, by considering how they are designed to build up the eventual pension, and broadly speaking, there are two different types: defined contribution schemes and defined benefit schemes. Occupational pension schemes may either be defined contribution schemes or defined benefit schemes (although on occasions, they may have the characteristics of both defined contribution schemes and defined benefit schemes, in which case, they are sometimes referred to as "hybrid schemes"). Personal pension schemes and stakeholder pension schemes are only ever defined contribution schemes.

8.2 Defined contribution pension schemes

These are sometimes known as money purchase schemes. Under a defined contribution pension scheme the individual member pays contributions at a specified rate and (if the individual's employer has so agreed) the employer also contributes at a specified rate (which may or may not be at the same rate as that paid by the member).[8] The contributions are paid into an account under the pension scheme in the member's name (sometimes colloquially referred to as the "member's money purchase pot") and the contributions so accumulated are invested.

---

[8] Strictly speaking, there is also the concept of a "cash balance" arrangement which may be considered a specialised type of money purchase scheme (and one that is distinct from "pure" defined contribution (DC) schemes). They differ from DC schemes in that in the case of a cash balance arrangement, the scheme employer will have provided some form of guarantee or promise in relation to the value of the members' retirement accounts which are used to provide the members' money purchase benefits. So, the value of a member's retirement account under a cash balance arrangement will not solely depend upon the payments made to it and the investment returns achieved by it. As they are specialised pension schemes (and considerably less common than defined contribution schemes), we do not consider cash balance arrangements in great detail in this book; further details may be found at www.hmrc.gov.uk/manuals/rpsmmanual/RPSM09202010.html

When the pension benefits come into payment the contributions so invested, and the accumulated investment returns which have built up over the years, are usually used to purchase an annuity for the benefit of the member (and, typically, his spouse or civil partner and dependants as appropriate). The annuity constitutes the pension provided by the defined contribution pension scheme.

The key thing to note about defined contribution schemes is that it is the individual members who bear the investment risk. The value of the resulting pension depends upon the return achieved by the invested contributions paid into the member's money purchase pot and (of course) investments can rise and fall in value. The value of the ultimate pension will also depend upon interest rates at the time of retirement, which influence the price of annuities. If the investment return is poor, the member's pension will be reduced accordingly, and the member (generally speaking) will have no claim to a larger pension than that which he (or she) actually receives. In particular, if the scheme has been "sponsored" by the member's employer, the member will generally be unable to require that his employer provides compensation for any investment losses which may be suffered by the member's money purchase pot. Similarly, if the scheme is operated by an insurance company or similar provider (e.g. if it is a personal pension scheme or stakeholder pension scheme) the member is unlikely to have a valid claim against the insurance company or provider if the ultimate pension is of a smaller amount than the member had hoped. This assumes of course that the employer (or provider) has not promised (or otherwise guaranteed) the member that he will receive a pension of a particular amount. Generally speaking, neither employers nor providers make such promises or guarantees.

Such a risk on the part of the member arises simply because of the nature of defined contribution schemes, and this is one of the reasons why defined contribution schemes have become popular (at least amongst employers) in recent years - from the perspective of employers, they can determine in advance what their likely future pension costs will be (since they know the rates at which they have agreed to pay contributions) and provided they pay their contributions promptly and in full, they will (generally) have fulfilled their legal obligations in relation to their employees' pension schemes. From an employer's perspective, defined benefit schemes (which we discuss below) do not offer the same degree of certainty.

8.3   Defined benefit pension schemes

Defined benefit pension schemes are generally regarded (at least by employees) as the "deluxe" version of pension schemes. They have a long history (Samuel Pepys, whilst working as a naval administrator in the 1660s reputedly established a form of defined benefit pension scheme for the benefit of his predecessor in office) and they became popular (in the private sector) after the Second World War, when many such arrangements were established. Similarly, defined benefit pension schemes dominated (and still dominate) the public sector - the Civil Service Pension Scheme, the Teachers' Pensions Scheme, the pension schemes operated for members of the Armed Services and other public sector schemes all operate on the defined benefit basis.

Defined benefit pension schemes were very common in the private sector until the 1990s, when rising pension costs, coupled with poor investment returns and increased regulation, led to increasing numbers of employers adopting the view that defined benefit schemes were becoming too expensive and too risky to operate. Over the last decade or so, there has been a swing away from the provision of defined benefit pension schemes to defined contribution pension schemes; nevertheless, large numbers of defined benefit pension schemes remain in existence although many are now closed to new entrants (i.e. new recruits to the employer's workforce), who will generally only be offered membership of a defined contribution pension scheme upon commencing employment. Nevertheless, some employers do still operate defined benefit pension schemes which remain open to new entrants, while anyone commencing work in the public sector may well find themselves having the opportunity to join a defined benefit pension scheme. For these reasons, and in order to understand the contrasts between defined benefit pension schemes and defined contribution pension schemes, it is useful to have at least an overview as to how defined benefit pension schemes work.

As discussed above, defined contribution pension schemes essentially operate on the basis that contributions are paid into a member's money purchase pot, and the value of the resulting pension depends upon how well these contributions are invested over the period until the member's retirement and the cost of providing a pension at retirement. There is (generally speaking) no guarantee as to the level of the ultimate pension which will be provided under a defined contribution pension scheme, and it is the individual members who bear the risk that the accumulated money purchase pots will be unable at the end of the day to fund adequate pensions. (On the other hand, if the investment returns are good and interest rates at retirement are favourable, then it is the member who benefits).

In contrast, as the name suggests, defined benefit pension schemes are operated on the basis that there is certainty as to the future level of pension benefits to be provided (although this does not, of course, mean that defined benefit pension schemes cannot (and do not) fail, leading to members ultimately receiving only a fraction of their promised level of benefits).

Typically, benefits are defined by reference to an accrual formula, which can vary depending upon the nature of the relevant pension scheme; however, a typical accrual formula would be:

$$P = 1/60 \times FPS \times PS$$

This is known as the "1/60ths" accrual basis.

P is the annual amount of the pension paid from the "normal pension date" or "NPD" (sometimes known as the "normal pension age"; i.e. the date upon which a member can retire and claim a pension as of right) - typically age 65 at present;

FPS is the retiring member's "final pensionable salary" at NPD (i.e. his salary at, or averaged over a period of time immediately prior to his NPD); and

PS is the retiring member's period of pensionable service, (that is the time during which the member has been actively accruing a pension under the defined benefit pension scheme - during this period, the member will usually be referred to as an "active member" of the pension scheme). Generally speaking, this will be the period during which the member pays contributions to the pension scheme (although some pension schemes do not require that the members pay contributions).

Worked Example

Suppose a member of a defined benefit scheme (providing benefits on a 1/60ths accrual basis) reaches his NPD after having been an active member of the pension scheme for 20 years. Suppose too that his final pensionable salary is £60,000 per annum and that at retirement, he takes his retirement benefits entirely in the form of a pension (i.e. he does not take part of his benefit entitlement in the form of a tax-free lump sum). In this case, the member's pension at NPD would be

1/60 x 20 x £60,000 = £20,000 per annum

As in the case of (occupational) defined contribution pension schemes, defined benefit pension schemes are funded by contributions from the employer (and usually, but not always, from member contributions), which are paid into the scheme, with the pensions ultimately being funded from the resulting "pension fund" either directly or indirectly by means of the purchase of annuities. However, unlike defined contribution pension schemes, the pension payable out of a defined benefit pension scheme is calculated by reference to the accrual formula, and not by reference to the value of the pension fund or the actual cost of purchasing annuities. Consequently, if there is a shortfall (i.e. deficit) in the pension fund (and over the last five to ten years, many defined benefit pension schemes have suffered serious deficits) then that shortfall must be addressed one way or another in order for the scheme to be able to provide the pensions as promised. Generally speaking, it will be addressed by reviewing the scheme's investment portfolio and (crucially) by increasing contribution rates (usually those of the employer), sometimes quite dramatically.

MONEY

This is probably an appropriate point to add that just as the funding level of a defined benefit scheme bears no direct relationship to the value of a member's accrued pension entitlement, the employer (and indeed, the employee) contribution rate also bears no (direct) relationship to the value of the entitlement. To put it another way, a member of a defined benefit pension scheme cannot gauge the value of his or her pension entitlement simply by considering the employer's contribution rate. That contribution rate may be high because the employer is seeking to reduce the size of a deficit in the pension fund. Alternatively, the employer contribution rate could be low (or even set at zero - this is commonly known as a "contribution holiday") because the scheme is in fact overfunded. Contribution holidays are unusual at the present time, when so many defined benefit schemes are in deficit, but were fairly common in the early 1990s, when many schemes were in surplus (and the Government of the day introduced financial penalties designed to discourage the overfunding of the defined benefit schemes).

It is worth noting that once in payment, pensions provided under a defined benefit occupational pension scheme must (with a few minor exceptions) be increased as follows:
- Any element of pension arising in respect of pensionable service on or after 6 April 1997 (and prior to 6 April 2005) must be increased by a minimum of the lesser of 5 percent each year and the increase in the retail prices index for that period (this is sometimes known as "limited price indexation");
- Any element of pension arising in respect of pensionable service on or after 6 April 2005 must be increased by a minimum of the lesser of 2.5 percent each year and the increase in the retail prices index.

(There is no requirement for the mandatory increase in pensions in payment arising under defined contribution schemes where the pension came into payment on or after 6 April 2005).

8.4 Early and late retirement

Regardless of whether an individual is a member of a defined contribution pension scheme or a defined benefit pension scheme, he will be able to claim his pension "as of right" when he reaches his NPD.

Usually, the member's NPD will be the same as his State Pension Age ("SPA"), although it is possible for these two dates to be different. Pension schemes are also usually designed to allow a member's pension to come into payment before or after NPD - although whether any particular member can actually afford to take early retirement even if he has the opportunity of doing so is a different matter. Pensions cannot generally come into payment before the member's 50th birthday (save where the member is suffering from a serious illness and is entitled to claim an "ill-health pension" from the pension scheme) - this minimum age requirement is due to rise to the member's 55th birthday by 2010.

Early and late retirement pensions generally pose few problems when provided under defined contribution pension schemes (since the pension to be provided will simply be funded out of the member's money purchase pot). However, it is usual for an early retirement pension from a defined benefit pension scheme to be reduced to allow for the fact that it will be (or at least is likely to be) in payment for longer than would have been the case if the pension had only commenced at the member's NPD[9]. Such a reduction (often known as an "actuarial reduction") will be dictated by the rules of the pension scheme and can in some cases be quite severe - actuarial reductions of 30% or more of the member's "original pension" are not unknown.

Similarly, delaying a pension for a period of time after NPD can lead to an increase in the value of a late retiring member's annual pension, usually by applying an actuarial enhancement reflecting the fact that the pension is likely to be in payment for a shorter period than was anticipated - although other methods of enhancement (for example permitting the member to continue to remain in pensionable service and thus accrue further pensions benefits after NPD) also exist.

---

[9] In other words, if it is anticipated that a member will survive (say) fifteen years after his NPD, then broadly the actual pension costs to the defined benefit pension scheme will increase if the member were to be allowed to retire five years early on an unreduced pension - since that member's pension will thus be in payment for twenty years rather than fifteen.

8.5 Death Benefits

Pension schemes are not only designed to provide retirement benefits for the actual member(s) but are also capable of providing pensions for the member's spouse (or civil partner) and dependants, (the latter generally meaning children and adults dependent upon the member, for example, by reason of disability). In the case of occupational defined benefit pension schemes, spouses'/civil partners' and dependants' pensions will come into payment upon the death of the member, and will be payable for life in the case of a spouse's/civil partner's pension or an adult dependant's pension. In the case of a child's pension, following recent changes to pension legislation, these may now be paid until the age of 23. The value of these pensions will depend upon the rules of the relevant pension scheme. Death benefits are also often available under defined contribution pension schemes; however, as such schemes generally provide their pensions via annuities, in order for spouses'/civil partners' and dependants' pensions to be provided, appropriate annuities capable of providing such benefits must be selected (and if selected, the member's own pension will be reduced accordingly since the member's pension pot must be used to fund not only the member's pension but also his spouse's/civil partner's and/or dependants' pensions). In the case of some defined contribution schemes, the member is given a choice as to whether or not he wishes to choose an annuity capable of providing a spouse's/civil partner's/dependant's pension.

Such pensions are usually paid regardless of whether or not the member had retired before death. However, if the member dies whilst in pensionable service, many occupational pension schemes also provide a lump sum benefit (typically from one to four times the deceased member's salary). Such lump sum benefits are usually paid by the trustees of the scheme to whomsoever they elect from a list of eligible recipients, but members are usually encouraged to nominate potential recipients. The trustees may have regard to the wishes of the deceased member as so expressed but are not bound by them. This is so as to ensure that any such lump sum payment cannot be deemed to form part of the deceased member's estate and thus enables the lump sum to be paid free of inheritance tax.

We should add that employers sometimes arrange for "lump sum death-in-service benefits" coverage to be provided for all employees, regardless of whether or not they are actually active members of the pension scheme - employees so covered who are not active members are often referred to as "life cover only members". Employers often provide such life cover through separate life assurance arrangements (rather than via pension schemes) for their employees. Life cover only members are generally not obliged to pay for the benefit of such life cover.

8.6 Member Nominated Trustees

If you join your employer's occupational pension scheme, you are likely at some point to be offered the opportunity to vote for one or more member nominated trustees (or "MNTs" as they are commonly known)[10]. You may even consider standing for election for the post of MNT yourself. It is useful therefore, to understand how MNTs operate.

MNTs were introduced by the Government in 1997, as it was felt that members of occupational pension schemes should have an opportunity to elect at least some of the trustees representing their interests under their occupational pension schemes. (The MNT legislation does not of course apply in relation to personal pension schemes or stakeholder pension schemes). Originally, the "MNT requirement" was that members had to be offered the opportunity to nominate and elect at least one-third of the trustees of an occupational pension scheme (although the MNT requirement did not (and does not) apply in relation to certain specialised types of occupational pension schemes (for example, non-registered pension schemes (as discussed in section 8.7) or schemes with fewer than two members); however, such schemes are rarely relevant to most employees). The one-third requirement remains the law.

---

[10] If your pension scheme has a trustee company (that is, a company which fulfils the duties of a trustee), rather than individual trustees, instead of voting for MNTs you will be asked to vote for "member nominated directors". However, regardless of whether you vote for "MNTs" or "MNDs", the principles remain the same, and in this section we shall simply refer to MNTs.

However, the MNT legislation as originally drafted permitted employers to "opt out" of the MNT requirement (with member consent) and many employers in fact did this, with the effect that the MNT legislation was disapplied in respect of many occupational pension schemes. In order to address this, the ability of the employer to opt out was abolished, and all current employer opt-outs are scheduled to lapse by no later than 31 October 2007.

It is the responsibility of the trustees of an occupational pension scheme to ensure that their scheme is in compliance with the MNT legislation. If a vacancy arises in relation to which you are eligible to vote (and/or nominate a candidate), they will write to tell you and specify the steps you should take if you wish to participate in the process. Generally speaking, all active members and pensioners will be eligible to vote for and nominate candidates. Deferred pensioners (that is, individuals who have a pension entitlement under the scheme, but have ceased to be in pensionable service without commencing receipt of their pension – they may, for example, be working for another employer or perhaps are now self-employed and may have entered into new pension arrangements) are not usually so entitled.

There are several other points which should be noted in relation to MNTs:

- At law, an MNT has the same duties and powers as any other trustee. Consequently, if an individual is elected as an MNT, he is under a legal duty to act in the best interests of all the beneficiaries of the pension scheme, in accordance with its governing provisions and the general law in exactly the same way as any other trustee.
- Although the minimum threshold for MNTs is one-third of the total number of trustees, it is possible for a greater number of MNTs to be elected into office, provided the employer so consents (in our experience, they seldom do).
- Non-members can be elected as MNTs, but (again) only if the employer so consents (and again, they seldom do).
- MNTs (and indeed any other employee who is a trustee) are offered certain legal protections. In particular they must be allowed time off work (without suffering any salary reduction) to perform their duties

and carry out trustee training. Moreover, they can claim unfair dismissal if they are dismissed by their employer if the reason (or primary reason) for the dismissal is that they carried out any act (or failed to act) as a consequence of being a trustee.

8.7 Tax advantages of pension schemes

We have already mentioned that pension schemes may be considered to be tax advantaged saving vehicles. This statement actually requires a degree of clarification: pension schemes (and the members of pension schemes) enjoy certain tax advantages if the pension schemes are "registered pension schemes" (which the vast majority of pension schemes will be) and provided the relevant individual member's level of "pensions savings" does not exceed certain limits[11]. Within the limits of these constraints registered pension schemes can confer certain tax advantages. It should be emphasised that this is a complex area; what follows is a brief general description of the tax advantages. Detailed descriptions of the various tax advantages and the circumstances in which they can be enjoyed can be found in HMRC's Registered Pension Schemes Manual
(www.hmrc.gov.uk/manuals/rpsmmanual/index.htm).

The tax advantages enjoyed by registered pension schemes include:
- Subject to the points we make below in relation to the "Annual Allowance", any contributions paid by the member to the pension scheme receive tax relief (i.e. they do not form part of the member's taxable income). Exactly how this relief is provided will depend upon the nature of the relevant pension scheme.
- Contributions paid by the employer will not be treated as "benefit-in-kind" - type payments upon which the HMRC will seek to tax the member.

---

[11] Pension schemes which are unregistered do not enjoy the tax advantages of registered schemes. They are however, relatively rare and you are unlikely to encounter them. Consequently, we do not discuss unregistered schemes in any great detail.

- With some minor exceptions, income and capital gains accrued by the pension scheme will not be taxed, allowing such income and capital gains to accumulate on a tax-free basis.[12]

- Pensions (once in payment) will be subject to income tax in the hands of the recipient; however, at retirement, members may take or "commute" (to use typical pensions jargon) part of the pension entitlement (generally not exceeding 25% of the member's money purchase pot, or 25% of the capital value of the member's pension entitlement in the case of a defined benefit scheme) in the form of a tax-free lump sum if the rules of the pension scheme so permit (which generally they will do), and provided the relevant Lifetime Allowance limits (discussed further below) are not exceeded.

- Even if an individual is not a taxpayer, he or she can still obtain tax relief on pension contributions up to £3,600 per year (including the benefit of tax relief granted by the Government).

As mentioned above, the tax advantages provided by a registered pension scheme only apply in respect of a member's pension savings below certain limits. Broadly speaking:

- An individual may contribute to a defined contribution pension scheme (or have contributions made on his or her behalf) up to 100% of his or her (taxable) earnings and enjoy tax relief on the contributions so made, subject to an annual limit (known as the "Annual Allowance"). In the case of a defined benefit pension scheme (where the pension contributions paid have no direct relationship to the pension benefits which are being built up), the Annual Allowance "test" is applied to the yearly increase in the amount of the accrued pension benefits. Most defined benefit pension schemes' accrual rates will not exceed the Annual Allowance and therefore the Annual Allowance is generally most relevant to defined contribution pension schemes. For the tax year 2007/2008, the Annual Allowance is

---

[12] Pension schemes are less tax efficient than they were, thanks to the Chancellor's decision in July 1997 to withdraw the ability of pension schemes to reclaim dividend tax credits. It has been estimated that this action has cost pension schemes over £5 billion each year since 1997.

£225,000; this is due to rise to £255,000 by the tax year 2010/2011, following which it is to be reviewed. Where the Annual Allowance is exceeded, the individual member (not the pension scheme) will be liable to an "annual allowance charge" of 40% of the excess.

- An individual's accumulated pension savings will also be subject to a "Lifetime Allowance" test when they come into payment (or at age 75, if earlier)[13]. The Lifetime Allowance has been set at £1.6 million in respect of the 2007/2008 tax year and is expected to rise to £1.8 million by 2010/2011 following which (as in the case of the Annual Allowance), it is to be reviewed. Special rules apply if you were lucky enough to accumulate pension benefits in excess of £1.5 million before 6 April 2006 ("A" Day) when these limits came into effect.

- If an individual's accumulated pension savings exceed the Lifetime Allowance when the test is applied (which will generally be when a benefit comes into payment – otherwise known as a "benefit crystallisation event") tax charges are levied on the excess. Such charges are in addition to any income tax charge arising in respect of any benefit in payment.

- If an individual has more than one registered pension scheme (for example, if he has more than one personal pension scheme), his accrued pension savings will be aggregated when applying the Annual Allowance and Lifetime Allowance tests.

8.8 Discrimination and pension schemes

Broadly speaking, it is illegal for a pension scheme to be operated on a basis which discriminates between male and female members.[14] This can be a surprisingly complex area, but means for example:

- Contributions paid by employers in respect of female members to defined contribution schemes (whether occupational pension schemes, personal pension schemes or stakeholder schemes) must be calculated

---

[13] Unless you happen to be a judge. The Lord Chancellor has decided that the judicial pension schemes should not be treated as registered pension schemes and thus are exempt from the Annual Allowance and Lifetime Allowance tests.

[14] There are a number of technical exceptions to this general statement.

at the same rate(s) as contributions paid on behalf of comparable male members. Similarly, the rate of contributions required to be paid by the members themselves cannot vary depending on whether the relevant member is male or female (although there is of course nothing to prevent individual members themselves voluntarily paying additional contributions if they so wish).

- In relation to defined benefit occupational pension schemes, normal pension dates (NPDs) of male and female members must be "equalised". Historically, this requirement (originally arising as a result of a decision of the European Court of Justice in 1990 in a case commonly known as "Barber") has posed many problems in relation to defined benefit schemes since many schemes established before 1990 did indeed operate on the basis of differing NPDs for men and women (typically male NPDs were age 65, whilst female NPDs were age 60, the intention being that retirement benefits from the occupational pension schemes should come into payment at the same time as pensions from the state pension scheme). There was initially some confusion following the Barber judgement as to how schemes should equalise their NPDs, but this was (largely) clarified in a subsequent series of decisions by the Courts, and certainly any pensions presently being accrued should do so on the basis of a common NPD for male and female members (typically, but not invariably, age 65).

- The exclusion from membership of pension schemes of part-time workers (and in certain circumstances, temporary workers) may constitute illegal indirect sex discrimination (since, for example, part-time workers tend more often to be female than male and thus the exclusion of part-timers may have a disproportionate effect on females as compared to males in a comparable situation).

Others forms of anti-discrimination laws also apply to pension schemes. For example, it would of course be illegal for an employer to deny an employee access to a pension scheme (or to offer membership on less favourable terms than other members) on the grounds of race, sexual orientation or disability.

The new anti-age discrimination legislation now also applies to pension schemes, although (in relation to pension matters) the legislation contains many exemptions which means that many practices which at first sight would appear to constitute age discrimination are in fact permissible. By way of example, the application of age-related actuarial factors and (in certain circumstances) age-related contributions will continue to be permissible. Nevertheless, broadly speaking, the effect of the new anti-age discrimination legislation will be that employees working after NPD whose employers offer pension scheme membership to comparable employees who have not yet attained NPD must now also be given the opportunity to continue to accrue pension benefits (and, where applicable, to continue to enjoy the benefit of death-in-service cover). We discuss the anti-discrimination legislation in greater detail in Chapter 11.

8.9 Stakeholder Pension Schemes

As a general rule, employers are not obliged under the general law to provide (or contribute to) a pension scheme for their employees. Under legislation introduced in 1999, they are however obliged to "designate" stakeholder pension schemes for the benefit of their employees provided certain conditions are met.

Stakeholder pension schemes were introduced by the Government in order to encourage individuals to save for their retirement. They are intended to be individual defined contribution arrangements (rather like personal pension schemes in fact), but with a low cost and simple charging structure. Providers of stakeholder pension schemes are not permitted to levy annual charges exceeding 1% of the stakeholder pension scheme's accumulated fund (although certain other "additional" charges are permissible); nor can they penalise members for transferring their accumulated money purchase pots in or out, or for varying their pension contributions.

As stated above, employers are obliged to designate stakeholder pension schemes in certain circumstances. "Designation" in this context means that the employer must provide details of the stakeholder pension schemes to its employees and permit any employees who wish to contribute to their stakeholder pension schemes to do so by means of deductions from payroll. Employers are not, however, themselves obliged to contribute to their employees' stakeholder pension schemes (although they may do so if this is agreed by the employer and employee).

The obligation to designate (and provide access to) stakeholder pension schemes applies to all employers, except for:
- Employers with fewer than five employees;
- Employers who offer their employees access to an occupational pension scheme (with a membership waiting period of 12 months or less, and with a minimum qualifying age of no more than 18 and a maximum qualifying age of no more than five years below the scheme's NPD);
- Employers who offer to contribute to a GPP (satisfying certain minimum requirements) at a rate of at least 3 per cent of the employees' basic pay;
- Employers whose workforces earn less than the National Insurance lower earnings limit.

Moreover, employers are not required to designate a stakeholder pension scheme in respect of any employee who could have joined their employer's occupational pension scheme but has declined to do so, and is now not eligible to join. Nor is an employer obliged to designate a stakeholder pension scheme in respect of any employee who has been employed for less than three months.

8.10 How do I join a pension scheme?
If you are an employee, the terms of any pension scheme available to you will usually be explained to you by your employer often at the commencement of your employment. Your employment contract is unlikely to say a great deal about your pension scheme - generally an employment contract will simply refer to the existence of a pension scheme, and state that you can elect to join subject to its governing provisions. More details will usually be found in your employer's staff handbook (assuming that there is one) and you may (should) be offered an explanatory booklet describing the terms of the pension scheme.

As regards the actual mechanism of joining the pension scheme, you will usually be asked to fill in an application form stating that you wish to join the scheme and agree that member contributions should be deducted from your salary (generally on a monthly basis). You may also be asked to sign a death in service nomination form. An employer may however, operate a pension scheme on the basis that all employees will automatically join the pension scheme, unless they "opt out". If your employer operates such a system, this should be explained to you. You cannot be forced to join and remain an active member of a pension scheme against your will. Your employer can however, provide death benefit cover for you without your consent.

Occasionally, you may find that you are obliged to have been employed by the employer for a period of time before you can join the pension scheme. You may also find that if you do not join the pension scheme at your first opportunity, you cannot later join the pension scheme without the consent of your employer (and possibly the trustees of the pension scheme if the scheme is an occupational pension scheme).

If you are self-employed (or if your employer does not offer a pension scheme), then selecting a suitable personal pension scheme is really up to you. We would recommend that you speak to an independent financial adviser (one who offers to charge by a fee arrangement rather than on a commissions basis), who should be able to recommend a suitable pensions provider to you. (In addition, you may also be eligible to contribute to a stakeholder pension scheme, as previously discussed).

8.11 What happens if I change jobs or want to leave a pension scheme for some other reason?

As we mention above, you cannot be forced to become an active member of a pension scheme and can cease to be in pensionable service (i.e. cease to be an active member) if you so wish, regardless of whether or not you remain an employee of the employer who has "sponsored" the pension scheme. (Of course, whether this is a wise course of action to take is another matter and we would urge you to take appropriate professional advice before taking any such step.) If you are a member of an occupational pension scheme and you leave your employment, you will

MONEY

almost certainly find that you must also cease active membership of the occupational pension scheme as well. If, however, you are a member of a personal pension scheme (e.g. one forming part of a GPP sponsored by your employer) or a stakeholder pension scheme, you may find that you can continue to contribute to that personal or stakeholder pension scheme - you should speak to the personal or stakeholder pension scheme provider in such circumstances, who will be able to advise you of any steps you may need to take.

If you have joined an occupational pension scheme and later on (before you reach your NPD) and without taking an early retirement pension, you cease to be an active member of the pension scheme, you will be deemed to be an "early leaver" under your pension scheme's governing provisions. Hopefully, you should have been given an explanatory booklet when you joined the pension scheme which will explain the rights you will have as an early leaver; in any event the pension scheme's rules must allow you the following options:

- If you have (or are treated as having) two or more years' accrued pension benefits under the pension scheme (sometimes referred to as the two year vesting period or the two years' qualifying service requirement), you will have the right to be treated as a deferred pensioner under the scheme. This means that your accrued pension benefits are retained under the scheme until they come into payment (for example, when you reach your NPD) or until you decide to transfer those rights to another pension scheme. We should add that strictly speaking, it is possible in certain circumstances for your accrued pension benefits to be transferred to another scheme without your consent - such transfers are known as "without consent transfers" and typically occur where (for example) an employer operating two pension schemes seeks to merge them together. The rules governing without consent transfers include certain provisions intended to protect accrued pension benefits which are the subject of a without consent transfer.

- Provided you have satisfied the two year vesting period requirement, in addition to having the right to be treated as a deferred pensioner, you will also have a statutory right to elect for the transfer of your accrued pension benefits to another registered pension scheme (for example, to a personal pension scheme) if that pension scheme is willing to accept the transfer of your accrued pension benefits; not all pension schemes are willing to do so. This statutory transfer right - commonly called a "cash equivalent" transfer right - is generally not available to individuals who are within one year of their NPD, or (in certain circumstances) if they ceased to be an active member of the pension scheme before 1 January 1986 or if the pension scheme is in the process of being wound up. Electing to take a cash equivalent transfer can have an adverse effect on the value of your accrued pension benefits if your pension scheme is a defined benefit pension scheme and you should consider taking independent financial advice before exercising your rights in this regard. Occasionally, you may be offered the opportunity to elect to take an "enhanced" transfer (i.e. a transfer calculated on more generous terms then a cash equivalent transfer) - again, we would recommend that you take independent financial advice before taking any final decision.

- If you wish to exercise your statutory right to a cash equivalent transfer, you should contact the trustees of your pension scheme who will explain the steps you need to take in order to make the election. They should offer you a transfer statement quoting the transfer value available and which will explain the various options available to you. Generally speaking, you have the right to request a transfer statement once a year. Transfer values can (and will) vary, depending upon the exact circumstances in which they are made and the type of scheme from which they are paid.

- If you have less then two years' qualifying service (i.e. you have not satisfied the two year vesting period) you do not have a (statutory) right to be treated as a deferred pensioner. (You may have an analogous right under the governing provisions of your pension scheme, although this is relatively uncommon). If, however, you have at least three months' pensionable service under your pension scheme (but no vested rights) you will be entitled to a "cash transfer sum" (effectively a transfer calculated in the same way as a cash equivalent transfer) or (where the rules of the pension scheme so permit) a refund of your contributions. Any refunded contributions will be taxable at the rate of 20% on the first £10,800 and at the rate of 40% of any excess. If, however, you have less than three months' pensionable service (and no vested rights), you will not have a statutory right to a cash transfer sum, although you may still be entitled to a refund of your contributions. Further details of your rights and options in this regard should be set out in your pension scheme's explanatory booklet.

If you are member of a personal pension scheme (or a stakeholder pension scheme) you will have also have the right to be treated as a deferred pensioner or to elect for a transfer value to be paid on your behalf (although the two year vesting period applicable to occupational pension schemes does not apply to personal pensions schemes or stakeholder pension schemes; i.e. there is immediate vesting, meaning you can become a deferred pensioner even if you have less than two years' worth of scheme membership). Should you wish to transfer your accrued pension benefits to another registered scheme, you should contact the manager of your personal or stakeholder pension scheme who will be able to advise you of the options available to you.

As we mentioned above, if you are an early leaver from an occupational pension scheme and have (or are treated as having) more than two years' worth of accrued pension benefits, you have the right to be treated as a deferred pensioner under your pension scheme. Historically, one of the problems associated with being a deferred pensioner under a defined benefit occupational pension scheme was the effect that inflation could have on the value of your deferred pension benefits over the period of time until your benefits came into payment. To address this issue (at least partially), the concept of the mandatory revaluation of deferred benefits was introduced, which provides a degree of inflation proofing to your deferred benefits.

Revaluation of deferred benefits under defined benefit occupational pension schemes is a complex area, with different methods applying depending upon the exact nature of the pension scheme. Broadly speaking, however, limited price indexation (which we mentioned previously in the context of mandatory increases to pensions in payment) will be applied to the deferred pension (although you will by now not be surprised to know there are exceptions to this general statement). Your explanatory handbook should provide you with further details as to how your deferred benefits under a defined benefit occupational pension scheme are calculated.

If you are a deferred pensioner under a defined contribution pension scheme (whether an occupational pension scheme, a personal pension scheme or a stakeholder pension scheme), revaluation is in practice less of an issue, since effectively your money purchase pot will remain invested and receive the benefit of any investment gains (e.g. dividends, capital growth etc) - and conversely, will suffer any investment losses which may arise in respect of the underlying investments.

8.12 Pensions and Divorce

For most people, their most valuable asset (with the possible exception of their home) will be the pension benefits which they have built up over the years. It is therefore not surprising that the Courts are empowered to take pension benefits into account when addressing the issue of financial settlements on divorce. Broadly speaking, there are a number of ways that pension benefits may be taken into account when dividing property on divorce:

- Earmarking. Under the earmarking procedure, the pension benefits are retained in the name of the relevant party; however, upon the benefits come into payment, the other party will receive a specified proportion of the benefits. An obvious disadvantage of earmarking is that the second party can only begin to receive his or her "share" of the benefits when they come into payment to the first party. This disadvantage means that earmarking has become less common in recent years.

- Pensions Sharing. Under this approach, the pension benefits are actually divided so that both parties have pension benefits which are held in their respective names subject to the rules of the relevant pension scheme. (It should, however, be noted that some schemes are designed so that the ex-spouse (or ex-civil partner) being granted a share of the member's accrued pension benefits will be obliged to transfer those granted benefits out of the pension scheme (for example, into a personal pension scheme)). The major advantage of pensions sharing is that both parties will have rights to pension benefits which are independent of one another. Pensions sharing is also available in relation to civil partners whose civil partnerships are dissolved or nullified.

- Offsetting. A third possible approach is to "offset" the value of one party's pension rights against the other financial assets available for the purposes of the settlement, so that for example, one party retains his or her full entitlement under the relevant pension scheme, whilst the other party may receive a larger cash sum, or a larger share of the house. Offsetting too is available in relation to civil partnerships.

8.13 Can my pension rights be taken away from me?

Or to put it another way, can your accrued pension benefits be "forfeited"? When we discuss forfeiture, we do not mean the "loss" of benefits as a result of earmarking or pension sharing upon divorce; nor are we referring to losses arising because a pension scheme has "failed" due to underfunding problems. Essentially, we are referring to the removal of your rights to the pension benefits you have earned, the loss of such rights being a "punishment" of some kind. Moreover, we are principally considering pension benefits which have accrued under an occupational pension scheme; the forfeiture of pension benefits is not usually an issue in relation to personal or stakeholder pension schemes.

Generally speaking, it is very difficult for pension benefits to be forfeited; forfeiture can only occur in very specific circumstances. For example, forfeiture is permitted if the member has been convicted of very serious offences, such as treason, or certain offences under the Official Secrets Acts. Moreover, rights to benefits can be lost if they are not claimed by the person who is entitled to receive them (who need not be the member, of course) within six years of them coming into payment. Benefits can also be forfeited if the person to whom they would otherwise be payable has caused a monetary loss to the pension scheme as a result of a criminal, negligent or fraudulent act (or omission) or (in the case of a trustee of the pension scheme) a breach of trust.

We should add that members are generally not supposed to assign, offset or charge their rights to pension benefits (since pension schemes are supposed to be used to build up funds to provide a retirement income, rather than be used for another financial purpose). Broadly speaking, an attempt to do any of these things will be void, but any such attempt may itself cause the forfeiture of the member's benefits. Having said that, it is possible for a member's benefits to be charged or subjected to an offset if the rules of the pension scheme so permit (and generally, they will do) and if the purpose is to allow the member's employer (or the pension scheme) to recover any amount owed to it as a result of any criminal, negligent or fraudulent act or omission on the part of the employee. Similarly, if the member is a trustee of the pension scheme and causes a loss to the scheme as a result of a breach of trust, the scheme can generally seek to recover the amount of the loss by way of forfeiture of the trustee member's benefits. It should be noted, however, that the amount of any charge, or set-off cannot be greater than the actual amount due or (if less) the value of the member's entitlement under the pension scheme (calculated in accordance with the relevant legislation).

8.14 Can my occupational pension scheme be changed?

Here, again, we are primarily considering occupational pension schemes. The basic answer to the question is yes, the terms of an occupational pension scheme may be changed. Generally speaking (as ever, this being a discussion of pension issues, there are exceptions) in order for a scheme's terms to be capable of change, the scheme's governing provisions must include an amendment power; it would however, be very unusual for such a power not to be included. Amendment powers are usually drafted so that the power is exercisable by the employer but only with the prior consent of the trustees (or vice versa). Moreover, there are legal restrictions which severely limit the ability to alter the terms of a pension scheme so as to reduce the "value" of the pension benefits which have accrued prior to the date of the exercise of the amendment power. In addition, employers (with more than 100 employees in Great Britain - this number is to be reduced to 50 in April 2008) and trustees are required to "consult" with affected members before making certain amendments (known as "listed changes" - these include changing the normal pension date, varying member contribution rates, closing the pension scheme and changing a defined benefit scheme into a defined contribution scheme). The consultation requirements also apply to personal pension schemes. The consultation exercise may take place with representatives of the employees (e.g. union officials) and whilst the consultation exercise must be carried out in good faith, the employer and trustees are not obliged to follow the wishes of the workforce. The consultation exercise must be carried out over a period of at least 60 days.

8.15 What if my pension scheme "fails"?

We have previously explained that a person's entitlement to a pension under a defined benefit pension scheme is dependent upon the scheme's benefit structure (and specifically, its accrual formula) and not the scheme's funding level from time to time. If a scheme has insufficient assets to meet its obligations, it is said to be in deficit, (although we should stress that there are various ways of measuring a deficit) and generally in such circumstances the trustees will look to the employer(s) participating in the pension scheme to remedy the deficit by increasing the rate of employer contributions payable to the pension scheme. If, however, the employer is unable to meet the additional funding costs so required, (for example, because the employer itself has become insolvent), the trustees may well have no choice but to wind up the scheme in deficit. Historically, if this occurred, the trustees' duty was to seek to realize the scheme's assets, and apply those assets to "secure" the members' benefit entitlements in accordance with the scheme's "winding-up priority rule". The purpose of the winding-up priority rule is to ensure that such assets as are available are applied for the benefit of the most vulnerable of members (typically pensioners). The net result however, is that in such circumstances, many members of the pension scheme (and people claiming "through" such members; e.g. spouses and dependants) could find their pension benefits cut back (perhaps drastically) because the scheme is simply unable to pay them.

As we say, this was the historic position, and it remains the case that a scheme wind-up can lead to the trustees applying the scheme's assets in this manner. However, the Government has recently introduced the

Pension Protection Fund ("PPF"), which is a statutory fund intended to provide some measure of protection for members of under-funded defined benefit pension schemes which meet certain criteria when the sponsoring employers suffer an "insolvency event" on or after 6 April 2005. If a scheme qualifies for entry into the PPF, the PPF essentially takes over responsibility for the scheme and members will receive benefits from the PPF.

Those benefits will not, however, necessarily be of the amounts to which the members were entitled under the rules of the pension scheme. Broadly speaking, beneficiaries who have already reached their scheme's NPD or (regardless of age) are in receipt of a survivor's pension (e.g. a spouse's pension) or an ill-health pension, will receive 100% of their pension.

Other beneficiaries' entitlements will be restricted to 90% of their accrued pension entitlement, subject to a maximum cap of £26,936 (for the year commencing 1 April 2007) at age 65. The cap will vary depending upon the recipient's age). In certain circumstances, dependants' pensions may be restricted even further.[15]

8.16 What if I have a complaint?

It may be that at some point, you encounter a problem in relation to your pension scheme membership. If this occurs (and, unfortunately, it does from time to time), there are a number of options available to you, depending on whether you are a member of an occupational pension scheme, or a personal or stakeholder pension scheme.

---

[15] In addition to the PPF, there also exists the Financial Assistance Scheme ("FAS") which was established to assist members of defined benefit occupational pension schemes which commenced wind-up after 1 January 1997 and before 6 April 2005. The FAS is (considerably) less generous than the PPF, and has been widely criticised for (so far) assisting only a small number of people. Further details of the FAS may be found at: www.dwp.gov.uk/lifeevent/penret/penreform/fas/

If you are a member of an occupational pension scheme, the trustees of the scheme should operate a system known as an "internal dispute resolution" procedure - or IDR. (There are some minor exceptions - for example, IDR is not required in relation to schemes with less then two members, or schemes whose members are all trustees. Such schemes are relatively rare, however, and we do not consider them here). IDR is essentially a mechanism which permits you to raise your concerns directly with the trustees of your pension scheme. Details of how you can present your complaint under IDR should be set out in your members' explanatory booklet. IDR should generally be regarded as the "first stage" when seeking to raise a complaint.

If you do not receive satisfaction under the IDR process, you may wish to seek the assistance of the Pensions Advisory Service ("TPAS"). TPAS is an organisation which provides access to volunteer pensions advisers who may be able to assist you by liaising with your trustees or employer or pensions administrator on your behalf. There is no fee for this service. As a general rule (there are occasional exceptions), you should have sought to address your concerns by means of IDR before approaching TPAS. However, if you have any doubts, contact TPAS in any event, and they will be able to advise you as regards a recommended course of action. Details of how to contact TPAS are set out in Appendix 1.

It is important to recognise that the role of TPAS is only to provide general assistance to individuals with pensions problems; TPAS cannot force any trustees or employer or pensions administrator to adopt any particular course of action. Moreover, TPAS is unable to provide financial advice or initiate legal proceedings. If TPAS is unsuccessful, and you still wish to pursue your complaint, you may wish to consider instructing a solicitor (although it must be admitted that this is likely to be a costly exercise. Legal aid is not available in relation to pension complaints).

As an alternative to instructing a solicitor, you may wish to consider lodging a complaint with the Pensions Ombudsman. The Pensions Ombudsman is able to hear complaints brought against employers, trustees and pensions scheme managers and administrators. Lodging a complaint is free, although some complainants do obtain legal or other professional advice when preparing their complaints. If a complaint is brought before the Ombudsman and he has jurisdiction to hear it, the Ombudsman will investigate the matter. Details of the Ombudsman's jurisdiction may be found on his website www.pensions-ombudsman.org.uk. The Ombudsman's jurisdiction is wide, but he cannot hear every complaint of a pensions nature. For example, as a general rule, he will not be able to hear complaints of a contractual "employment nature" which should more properly be raised before an employment tribunal.

Typically, if you bring a complaint before the Ombudsman which is within his jurisdiction, he will seek to contact the party against whom you have lodged a complaint, with a view to hearing "their side of the story". Both sides will be asked to provide any relevant information in their possession (for example, scheme documentation). Both sides will be allowed to comment on the other's arguments and once the Ombudsman is satisfied that no further enquiry is necessary, he will issue a "Determination" or ruling which is legally binding on both parties. Decisions of the Ombudsman may be appealed to the High Court, and from there to the Court of Appeal (but only on issues of law).

It is important to note that complaints must usually be brought before the Pensions Ombudsman within three years of the act (or omission) that is the subject of the complaint. The Pensions Ombudsman will only listen to complaints brought outside the three year period if he thinks it is reasonable to do so in the circumstances. Moreover, in most cases, the Pensions Ombudsman will be unwilling to hear a particular matter unless you have at least attempted to resolve it by means of the IDR/TPAS route.

The Ombudsman is also empowered to hear complaints (falling within his jurisdiction) arising in respect of personal pension schemes and stakeholder schemes.

8.17 The Pensions Tracing Service

If a person changes jobs a number of times during the course of his or her working life, it is surprisingly easy for them to lose track of their pension entitlements under the various pension schemes they may have joined over the years, particularly if their former employers or schemes have merged or changed names with the passage of time.

In order to address this problem, the Pensions Tracing Service was established, which maintains a register of occupational and personal pension schemes, the purpose of which is to assist people to trace their pension rights. Many (but not all) of the country's pension schemes are listed on the register. Details of how the Pensions Tracing Service operates and how it may be contacted, may be found at www.thepensionservice.gov.uk.

8.18 Who is the Pensions Regulator?

The Pensions Regulator is the new body created by the Government to "police" private sector pension schemes in the United Kingdom. He has widespread powers to monitor and if necessary intervene in the affairs of pension schemes and their employer(s) and one of his primary responsibilities is to encourage good governance and the prudent funding of pension schemes, so as to minimize the possibility of scheme failures. As we say, his powers are wide; he can for example become involved in the setting of pension scheme contributions and (in certain circumstances) he can require employers (and other members of the employers' corporate group) to remedy pension scheme deficits. Further details of the Pensions Regulator's role, and the approaches he adopts in relation to pensions issues may be found on his website at: www.thepensionsregulator.gov.uk.

8.19 The State Pension Scheme

The State Pension is paid to individuals who have made sufficient national insurance ("NI") contributions to qualify for an entitlement to it and who have reached the State Pension Age ("SPA"). At the moment, the SPA is age 60 for women and age 65 for men; however this discrepancy is due to be phased out by increasing the female SPA from 2010, so that by 2020, the SPA will have equalised at age 65 for men and women. In addition, as we have commented elsewhere, it is likely that the SPA will be increased (in stages) to age 68 between 2044 and 2048.

The State Pension (broadly speaking) is made up of two elements, the Basic State Pension and the State Second Pension (commonly known as "S2P").

8.19.1 The Basic State Pension

The Base State Pension is a flat rate pension paid by the State. The full Basic State Pension is increased each year; for the year 2007/2008, it is £87.30 per week for a single person. In order to qualify for a Basic State Pension, an individual must have paid (or otherwise been credited with) sufficient NI contributions. Broadly speaking, in order to qualify for a full Basic State Pension, an individual must have paid (or been credited with) NI contributions for approximately 90% of his working life (where an individual's working life is deemed to start on 6 April immediately preceding his sixteenth birthday, and end on 5 April immediately preceding his SPA).

If an individual's NI contributions record falls short (but exceeds 25% of the target), the individual will receive a reduced Basic State Pension. However, an NI contributions record which does not exceed 25% of the target will generally mean that the individual will not receive any Basic State Pension at all.

8.19.2 The State Second Pension

The Second State Pension - S2P - is (presently) a salary-related pension which is paid in addition to the Basic State Pension. S2P replaced an earlier earnings-related pensions system known as the State Earnings Related Pension Scheme ("SERPS") in April 2002, with the intention of improving state pension provision for employees on low and moderate incomes. It is anticipated that S2P will eventually become a flat rate pension scheme (rather than salary related).

The self-employed do not qualify for S2P pensions.

8.19.3 Contracting-Out

Contracting-out is a mechanism whereby employees who are members of a "contracted-out" pension scheme effectively waive their entitlements to pensions under S2P. Contracted-out pension schemes must satisfy certain criteria.

In exchange for waiving his or her entitlement to a S2P pension the employee and his employer pay NI contributions at a lower rate (the amount of the reduction being known as the "contracting-out rebate" if the employee is a member of an occupational pension scheme. (If the scheme is a defined benefit scheme, its benefit structure must satisfy certain criteria; if the scheme is a defined contribution scheme, the employer's contributions must be at least equal to the contracting-out rebate). Alternatively, if the employee "contracts-out" by means of a personal pension scheme or a stakeholder pension scheme, the employee (and his employer) will continue to pay NI contributions at the full rate, but the Government will pay a "rebate" of part of the NI contributions so paid to the provider of the personal pension scheme or the stakeholder pension scheme.

It is worth noting that even if an employee does not have access to a contracted-out occupational pension scheme (for example, because the pension scheme does not satisfy the contracting-out criteria, or because the employer does not offer any pension scheme at all), the employee can still contract-out by means of a "minimum contribution only" personal pension scheme (which can only accept the rebated NI contributions).

Whether or not it is a good idea to contract-out (or remain contracted-out) is a complex question and one which we would always suggest should be referred to an independent financial adviser.

8.19.4 The Pensions Credit

Poverty in old age is a major (and growing) problem. In an attempt to address this, the Government introduced a system known as "Pensions Credit" in 2003, which is intended to ensure that pensioners have at least a minimum income level. The system is complex, but effectively consists of two elements: "Guarantee Credit" and "Savings Credit" and (broadly speaking) is available to individuals in the UK aged 60 and over whose income and savings fall below certain thresholds (or in the certain circumstances, care for a disabled person).

Further details of the Pensions Credit system may be found at:
www.thepensionservice.gov.uk/pensionscredit/home.asp.

8.19.5 The Over 80 Pension

The Over 80 Pension is a pension provided by the state to people living in England, Wales and Scotland aged over 80 and who do not receive a full state pension (for example, because their NI contributions history is insufficient) or other social security benefits. At present, the Over 80 Pension is £52.30 per week if you do not get the state pension.

Further details may be found at:
www.thepensionservice.gov.uk/atoz/atozdetailed/over80.asp

8.20 The Future

It would be wrong to conclude our discussion of pensions without mentioning the Government's proposals for pensions reform.

These proposed reforms follow the report in December 2005 of the Pension Commission chaired by Lord Turner. Key aspects of the Government's proposals include:

- The increase of the SPA in stages to age 68 between 2044 and 2048;
- The gradual change of S2P into a flat rate pension, probably by 2030;
- A reduction in the period needed to qualify for a full state pension to 30 years;
- A restoration of the index linking of the state pension on an average earnings basis (so that the state pension will rise (approximately) in line with average earnings rather than in line with rises in the retail prices index);
- The eventual abolition of contracting-out in respect of defined contribution schemes;
- The creation of a new (defined contribution) National Pensions Savings Scheme providing "personal accounts" by 2012 into which all employees (aged over 22 and below State Pension Age and earning above £5,000, per annum) will automatically be enrolled unless they opt out. As at the time of writing, it is proposed that there will be mandatory minimum contributions calculated by reference to earnings between £5,000 and £33,500 (this band being revalued annually in line with earnings); individuals will contribute at the rate of 4%, employers will contribute at the rate 3% and the state (by means of tax relief) at the rate of 1%. Contributions in excess of the minimum employee and

employer limits may be paid subject to a maximum contribution limit of £3,600 per annum (which will also be revised annually). Employers will be exempt from the contribution obligations if they offer alternative private pension provision for their staff which satisfies certain criteria. Further details as to how the personal accounts will operate are expected to be released in due course.

PART TWO: WORK

9 Jobs

Employment Status –
    am I an employee?
    do I have employment rights?

9.1 The job life-cycle

We now move from the Money Section to consider various aspects of the working world. Before getting into the details, however, we should take a brief look at the lifecycle of a job. You may, of course, have several jobs during the course of your working life (and possible more than one at any time); this is becoming more common, partly due to increased lifespans but also because employment mobility is an accepted phenomenon in the modern working world (this was not always the case). Nevertheless, no matter how many jobs you may (ultimately) have, they will all have distinct phases, which may be described as follows:

- Phase 1 - Getting the job
- Phase 2 - Working
- Phase 3 - Leaving the job

Phase 1 of course involves the process of identifying potential employers, preparing your curriculum vitae (which is essentially a summary of your work experience and qualifications and commonly abbreviated to "CV") and job application forms, attending interviews and so on. There are numerous guides available which can provide advice on issues such as CV preparation and interview technique; the one point we would stress is the need to ensure accuracy in both your CV and your subsequent interviews. The provision of inaccurate information to a prospective employer (for example, errors as regards previous work experience or academic grades) may give the employer grounds for summarily dismissing you once the inaccuracy is discovered. Employers do carry out checks on the contents of employees' CVs, especially employers within highly regulated environments such as the legal and financial world. Dismissal is particularly likely if the error was deliberate (and indeed the provision of false information to a prospective employer could potentially constitute a criminal offence).[16]

Assuming that the prospective employer wishes to employ you, a job offer will be made to you. This will usually be made by means of a written offer in the form of a letter (although the offer could be oral); generally speaking an offer letter will summarise the most important employment terms (salary, available employee benefits, holidays, hours of work and so on) but will usually be subject to you entering into a formal written contract with the employer before or upon commencing work. (We discuss employment contracts and the terms they may contain below).

Phase 2 is the period during which you actually work for your employer, (and this can overlap with the period of Phase 3). During the course of your employment, you will be legally required to carry out your employment duties in accordance with the provisions of your contract of employment and general employment law; in return, your employer must satisfy its obligations under the contract (for example, paying your salary) and furthermore must meet any obligations imposed on it as a result of being an employer (for example, in respect of health and safety issues).

Phase 3 arises when you (or your employer) decide that your term of employment should end. The period following this decision until you actually leaving employment may not be long (indeed, leaving can be instantaneous, for example, in a situation where an employee is summarily dismissed or conversely, where an employee concludes that an employer's actions constitute constructive dismissal (see Chapter 10)). Generally, however, Phase 3 will last for several weeks or months and will usually commence upon the date on which the employee or employer gives the other party notice that the employment relationship is to terminate. (This assumes that the relevant employment contract is not a fixed term contract, which will automatically come to an end (unless

---

[16] For example, obtaining money (i.e. salary) by deception.

extended by the agreement of the parties) after a specified period of time).

As discussed below, in the case of an employment contract which is not for a fixed term, the party wishing to terminate the employment relationship must normally give the other "notice", although this requirement can be waived by agreement.

During a notice period, you will still be an employee and must continue to fulfil the contractual obligations under your employment contract. In particular, any restrictive covenants will continue to apply (indeed, they may continue to apply for a period of time after the employment relationship has come to an end), as will the general obligation on both you and the employer to act towards one another "in good faith". Although the employer may be quite happy for you to continue to carry out your normal work during your notice period, if your contract so permits, the employer would be within its rights to ask you to spend your notice period "on gardening leave"(see section 10.1.3 below).

When the employment relationship comes to an end, your employer should give you a P45 tax form (see section 7.6) which provides details of your pay and the tax you have already paid in the current tax year. The P45 form has four parts (Parts 1, 1A, 2 and 3); Part 1 is sent to HMRC by the employer, Part 1A should be retained by you, and Part 2 and 3 should be given to your new employer if you are moving to a new job. If you are a member of a pension scheme, you may have various options available depending on your pensions history and the nature of your pension scheme, as previously mentioned in Chapter 8.

If your departure from employment is acrimonious, you may consider taking legal action against your former employer (for example, brining a claim before an employment tribunal for wrongful and/or unfair dismissal). We discuss such matters in greater detail in Chapter 16.

9.2 Contractual Issues

We now turn to the issue of legal rights within the employment arena. On getting a job, not only does a new chapter in your life begin, but a whole new legal relationship is established with a new 'person' in your life, namely your employer. Whether you are an employee or not is now very important, and is critical to your rights and obligations, since employees have the benefit of employment protection legislation which is not available to the self-employed.

In the vast majority of cases, of course, there will be no doubt that you are an employee; just occasionally, however, doubts may arise. For this reason, it is useful to consider the criteria which apply in determining whether or not a person is, in fact, an employee.

An employee is a person who is employed under a "contract *of* service" or a "contract *of* employment" or a "contract *of* apprenticeship". For present purposes, we shall simply refer to a contract of employment.

In contrast, an independent contractor or self-employed person works under a "contract *for* services". The distinction between these two different types of relationship lies in the nature of the obligation undertaken.

A contract of employment can be "express" (that is, specifically and explicitly agreed between the employer and the employee) or implied (that is, arising "automatically", even if the parties have not expressly agreed the terms of the contract. See section 10.1.4 below). An express contract may either be "oral" (without a written document) or, more usually, in writing.

Contracts for services are not so well defined. Essentially, they will be contracts for the provision of services between two parties who do not form part of an employer-employee relationship; for example, the relationship between a householder and a window cleaner, or the relationship between a company and an engineer whose services are "hired" on a consultancy basis, but who is not an employee of the company.

9.3 The tests

In order to distinguish the potential confusion between contracts of employment and contracts for services, a number of legal tests have evolved. These tests are commonly known as the "Multiple Test", the "Mutuality of Obligation Test" and the "Tax Test". Perhaps the best way of understanding these various tests is to consider the following case histories which explain how the various tests have been applied by the courts in real life.

9.3.1 The Multiple Test

The Multiple Test means that the question of whether or not an individual is employed will depend on several factors. The test derives from a court case known as Ready Mixed Concrete which concerned the question of whether the driver of a lorry was employed or self-employed. Under the driver's contract:

- he bought the lorry he was to drive on a hire purchase agreement;
- he was obliged to wear the company's colours and company insignia;
- the lorry was to be painted in the company's colours along with the company insignia;
- use of the lorry was for company business only;
- the driver agreed to obey all reasonable orders 'as if he was an employee';
- the company could request that the vehicle be repaired, with the driver being responsible for all running and repair costs; and
- the driver was not obliged personally to drive the lorry, but was allowed to use a substitute driver.

Having heard all the evidence presented, the Court decided that the arrangement was not consistent with an employer-employee relationship, and that the driver must be self-employed. The Court reasoned that a contract of employment exists if the following three conditions are fulfilled:

- The employee must agree that in exchange for a wage or other remuneration he will provide his own work and skill in the performance of some service for his employer.
- The employee must agree (expressly or impliedly) that in the performance of that service he will be subject to the other's control to a sufficient degree to make the other "the employer".
- The other provisions of the contract must be consistent with its being a contract of employment.

A second example of the application of the Multiple Test arose in a case involving qualified gymnastic instructors working at sports centres operated by a Council. If an instructor could not take a class, she would arrange for a replacement from a register of coaches maintained by the Council. The replacements were paid by the Council and not by the relevant instructor. The Court held "The individual there, at his own choice, need never turn up for work. He could, moreover, profit from his absence if he could find a cheaper substitute." He could choose the substitute and then in effect he would be the employer. This was held to be inconsistent with the instructors being employees of the Council and therefore the instructors were held to be self-employed. Consequently, the instructors were not employees of the Council.

Therefore, in order for an individual to be an employee of another person (or company etc.), the relationship between the parties must be consistent with an employer-employee relationship.

9.3.2 The Mutuality of obligation test

For an employer-employee relationship to exist, there must be a "mutuality of obligation"; in other words, both the employer and employee must have obligations in respect of one another arising as a result of the existence of a contract of employment. The Mutuality of Obligation Test can be demonstrated by considering the approach adopted by the Court when deciding whether 'regular casuals', called in to work at banquets at a hotel, were employees.

Although in this case, there were a number of reasons to suggest that the casual workers were in fact employees (for example, that they were not in business on their own account, the hotel had a significant amount of control over the workers, there was a discipline and grievance procedure, and that permission was required in order to take time off from roster duties), the fact that the workers had no contractual right to claim compensation if they were not offered work, and equally, that they were under no obligation to accept work which was offered, indicated that they were self-employed. There was no mutuality of obligation between the casual workers and the hotel. The casual workers were effectively on 'standby' unless and until they were asked to come in and assist with a particular banquet. Consequently, the Court concluded that the workers were not employees and therefore could not benefit from employment protection legislation (specifically, they could not bring a claim for unfair dismissal).

The issue of casual staff was again considered by the highest court, the House of Lords, in 1999. The facts of this case were that the casual staff worked as power station tour guides for the Central Electricity Generating Board. At the time they were offered the work, they were required to sign a statement which read: 'I am pleased to accept your offer of employment as a station guide on a casual as required basis'. The casual staff received payment calculated by the number of hours they worked, less deductions made for income tax and NI contributions. Due to their position as 'casual as required', they were not obliged to take any work, and the CEGB did not guarantee that work would be available. The casual staff claimed to be entitled to a written statement of particulars, (a right which they would only have if they were employees). The House of Lords concluded that the guides were not employees as neither party incurred any obligations to accept or provide work. The guides had only agreed to be available for casual work as and when their services were required, and this arrangement did not amount to the degree of mutual obligation necessary to create a contract of service.

9.3.3 The Tax Test

Thirdly, we have what is known as the "Tax Test" under which the process of deciding whether a person carries on business on his or her own account or as an employee is determined by reference to fiscal (tax) matters. How the Tax Test works is best demonstrated by the case concerning a skilled television technician who worked for various (separate) companies on a series of short-term engagements. He made use of the equipment of the television company to which he provided his services at any particular time. Payment to him was made in the form of a lump sum (i.e. he did not receive a regular salary), plus travel expenses for each job that he undertook. Establishing his employment status was important for determining the basis on which he would pay income tax. On the facts, the Court decided that the technician was self-employed, but stressed that employment status should not be determined simply by running through some form of checklist; instead all the circumstances should be considered and evaluated. Accordingly: 'The whole picture has to be painted and then viewed from a distance to reach an informed and qualitative decision in the circumstances of the particular case.'

In summary, there is no "one test" which can be used to determine whether or not you are an employee. That said, the following factors are the most important in painting a picture of a person's work activity:

- the contractual provisions (for example, fees, expenses and holiday pay);
- the degree of control exercised by the "employer";
- the obligation of the "employer" to provide work;
- the obligation on the person to do the work;
- the provision of tools, equipment, instruments and the like;
- the arrangements made for tax, National Insurance contributions, sick pay and VAT;
- the opportunity to work for other employers;
- whether an arrangement in which a person is a self-employed independent contractor is genuine or whether it is designed to avoid the employment protection legislation.

9.4   Employment Status Checklist

EMPLOYED	SELF-EMPLOYED
Pays tax and national insurance contributions as an employed individual	Pays tax and national insurance contributions as a self-employed individual
Mutuality of obligation	NO mutuality of obligation
Controlled	Business on own account (own equipment/tools) – NOT controlled

Once you have ascertained and/or checked your employment status, as described above, if you are an employee, you have rights!

10 Rights and obligations at work

Employment rights/obligations –
    what rights do I have?
    what obligations have I agreed to?
    what are statutory rights?

10.1 Employment Contract

When you become an employee, you enter into a legally binding contract with your employer. An understanding of the terms of your contract is therefore important, if you want to understand what your rights and obligations are in respect of your employer (and what your employer's rights and obligations are towards you).

The main source of your rights and obligations will be the express terms contained in the contract itself (see section 10.1.2 below). Employers are legally required to give their employees "written statements of particulars" of many of the more important terms of their contracts within eight weeks of the employee starting work. Many employers, of course, provide their employees with formal contracts, rather than simply giving them the written particulars of the more important terms. Terms may be expressly incorporated by a reference in the contract to another document, such as a collective agreement (see section 15.2), but not all such terms are appropriate for incorporation; other documents may also be impliedly incorporated.

10.1.1 Statutory Written Statements

If you are given a written statement of particulars, it should contain the main terms of the contract, covering such matters as: pay, hours of work, holidays, sick pay, notice entitlement and the like.

The following particulars must all appear in a single document:
- the name of the employer and employee,
- the date of the start of employment with the employer,
- the date of the start of continuous employment, and
- the details relating to pay, hours of work, holiday entitlement, the employee's job title and the employee's place of work.

If the employer fails to provide a written statement, then, as a last resort, an employee may enforce his or her right to be given a written statement before an Employment Tribunal. (This is in addition to the employee's right to sue the employer for breach of contract before the ordinary courts or, where appropriate, the Employment Tribunal). Specifically, the employee may ask the Tribunal to decide which particulars ought to have been included, in cases where either no statement has been given or the statement does not comply with what is required. Where a statement has been given but there is a dispute as to what particulars ought to have been included or referred to in it, the employer or the employee may refer the matter to the Tribunal, which has the power to determine what particulars ought to have been included, or whether any particulars which were included should be confirmed, amended or substituted.

10.1.2 Express Contractual Terms

We have already noted that a contract of employment can be express (that is, it contains "express terms").

Express terms are the principal sources of contractual obligations, so the starting-point for determining the respective rights and obligations of the parties is the contract or written statement of particulars. The best evidence of an express term is a written term forming part of a written contract of employment, although, as noted above, a contract may be oral, or partly written and partly oral. However, in the absence of a written contract, the statutory written statement of particulars given to an employee is likely to provide the best evidence (though it is not conclusive evidence of the terms agreed).

Express terms of the contract may also be found in documents expressly or impliedly incorporated into the contract, such as collective agreements or staff handbooks. Express terms which are unreasonable may be declared voidable by the Courts.

10.1.3 Specific express terms

Some of the most common express terms are found in clauses dealing with the following matters:

- mobility
- working time

- pay
- benefits in kind
- holidays
- 'garden or gardening leave'
- notice and pay in lieu of notice

and are discussed below.

Mobility

The written statement of particulars must specify the place of work, or where the employee is required or permitted to work at various places, must give an indication of those places. A mobility clause is, effectively a clause which allows an employer to require its employees to work in various locations, and is often included in the contract of employment.

Working Time & Holidays

The arrangements for working time will depend upon the nature of the employer's work. For example, the employer may operate a shift system for production staff and flexitime arrangements for administrative staff; field sales staff and managers may have fixed hours.

Until recently there was very limited regulation of holiday rights, and in practice an employee's entitlement to holiday depended upon the terms of his employment contract. However, since 1998, under the Working Time Regulations, the law entitles workers to a minimum of four weeks' annual paid leave in each leave year (this is inclusive of bank holidays, but may change in due course).

In practice, of course, many (but by no means all) employees have holiday entitlements which exceed the statutory minimum.

'Garden leave' clauses

A 'garden leave' clause is a clause in which the employer reserves the right to require the employee not to perform his or her duties as an employee but agrees that in the event of the employer exercising this right, the employee will continue to be paid. Such clauses are often found in the employment contracts of executives and other professionals, and may be invoked in situations where an employee is working out his notice.

It is worth noting that an excessively long period of notice linked with garden leave might be held to be in restraint of trade and thus be void and unenforceable.

Notice

Broadly speaking, the parties to an employment contract are free to agree whatever notice provision they like. If, however, the contract of employment does not specify a notice period, a reasonable period of notice will be implied subject to the statutory right to a minimum period of notice. For instance, those continuously employed for one month or more but less than two years are entitled to at least one week's notice. After two years' employment, they are entitled to one week's notice for each year of continuous employment, but, if they have been employed for more than 12 years, their statutory entitlement will not exceed 12 weeks.

10.1.4 Implied terms

As we have previously noted, terms may be implied into a contract of employment, even though they have not been expressly agreed by the employer and employee. In particular, even if the employer complies with his legal obligations and provides a written statement of particulars or decides to give an employee a full written contract of employment, there may be areas in the contract which are not covered by express terms and where a Court or Tribunal will have to consider resorting to implied terms to fill the apparent gap. A term, however, will only be implied where there is no express term governing the matter over which there is dispute, and if a term is implied it will be no wider than is necessary to allow the contract to operate. Moreover, an express term may in some cases be qualified by an implied term.

Constructive Dismissal

A breach by either party of an implied term may give the other party the right to terminate the contract without notice. Thus, a breach of an implied term by the employer may give the employee the right to resign and argue that the breach was so significant as to amount to a repudiation of the contract by the employer and to entitle the employee to treat the contract as at an end. In the context of the statutory right not to be unfairly dismissed this is usually called a "constructive dismissal".

RIGHTS AND OBLIGATIONS AT WORK

It is important to note that both parties to the employment relationship have well established implied terms with which they must comply. These will be considered more fully under their respective sub-headings below, but in summary the employee has the following terms automatically implied into their employment contract:

- The duty to obey lawful and reasonable instructions given by the employer.
- The requirement that he or she is reasonably competent to do the job.
- The duty to take reasonable care in the performance of his or her duties under the contract.
- The duty of loyalty and fidelity to his or her employer.
- The duty not to disclose confidential information.
- The requirement to maintain mutual trust and confidence.

Implied terms which impose obligations on the employer include:

- The duty to pay wages. It must be noted that generally this does not extend to the provision of work.
- A duty of care in respect of an employee's health and safety.
- A duty to take care when producing an employee's reference.
- The requirement to maintain mutual trust and confidence.

10.2 Employees' obligations

As an employee, you will be under an obligation to obey lawful and reasonable instructions given by your employer. This is a fairly wide obligation, which in effect underlines the employer's authority over the employee. It extends beyond the normal situation of obedience to instructions given in the workplace to such issues as mobility and the need to adapt to changes in working practices.

Similarly, as an employee, you impliedly agree to take reasonable care in the performance of your duties under your contract of employment. If a person has suffered loss or damage as a result of the negligent actions of an employee while carrying out his or her employer's business, that person may be able to pursue a claim for negligence against the employer notwithstanding that it was the employee who was negligent. This is known as vicarious liability. Theoretically, the employer may sue a negligent employee for breach of the duty of care in such a case. In

MONEY AND WORK: AN ESSENTIAL GUIDE   189

appropriate circumstances, carelessness on the part of an employee may justify summary dismissal, although in practice, this would be very unusual - the carelessness would have to be so serious as to amount to a repudiation on the employee's part of his or her contractual obligations.

10.3 Employers' obligations

The general rule is that an employer is not obliged to provide work for the employee to do but only to pay the wages due under the contract.

There are, however, exceptions to the general rule which have arisen in cases where the law has recognised that in certain types of contract it is essential that the employee is given the opportunity to work. So, for example, it will be a breach of contract to fail to provide work for an employee paid on a piecework or commission basis. Moreover, "professional" employees (for example, doctors, dentists, lawyers, accountants) must be provided with appropriate opportunities to maintain and develop their professional skills.

Another group of exceptions arises in cases where the nature of the work is such that the opportunity for publicity is as important as the remuneration paid to the employee. This applies to performing artists if they are not self-employed.

The employer's obligation to pay the employee the wages which are due is at the heart of the employment contract. Normally, the contract will contain express provisions dealing with the remuneration due, and it is a statutory requirement that details of the scale, rate or method of calculation of the remuneration should be given to the employee in writing. Employees also have a statutory right to receive an itemised pay statement upon payment of wages or salary.

The employment relationship between employer and employee imposes upon the employer the important duty to care for the employee's health and safety and the duty to take care in the compilation of references for the employee.

10.4 Minimum wage

Since 1999, the UK has had a national minimum wage, and most workers in the UK (which excludes workers in the Channel Islands or the Isle of

Man) are entitled to the protection it offers, including workers employed by an agency, casual workers and workers on short-term contracts. However, you will not be entitled to the protection of the national minimum wage legislation if you are:

- self employed;
- under the school leaving age (currently 16);
- an au pair;
- a member of the military;
- a voluntary worker; or
- an apprentice aged under 19, or an apprentice aged over 19 and in the first year of your apprenticeship.

There are three national minimum age rates: the Adult Rate, the Development Rate and the 16-17 Year Old Rate.

From 1 October 2007:

- The Adult Rate of the minimum wage (for workers aged 22 and over) is £5.52 an hour. The Development Rate (for workers aged 18 - 21 inclusive) is £4.60 an hour.
- The Development Rate can also apply to workers aged 22 and above during their first 6 months in a new job with a new employer and who are receiving accredited training.
- The 16 - 17 year old rate is £3.40 an hour.

Further details are provided on the Low Pay Commission's website at: www.lowpay.gov.uk/

11 Discrimination & harassment at work

Discrimination at work!
what if I am discriminated against or bullied?
what action(s) can/should I take?
what remedies can I get?

Discrimination and harassment in the workplace is a very serious problem in the modern world and can give rise to very sensitive and difficult problems. In this section, we identify the different forms of discrimination which may be suffered. We also set out some basic steps that a person who is being discriminated against, harassed or bullied may wish to consider, and provide references for further reading on the topic.

Discrimination under English law covers:

- sex (gender, including sexual orientation and a change of sex, i.e. gender reassignment)
- race
- disability
- religion or belief, and
- age.

11.1 Gender and Race Discrimination

Distinct types of discrimination are recognised under both the Sex Discrimination Act 1975 ("SDA") and the Race Relations Act 1976 ("RRA"), with similar definitions:

- direct discrimination
- indirect discrimination
- harassment
- victimisation

11.1.1 Marital Status

It is unlawful for an employer to discriminate against a married person, for example promote one employee instead of another, on the ground that the individual not chosen was married and the other was not.

11.1.2 Discriminatory grounds: sex, race, colour, nationality, ethnic or national origin

As the sex discrimination legislation prohibits discrimination on grounds of sex and marital status, so the RRA prohibits discrimination against a person on grounds of colour, race, nationality and ethnic or national origin. The difficulty is determining what these terms mean.

In one case, a Sikh boy was refused entrance to a private school because he could not comply with the school's uniform requirements (as he wore a turban). As part of the ruling, the House of Lords defined the term 'ethnic group'. To be regarded as an ethnic group, the group had to regard itself, and be regarded by others, as a distinct community by virtue of certain characteristics. Two were essential: a long, shared history, and a cultural tradition of its own. Other relevant characteristics include either a common geographical origin or descent from a small number of common ancestors; a common language, literature or religion; and/or a sense of being a minority (or oppressed or dominant) group. The House of Lords held, applying these tests, that Sikhs were indeed a distinct ethnic/racial group. Therefore, the Court concluded in this case that there had been racial discrimination.

11.2 Direct discrimination

Direct discrimination is defined as less favourable treatment on the ground of sex, marital status, or gender reassignment, or on racial grounds.

The motive of the discriminator responsible for the direct discrimination is irrelevant, as demonstrated by a case involving a married couple, who were both aged 61. The problem arose when the couple visited a local authority swimming pool. The wife gained free admission, but the husband did not, since he had not reached the state pension age of 65. There was no intention to discriminate on the part of the local authority, it was merely giving concessions to pensioners, for which the husband did not qualify. He contended that this was direct discrimination based solely on the grounds of sex. The Court held that the test in cases of direct discrimination is objective, so there had been direct discrimination.

DISCRIMINATION & HARASSMENT AT WORK

Determining whether a person has suffered "less favourable treatment" requires a comparison to be carried out. The complainant must be treated less favourably than a person of the opposite sex is treated or would be treated or a person not of the same race. This means that an actual or a hypothetical comparator must be used when considering whether this test has been satisfied. Unsurprisingly, this requirement can cause problems when considering pregnancy-related sex discrimination claims.

Less favourable treatment alone is insufficient to found a claim for direct discrimination: the complainant must go on to show that he or she has suffered a detriment (which means being put at a disadvantage). Often it is not difficult to find that the complainant has been put at a disadvantage, e.g. by not being appointed to the post applied for, by not getting the promotion or transfer, and so on. The test should be objective, i.e. whether a reasonable worker would consider that they had suffered a detriment? Further, it is not necessary to identify an economic or physical disadvantage in order to establish that a detriment has occurred.

Harassment
Sexual and racial harassment are acts of direct discrimination, being forms of detriment based on the prohibited grounds. See sexual harassment below.

Vicarious liability of employers
Employers may be liable for acts of harassment committed by employees in the course of their employment. The test to determine whether an act was done 'in the course of employment' has been widened to include acts of sexual harassment or bullying taking place outside working hours and away from the employer's premises in a social setting (for example during drinks after work).

Racial harassment
Racial harassment occurs where, on the grounds of race or ethnic or national origins, a person engages in unwanted conduct which has the purpose or effect of (a) violating a person's dignity, or (b) creating an intimidating, hostile, degrading, humiliating or offensive environment for him or her. There are both objective and subjective elements to the definition because conduct is to be regarded as having that effect 'only if,

having regard to all the circumstances, including in particular the perception of that other person, it should reasonably be considered as having that effect.' The definition applies only to harassment on grounds of race or ethnic or national origin.

Sexual harassment

There is currently no express provision under the sex discrimination legislation concerning sexual harassment. As sexual harassment is a form of direct discrimination, being less favourable treatment on the ground of sex, it is necessary to establish that (a) the treatment suffered was on this ground; and (b) that the complainant has suffered a detriment judged from the complainant's perspective. A single act, if it is sufficiently serious, may amount to harassment by itself. However, a series of incidents, no one of which taken on its own amounting to harassment, may be sufficient, when considered "in the round".

Victimisation

Victimisation is itself a form of direct discrimination, i.e. it is less favourable treatment of a person by reason that they have brought proceedings, given evidence or information, or alleged a contravention of the SDA, the RRA or the Equal Pay Act, ('the protected acts') or where the discriminator knows or suspects that that the person victimised intends to do any of those things, or suspects the person has done, or intends to do, any of them.

The allegation of victimisation must be true and made in good faith. The alleged motive of the discriminator is not relevant – indeed, it may be unconscious or sub-conscious.

11.2.2 Indirect discrimination

Indirect discrimination is the application of an apparently gender-neutral or race-neutral requirement which places persons of one sex or persons of one colour, racial group, ethnic or national origins, at a disadvantage, and which cannot be objectively justified.

For example, in one case the Court was asked to consider an age requirement for a Civil Service post (the successful applicant had to be between 17 and 28). The complainant, who was 32, succeeded in her claim that this was indirect sex discrimination as it disadvantaged women, who would be more likely to be over this age as they often took time out of their career for childbirth and child-rearing. This sort of recruitment policy would now be illegal on grounds of age discrimination (see section 11.6 below).

11.3 Bullying

Bullying is sadly far too common in the modern workplace. The Health & Safety Executive has estimated that bullying costs UK employers 80 million work days and up to £2 billion of lost revenue every year. It also causes staff morale problems, ill-health (both mental and physical), high staff turnover and damages the reputation of the employer.

One of the difficulties which can arise in relation to bullying is that it may be difficult to show that the act(s) constituting the bullying falls within one of the identified classes of discrimination. Nevertheless, employers are legally obliged to provide a safe system of work for employees (this, as we have noted above, being a term which is implied by law into all contracts of employment). If an employee suffers injury because of breach of this implied term as a result of bullying then the employer may be liable (even if it did not condone the bullying). Injury in this context covers psychiatric injury as well as physical injury.

There is no comprehensive list as to what may constitute bullying behaviour, but generally accepted examples include:

- Competent staff being continually criticised and demeaned in public or private;
- Being unfairly denied promotion;
- Shouting at, or otherwise behaving unreasonably in relation to staff;
- Giving a member of staff unreasonable (or inadequate) amounts of work, inappropriate work, or setting impossible deadlines.

What should you do if you are bullied (or someone you know is bullied)? There are various sources which can provide you with detailed advice - in particular, the TUC (see www.tuc.org.uk/index.cfm) and ACAS (see www.acas.org.uk/index.aspx?articleid=30), and if you feel you are being bullied, you should investigate these (or similar) sources. Both the TUC and ACAS provide booklets on the topic of bullying. Generally speaking, however, possible courses of action open to you include:

- Confronting the bully. Sometimes, this is all that is required to address the problem;
- Tell a friend or colleague about the situation. You may well find that you are not alone in being bullied;
- Keep detailed written notes of every bullying incident. The importance of this cannot be overstated;
- If you are in a union, tell your union representative. Alternatively, (or in addition), you may wish to raise the matter with your employer's HR Department. A good employer should be anxious to address and resolve all instances of bullying as soon as possible.
- Consult your local Citizens Advice Bureau;
- Ultimately, it may be necessary for you to file a complaint under your employer's grievance procedures. (We discuss the grievance procedures in Chapter 14);
- In extreme cases you may wish to consider consulting a solicitor.

Whatever happens, however, there is no need for you to suffer the bullying. Bullying is against the law and remedies are available to you.

11.4 Disability Discrimination

Legislation outlawing discrimination on the ground of disability is presently set out in the Disability Discrimination Act 1995 ("DDA") and related legislation. There is also a Code of Practice giving practical guidance on matters relating to the elimination of disability discrimination in employment, encouraging good employment practices in relation to the disabled, and on reasonable adjustments.

The DDA applies to those working under a contract of employment or apprenticeship, and those who work under 'a contract personally to do any work'. The employment provisions of the DDA apply to work in an "establishment" in the UK. Originally, some forms of employment, e.g. police officers, fire-fighters, partnerships, barristers and prison officers were not covered by the Act; however the scope of the Act was extended in 2004 to cover these. Nevertheless, members of the armed forces members are still excluded from the scope of the Act.

Since 2004, coverage has been extended to ex-employees, who claim disability discrimination within three months of their departure.

11.4.1 Meaning of disability

The DDA takes the 'medical model', rather than the 'social model', of disability. Essentially, medical evidence determines whether a person is disabled.

A person has a disability for the purposes of the DDA if he has a physical or mental impairment which has a substantial and long-term adverse effect on his ability to carry out normal day-to-day activities. It is worth noting that the DDA's definition of a "disabled person" extends to cover a person who has had a disability in the past but who is no longer suffering any effects, for example, if an individual was refused promotion because of his absenteeism record in the past, which was caused by his previous depression, this could amount to discrimination. The key points to note about this definition are:

- a person must have a physical or mental impairment, and
- that impairment must have an adverse effect on his or her ability to carry out normal day-to-day activities, and
- that effect must be substantial, and
- that effect must also be long-term.

Mental impairments include learning, psychiatric and psychological impairments. If the impairment results from or consists of a mental illness, it must be clinically well-recognised to come within the definition. However, psychopathic or anti-social disorders (e.g. kleptomania, pyromania and paedophilia) are excluded. Spectacles wearers and hay-fever sufferers are also outside the definition of disability.

'Normal day-to-day activities' (not necessarily those concerning the job the employee is or will be doing) must be affected i.e.:
- mobility;
- manual dexterity;
- physical coordination;
- continence;
- ability to lift, carry or otherwise move everyday objects;
- speech, hearing or eyesight;
- memory or ability to concentrate, learn or understand; or
- perception of the risk of physical danger.

11.5 Sexual Orientation; Religion or Belief

Protection against discrimination on the grounds of sexual orientation, religion or belief and age has been introduced in recent years, with new rules on age discrimination being implemented in 2006 (see section 11.6 below).

11.5.1 Sexual orientation

Until recently, there was no protection in Great Britain concerning discrimination on the ground of sexual orientation, but this is now covered by anti-discrimination legislation similar to that for race, sex and disability discrimination.

11.5.2 Religion and Belief

There are four forms of unlawful discrimination relating to religion and belief: direct, indirect, harassment and victimisation. The definition of direct discrimination is less favourable treatment on the grounds of religion or belief, which does not necessarily have to be that of the complainant. For example, an individual could be discriminated against because of his or her friendship or support of another individual wit a particular religion or belief. Indirect discrimination involves, broadly, treatment of a person or group of people which would put another person or group of people who had a different religion or belief at a disadvantage.

11.6 Age

The Age Regulations came into force on 1 October 2006 (other than in relation to pension schemes, in respect of which they come into force on 1 December 2006). The central provisions of these Regulations closely follow the approach adopted on sexual orientation and religion or belief. The Age Regulations apply to discrimination on the ground of age (at whatever age it may strike). The Regulations do not affect the State Pension Age, which will remain (for the moment) at age 60 for women and 65 for men. However, all retirement ages under 65 are unlawful, unless objectively justified (This "default" retirement age of 65 is expected to be reviewed in 2011). Any such justification by the alleged discriminator must establish that the treatment or 'provision, criterion or practice' is a 'proportionate means of achieving a legitimate aim'.

Justification is not required in the following circumstances: requiring retirement at age 65 or more; linking the provision of benefits to length of service, although in the case of an employee with more than five years' service, the employer must establish that it 'reasonably appears' to him that the length of service condition 'fulfils a business need', e.g. it encourages loyalty or motivation, or rewards experience; linking pay to the national minimum wage where the employees in the lower age group (below age 22) are paid less than the adult minimum wage. The exemption from the requirement to justify does not cover all pay differences based on the national minimum wage age bands.

Positive discrimination is lawful where it provides special help to persons of a particular age or age group in relation to particular work if this 'prevents or compensates for disadvantages linked to age suffered by persons of that age or age group doing that work or likely to take up that work'.

The Age Regulations cover, among others, employees, workers and job applicants. The prohibited forms of discrimination are direct and indirect, harassment and victimisation. Except in cases of retirement is by mutual agreement, the 'duty to consider' procedure applies whenever an employer requires an employee to retire, whatever age, including retirements at age 65 or above. The duty to consider is based on the same procedure to request flexible working, which applies to parents of young children (see section 12.5).

The Age Regulations provide that not more than a year and not less than six months before an employee is dismissed by reason of retirement the employer must give a written notice to the employee concerned telling him (a) that he has the right to make a request not to retire on the intended retirement date and (b) the date on which he intends the employee to retire.

Employees dismissed for an age-discriminatory reason are able to claim for both age discrimination and unfair dismissal, although employees over the age of 65 do not have a right to claim for unlawful age discrimination.

11.7 Defences to Discrimination Claims

A discrimination claim can be defeated if the discriminator (e.g. the employer) can demonstrate that the act of discrimination complained of is 'objectively justified'. For example, the employer must show that the discriminatory act (e.g. a discriminatory clause in a contract of employment):

a.   corresponds to a real need on the part of the employer;

b.   is appropriate with a view to achieving the objective pursued; and

c.   is necessary to achieving that end result.

This means that an objective balance needs to be struck between the discriminatory effect of the provision and the employer's legitimate business needs.

11.7.1   Genuine occupational qualification

Where sex or race is a genuine occupational qualification for the job, less favourable treatment is allowed. This exception comprises a fairly narrow range of reasons, for example:

- Where the essential nature of the job calls for a man for reasons of physiology (excluding physical strength or stamina) or, in dramatic performances or other entertainment, for reasons of authenticity, so that the essential nature of the job would be materially different if carried out by a woman;
- The job needs to be held by a man to preserve decency or privacy because:
    - i)   it is likely to involve physical contact with men in circumstances where they might reasonably object to its being carried out by a woman, or
    - ii)   the holder of the job is likely to do his work in circumstances where men might reasonably object to the presence of a woman because they are in a state of undress.
- The job is likely to involve care of an elderly or disabled person, and it is more appropriate for the carer to be of the same sex as the person requiring care.

11.7.2 Justification in Disability Discrimination claims

Apart from direct discrimination, discriminatory treatment may be justified where the reason for it is both 'material to the circumstances of the particular case and substantial'. The test is objective, namely whether on the facts of the case, reasonable adjustments could be or could have been made, and if so, whether the employer was reasonable in not carrying them out.

11.8 Remedies – what can I get?

An individual may make an application to an Employment Tribunal within three months of the alleged act of discrimination, although the Tribunal may extend this where it considers it is just and equitable to do so. The Equal Opportunities Commission (EOC) and the Commission for Racial Equality (CRE) have powers to assist applicants where the case raises matters of principle or it is unreasonable to expect the applicant to deal with the case without support.

If the complaint is upheld, the Tribunal may:

• Make an order declaring the rights of the parties;
• Award compensation (which is unlimited);
• Make a recommendation that the employer takes action within a specified period to obviate or reduce the effect of the discrimination.

Compensation for injury to feelings may be awarded, and often comprises a major part of the package. There is no statutory cap on compensation awards in discrimination cases.

12 Family rights

What if I have a family? –
    what rights do I have?
    what obligations have I agreed to?
    What statutory rights exist?

Over recent years, employees who are (or about to become) parents have seen a steady widening of the protections and rights afforded to them under the law. In this section, we discuss maternity rights, paternity leave, parental leave, flexible working and related issues.

12.1 Maternity rights

Female employees have the following rights in relation to pregnancy/childbirth:

- The right to maternity leave;
- The right to maternity pay;
- Time off for ante-natal care;
- Protection from detriment or dismissal on the grounds of pregnancy or childbirth.

In 2004, the Government announced its 'family friendly strategy' for the following ten years. This contained a number of proposals, including:

- The introduction of a Childcare approval scheme, which provides families on incomes not exceeding £59,000 with Tax Credit support to help pay for home childcare;
- The introduction of paid maternity leave of 12 months by the end of 2007 (9 months from April 2007);
- The introduction of legislation by the end of 2007 to give mothers the right to transfer a proportion of their pay and leave to the child's father;
- Consultation on extending the right to request flexible working to parents of older children;
- An out-of-school childcare place between the hours of 8am and 6pm each weekday by 2010 for all children aged 3 to 14;

- Access to integrated services for every family through Children's Centres in their local community, with a goal of 3,500 Centres by 2010.

Of these proposals, the Work and Families Act 2006 has introduced a number of enhancements of rights for working parents, including extending the right to statutory maternity pay and statutory adoption pay from six months to nine months by April 2007, with the goal of one year's paid leave by the end of the next Parliament.

European law requires that women workers have the right to at least 14 weeks' maternity leave. Maternity rights in the United Kingdom are more generous, and some employers may offer maternity rights which are more generous still than the statutory rights set out below.

12.1.1 Ordinary maternity leave (OML)

Women are entitled to a period of ordinary maternity leave (OML) of 26 weeks (without the need to accrue a qualifying period of continuous employment).

There are detailed notification requirements to be followed, failing which the right to (OML) maternity leave may be lost. The employee must notify her employer no later than the end of the 15th week before the expected week of childbirth (EWC) – or as soon as reasonably practicable - of the fact that she is pregnant, the expected date of childbirth and the date on which she intends to commence her OML. This date may be varied by notifying the employer at least 28 days before the original planned commencement date or the new date, whichever is earlier. The employer must then give the woman notice of the date on which her OML will end. If the employer fails to do this, she may return early and she is protected from detriment or dismissal if she does not return on that date.

After her OML, a woman has the right to return to the job in which she was employed before her absence, on terms no less favourable than she would have enjoyed had she not been absent.

12.1.2 Unfair dismissal and protection from detriment

It is an automatically unfair dismissal to dismiss a woman for a reason connected with pregnancy, childbirth or maternity leave rights. There is one exception to this provision: it is not automatically unfair to dismiss a woman (for a reason other than redundancy) if it is not reasonably practicable to allow her to return to a suitable job and she has accepted or unreasonably refused the offer of a suitable alternative job made by an associated employer.

12.1.3 Additional maternity leave (AML)

A woman who is entitled to OML and who has been continuously employed for a period of 26 weeks by the 14th week before the EWC is entitled to period of additional maternity leave (AML) of 26 weeks. This gives qualifying female employees a total maternity leave entitlement of one year. However, maternity leave only attracts statutory maternity pay for the first 26 weeks of leave (see section 12.1.4 on statutory maternity pay), which means that, in practice, women will only wish to take the full 52 weeks of leave if there is a contractual entitlement with the employer to maternity pay covering the last half of the leave year. A woman returning from AML has the right to return to the job in which she was employed before her absence, on terms no less favourable than she would have enjoyed had she not been absent, but there are two exceptions to this right to return (see section 14.4.2 on unfair dismissal).

12.1.4 Statutory maternity pay

A woman with 26 weeks of continuous employment by the 15th week before the EWC with average earnings at or above the lower earnings limit for NI contributions (£87 per week from 6 April, 2007) is entitled to statutory maternity pay (SMP). For the first six weeks, it is paid at the rate of 90% of the woman's normal weekly earnings. For the remaining 20 weeks it is paid at the rate of statutory sick pay, which from April, 2007 is £112.75 per week. As mentioned above in relation to the starting date for OML, a woman must give 28 days' notice of the day SMP should start.

Time off for ante-natal care

A pregnant employee may request paid time off work to attend an ante-natal appointment, which may not be unreasonably refused by the employer. The employer may request written proof of the pregnancy and ante-natal appointment. The amount of pay is the normal hourly rate. The employee may complain to an Employment Tribunal that her

MONEY AND WORK: AN ESSENTIAL GUIDE   207

employer has unreasonably refused time off or has failed to pay her for the time off. The Tribunal may make a declaration and order the amount of pay due. Dismissal or subjection to a detriment because the employee has exercised her rights under these provisions will give her the right to claim under the maternity protection legislation, and to complain of unfair dismissal (as well as sex discrimination).

12.2 Maternity Rights Checklist:

	Ordinary Maternity Leave (OML)	Additional Maternity Leave (AML)	Statutory Maternity Pay	Ante-natal care rights
Pregnant worker rights	Up to 26 weeks, providing the correct notice is given.	Up to 26 weeks, so long as she has been continuously employed for 26 weeks by the 14th week before the expected birth date.	Only entitled to this payment in respect of OML. This is set at 90% of normal weekly earnings for the first six weeks, and at the rate of statutory sick pay for the remaining 20. To qualify, average earnings must reach the lower earnings limit for NI contributions.	Request may be made for paid time off to attend anti-natal classes. The employees normal hourly rate applies. This request can not be unreasonably refused.

12.3 Paternity leave

Male employees now have rights in relation to paternity leave (PL). These concern the two categories of PL:

1) paternity leave: birth, and
2) paternity leave: adoption.

Although the provisions relating to these two categories are similar, there are some differences and these two forms of leave are treated separately below. Where the employment contract also gives a right to paternity leave, an employee may not operate both rights separately but may choose whichever right is more favourable, i.e. he may choose either the contractual right or the statutory one, but not both.

The statutory right to paternity leave applies to fathers of children born on or after 6 April 2003 and who have been continuously employed for not less than 26 weeks ending with the week immediately preceding the 14th week before the expected week of the child's birth. However, the legislation refers to "partners" rather than fathers and the interpretation of "partner" under the legislation defines a partner as, "...a person (whether of a different or the same sex) who lives with the mother ... and the child in an enduring family relationship but is not a relative of the mother...". This is clearly wide enough to apply to a woman, despite the fact that the leave is called paternity leave. This means, for example, that the right to paternity leave could also apply (if the relevant requirements are met) to the female partner of a woman in a lesbian relationship where that woman has had a child. However, the masculine form will be used in this description of paternity leave, which (as lawyers like to say) should be read as also importing the feminine.

The entitlement is for up to two weeks' paid leave, which must be taken together - there is no right to take separate days of leave, although an employee may choose to take either one week's leave or two consecutive weeks' leave – and it must be taken within 56 days of the birth. The employee is entitled to Statutory Paternity Pay (SPP), which is paid at the same rate as SMP (provided his earnings equal or exceed the lower earning limit of £112.75 per week from 6 April, 2007). The statutory entitlement is 90% of average weekly earnings if earnings are less than the lower earnings limit. Step-parents and foster parents are not usually entitled to SPP.

12.4 Parental leave

European law established two 'family-friendly' rights:

(i)   the right to parental leave to care for young children (up to 8 years of age); and

(ii) the right to time off work to care for dependants in family emergencies.

This section deals with the former right, while the latter is considered in a subsequent section.

Under the legislation, both male and female employees, whether full-time or part-time, are entitled to unpaid parental leave of up to 13 weeks (per parent, per child) if they have one year's continuous employment and have (or expect to have) responsibility for the child. An employee has responsibility for a child where he or she has 'parental responsibility' (including responsibility for an adopted child) or where the employee has been registered as the parent on the child's birth certificate. There is a separate entitlement for each parent. The period of 13 weeks' leave must be taken in periods of a week or multiples of a week, except for parents of disabled children who may take leave of a day or multiples of a day (the limitations of this provision are discussed below), during the first five years of the child's life or, in the case of an adopted child, within five years of the placement for adoption or before the child's eighteenth birthday, whichever is the earlier.

This maximum leave period is extended to 18 weeks in the case of employees with a child who is entitled to disability living allowance. The leave is 'for the purpose of caring for that child'.

Employers and employees may make their own agreements on how to implement the parental leave right by adopting individual, collective or workforce agreements. This would allow them to agree, for example, that parental leave could be taken in units of days rather than weeks, which may be more convenient for the employee.

Employees must give at least 28 days' notice of their intention to take parental leave. In the case of employees giving this notice before the expected week of childbirth or placement for adoption, the employer must allow the leave. Apart from those two situations, the employer may postpone the leave for up to six months where he 'considers that the operation of his business would be unduly disrupted' if the employee took the leave, but must give the employee seven days' notice in writing of the postponement.

An employee may complain to an Employment Tribunal that the employer has unreasonably postponed a period of parental leave or prevented or attempted to prevent him from taking it.

An employee is entitled to certain terms and conditions of employment which apply during the period of parental leave, apart from the right to pay. These are: the implied term of trust and confidence; notice of termination of the contract; compensation upon redundancy; and the disciplinary and grievance procedures. During leave, the employee is bound by: the implied obligation of good faith and any terms relating to: notice of termination; disclosure of confidential information; the acceptance of gifts or other benefits; or participation in any business.

Employees returning after parental leave of four weeks or less are entitled to return to the job they were doing before going on leave. Employees taking longer periods of leave are entitled to return to the job they were doing before going on leave or, where that is not reasonably practicable, to a suitable and appropriate job. Upon return, the employee's rights to remuneration, seniority, pension rights and other similar rights must be no less favourable than they were before taking leave.

12.5 Flexible Working

Flexible Working allows an employee to do his or her job in an alternative way to what is initially proposed by or agreed with the employer. Employees who satisfy certain criteria have the right to request to work flexibly (i.e. a right to request a contractual variation), rather than an automatic right to do so. Any change proposed by an employee seeking to work flexibly must relate to hours or times and place of work.

To qualify for this right, the employee must:

- be a qualifying employee, i.e. with at least 26 weeks of continuous employment; and
- have or expect to have responsibility for the upbringing of a child aged under 6 (or under 18 if the child is disabled); and
- be either the parent, foster parent, guardian, or adopter of the child, or the husband, wife or partner of such a person.

The employer must hold a meeting within 28 days of the request to work flexibly being made, and inform the employee of his decision within 14 days of the meeting. The employee may be accompanied in the meeting by a fellow worker. The employee may appeal against the decision within 14 days and, if an appeal is made, an appeal meeting must be held within 14 days of the appeal being lodged, unless the appeal is upheld within 14 days of the appeal being lodged.

12.5.1 Grounds for refusal

The employer may only refuse a request to work flexibly made by an employee who satisfies the criteria referred to on 'business grounds'. These are:

- burden of additional costs;
- detrimental effect of the ability to meet customer demand;
- inability to reorganise work among existing staff;
- inability to recruit additional staff;
- detrimental impact on quality or performance;
- insufficiency of work during periods that the employee proposes to work planned structural changes.

12.5.2 Time off to care for dependants

Employees have a statutory right to take time off work (unpaid) for urgent family reasons. No qualifying period of employment is necessary for entitlement to the right. A 'dependant' is the employee's wife, husband, civil partner, child, parent, or someone living in the same household (but not a person who is the employee, tenant, lodger or boarder of the employee seeking to exercise the right). This is wide enough to include partners of the opposite or the same sex as the employee, a person who reasonably relies on the employee for assistance when they fall ill, are injured or assaulted, or who relies on the employee to make arrangements for the provision of care in the event of illness or injury. Where there is unexpected disruption or termination of arrangements for the care of a dependant, the definition also includes any person who reasonably relies on the employee to make arrangements for care.

12.5.3   Part-Time Workers- a case for special protection

Part-time workers are also protected under the law. "Part-time" usually means working less than 37 hours per week.

In particular, a part-time worker has the right not to receive less favourably treatment from the employer compared with full-time workers. For example, part-timers must have the same entitlements to maternity leave (and maternity pay), parental leave, and time-off for dependants, on a pro-rata basis, as comparable full-time workers. Therefore, part-time workers are entitled to the same treatment pro rata as full-timers doing similar work unless less favourable treatment can be "objectively justified". This means that the employer must show that the less favourable treatment must be intended: is to achieve a legitimate objective, (for example, a genuine business objective), be necessary to achieve that objective; and is an appropriate way to achieve the objective.

13 Pay discrimination?

What if others doing the same job as me, are on more pay –
    what protections do I have?
    what rights do I have?
    how can I challenge it?

Over the years, equal pay legislation has been introduced with the intention of eliminating sex discrimination from pay systems, and to close the so-called 'gender pay gap', i.e. the difference in pay between men and women who do equal work. The overriding legal principle is that men and women should receive equal pay for the same work of equal value, and is enshrined in European Law. The Equal Opportunities Commission has issued a Code of Practice on Equal Pay ('the Code') which can be used in evidence in legal proceedings relating to equal pay claims.

13.1 What is equal pay?

The Equal Pay Act 1970 seeks to eliminate gender-based pay discrimination, although differences in pay between men and women are allowed, provided they are due to factors other than sex, e.g. performance-related pay or pay to reward qualifications achieved (see the discussion of the genuine material factor defence below).

13.2 Bringing an Equal Pay claim

To bring a successful equal pay claim, the woman[17] must establish that she is in the same employment (or working for an associated employer) as a selected but actual (not hypothetical) comparable male worker(s), who is/are engaged in one of the following three situations:

(i)   like work,

(ii)   work rated as equivalent, i.e. work which has been given an equivalent rating under a job evaluation study, or

---

[17] A man can of course bring an equal pay claim if he is in fact the disadvantaged party. Unsurprisingly, however, the majority of equal pay claims are brought by women, and for present purposes, we shall assume that claimants are female.

(iii)   work which is of equal value.

Where a woman's contract of employment contains a term (or terms) less favourable than the analogous term(s) in the comparator's contract, the Equal Pay Act, as amended, introduces an "equality clause", which has the effect of modifying the woman's contract so as to remove the discrepancy, thus legally entitling her to the same level and type of benefits as her comparator.

13.3 Like work

One of the situations in which a woman may bring an equal pay claim is where she is engaged in like work to that of her comparator. 'Like work' is work that is of the same or a broadly similar nature, and where any differences from that of the comparator are not of practical importance in relation to terms and conditions of employment, taking into account how frequently any such differences occur in practice.

For example, in one case an employer claimed that male counter-staff at its betting shop were paid a higher hourly pay than female counter-workers because of risk of robbery, and the men were employed for security reasons. In fact, the men had never been called upon to perform any security function, and the Court held that, as the men had never been required to deal with any disturbance or attempted violence, the jobs were essentially the same.

13.3.1 Genuine Material Factor Defence

If a claimant establishes that she is paid less than her male comparator who is engaged on like work, work rated as equivalent, or work of equal value, the employer may say that the difference in pay is not due to sex discrimination, and that there is a material difference between the claimant's case and that of the comparator. This is the genuine material factor defence (GMF). If the employer succeeds in this defence, he will not be breached the equal pay legislation.

In the GMF defence, the employer must identify a factor which is (a) the genuine cause of the difference in pay; and (b) material. In other words the requirement of genuineness means that the reason put forward by the employer must not be a sham or a pretence or trivial.

13.4 Putting right the wrong? - remedies for equal pay

All equal pay claims must be brought in the Employment Tribunal, and in bringing a claim the claimant may rely upon both European and domestic legislation. Employers may also apply to the Employment Tribunal for a declaration where there is a dispute over the effect of an equality clause. The Government may also bring proceedings where it appears that the employer of any women is or has been in breach of a term modified or included by an equality clause, and it is not reasonable to expect the women themselves to bring proceedings (e.g. because they do not have a union to support their claim). The Equal Opportunities Commission can also seek a ruling from a Tribunal in certain circumstances.

It is very important to note that equal pay claims must be brought during or within six months of leaving the employment to which the claim relates. Failure to do so means that the equal "pay" claim will almost certainly be "out of time".

14 Dismissal and Redundancy

What if I am sacked (dismissed)? –
   what rights do I have?
   what procedure should be followed?
   what compensation can I get?
What is redundancy?
   What am I entitled to?

If you are dismissed from your job, you may be able to claim to have been:

* dismissed in breach of contract (wrongful dismissal); or
* dismissed in breach of your statutory rights (unfair dismissal or redundancy).

14.1 Distinguishing wrongful and unfair dismissals

It is important to distinguish between wrongful dismissals and unfair dismissals. A wrongful dismissal will occur if an employee is dismissed in contravention of the terms of his or her contract of employment; so, for example, if a person is dismissed without notice in circumstances where he or she should have been given (say) three months notice, the dismissal would be "wrongful", and the dismissed employee will be able to bring a legal claim against the employer for breach of contract.

If, however, the employee did receive the necessary notice (and assuming there has been no other breach of contractual term by the employer), the dismissed employee will not have a valid claim for *wrongful dismissal*, because there will quite simply have been no breach of contract by the employer. Nevertheless, the employee may still have a valid claim against his (former) employer for *unfair dismissal*, that is, a breach of the employee's statutory right not to be unfairly dismissed. Demonstrating a breach of this statutory right does not require the employee to show that there has also been a breach of contract. Thus, it is perfectly possible for an employee to be dismissed in accordance with his or her contract of employment but in a way which contravenes the employee's statutory rights. In such a case, a wrongful dismissal claim will fail, whereas an unfair dismissal claim will succeed. It is important to bear in mind that the terms 'unfair' and 'wrongful' cannot be used interchangeably.

Determining whether a dismissal has in fact taken place, and at what point in time this occurred, is often a complex question. However, the examples below might help to explain it:

14.1.1 Expiry of a fixed-term contract

Fixed-term contracts may take a number of forms. The contract may specify that it is to continue for a stated period (e.g. five years from January 1, 2006). In that case, it cannot be terminated before the expiry of that period, unless the terms of the contract empower the parties to terminate it earlier or they both agree to bring it to an end.

There are legal restrictions which prevent less favourable treatment of fixed-term employees by comparison with permanent employees and there are statutory provisions to convert fixed-term contracts into permanent "ongoing" contracts in the case of employees continuously employed for four years or more.

14.1.2 Frustration

Frustration occurs when circumstances beyond the control of either party to a contract make it incapable of being performed in the form originally agreed. If a contract is frustrated, the contract will terminate automatically and (in the context of an employment contract) the frustrating event will not be treated as a dismissal for the purposes of any dismissal claim. This is known as the "doctrine of frustration". The most common examples of frustration are illness and imprisonment. The death of either party may also be treated as a frustrating event. It is clear that the doctrine of frustration can, in appropriate circumstances, be applied to a fixed term contract terminable by the employer by short notice.

14.1.3 Mutual consent

Generally speaking, the parties to a contract are free to enter into an agreement that the contract should terminate. It is also open to them to agree in advance that, if certain specified events occur (e.g. a fixed-term contract being brought to a premature end by the employer), the employer will pay to the employee an agreed sum to settle any claims that he or she may have.

14.1.4   Dismissal with notice

Termination occurs when either party informs the other clearly and unequivocally that the contract is to end, or the circumstances are such that it is clear that termination was intended or that it can be inferred that termination was intended. The words used to terminate the contract must be unambiguous. The principles are the same regardless of whether the termination consists of a dismissal by the employer or a resignation by the employee.

In the case of a dismissal by the employer, phrases such as 'I hereby give you notice of dismissal' are clear. Problems arise, however, where there is an argument between the employer and the employee and words are used in the heat of the moment. If the words used by the employer are not ambiguous or could only be interpreted as amounting to words of dismissal, then the conclusion is clear. If, on the other hand, the words used are ambiguous and it is not clear whether they do amount to words of dismissal (e.g. 'You're finished with me'), it is necessary to look at all the circumstances of the case, particularly the intention with which the words were spoken, and consider how a reasonable employee would, in all the circumstances have understood them.

14.1.5   Dismissal without notice

A dismissal without notice – usually called 'summary dismissal' – is on the face of it a breach of contract, since the employee has been denied his or her contractual entitlement to termination of the contract by notice (or to the expiry of a fixed term contract). In some circumstances, the employer might seek to argue in his defence that the employee had himself committed a breach of the contract sufficiently serious to justify dismissal without notice. In effect, therefore, the issue in a summary dismissal case is not whether the employee was dismissed but whether the dismissal was in breach of contract and thus 'wrongful'.

14.2 Resignation

The requirements for an effective resignation by an employee are very similar to those for a dismissal. It is important for employers to know whether an employee has resigned, since if they erroneously treat the employee as having resigned, they themselves may be held to have dismissed the employee.

Constructive Dismissal

If the employee's resignation is prompted by a breach of contract by the employer, that may be treated as a constructive dismissal by the employer. In effect, this means that the employee's resignation was prompted by an action by the employer which may be categorised as a breach of contract. The critical legal test is:

'If the employer is guilty of conduct which is a significant breach going to the root of the contract of employment, or which shows that the employer no longer intends to be bound by one or more of the essential terms of contract, then the employee is entitled to treat himself as discharged from any further performance ... [T]he conduct must ... be sufficiently serious to entitle him to leave at once...'

In the case in which this test was first laid down, the applicant was suspended without pay by the employer as a disciplinary sanction after taking time off work without permission. Due to the severe financial difficulties this placed the applicant in, he then asked his employer for his accrued holiday pay, and when this was refused he asked for a loan, which was also refused. He then resigned, and pursued a claim for constructive dismissal based on unreasonable conduct on the part of the employer. The Court held that the employer's conduct was inappropriate and therefore had breached the contract. The applicant's claim was successful.

The "last straw"

More recently, the courts have sought to clarify the concept of constructive dismissal, and in particular the idea of 'last-straw' offences. One example concerned an employee of a local authority, who during a 30 month period had issued five separate sets of proceedings in the Employment Tribunal against his employer. Finally, the employer refused to pay the employee's full salary when he was absent attending one of these hearings, which was in accordance with the employer's policy requiring employees to apply for unpaid or annual leave to attend Tribunal hearings. As a result the employee resigned, and claimed in his resignation letter that there had been a breach of his trust and confidence in the employer, that this was "the last straw in a series of less favourable treatments that I have been subjected to over a period of years". Along with other claims brought before the Employment Tribunal on these events, his claim for constructive dismissal was thrown out.

The Court held that the essential requirement for the "final straw" defence is that it should contribute to a breach of the implied term of trust and confidence. The test of which is an objective one.

14.3 Wrongful dismissal

A contract of employment is terminable by notice, express or implied, unless the contract is for a fixed term or for the completion of a specific task or contains an exhaustive enumeration of the grounds upon which it may be terminated. As we have previously noted, if either party terminates the contract summarily, (i.e. without notice), the other party has the right to sue for breach of contract. If the employer's summary termination of the contract was a response to an action on the part of the employee, a defence may be available.[18] But the employee must be able to show that the employer's behaviour amounted to a breach of a serious term of the contract or a repudiation of the contract which entitled him or her to terminate the contract summarily.

If the summary dismissal by the employer is not justified, the employee will be treated as having been wrongfully dismissed; if the employer's conduct causes the employee to resign and that conduct is held to be in breach of contract, the employee's contract will be treated as having been breached.

---

[18] Technically, of course, it could operate both ways; i.e. it could be the employee who summarily (illegally) terminates the employment relationship in breach of contract. If this happened, the employer could sue the employee for breach of contract. For present purposes, we assume that it is the employer who has summarily dismissed the employee.

An action for wrongful dismissal or breach of contract is heard in the County Court or High Court; the Employment Tribunals can also now hear such cases where damages are claimed.

14.4 Unfairly dismissed?

Potential claimants must fulfil certain requirements before being able to make a complaint of unfair dismissal. These are:

- they must be an employee;
- they must have been 'continuously employed' for one year;
- they should not be in one of the excluded classes (which we discuss further below);
- they must present their complaint of unfair dismissal within three months of the 'effective date of termination'; and
- they must have been 'dismissed'.

14.4.1 Qualifications

An employee has the statutory right not to be unfairly dismissed by his or her employer. This right is made subject to certain caveats (for example, the right is not available to those who have reached 'normal retiring age' or who are over 65). Thus, the right not to be unfairly dismissed only extends to "qualifying" employees; it is not available to those who are self-employed or those who do satisfy the qualification criteria.

Excluded categories

The following categories of employee are excluded from the legislation:

- Employees employed under illegal contracts.
- Those covered by diplomatic or state immunity.
- Employees of international organisations.
- Crown employees.
- Parliamentary staff.
- Employees over retirement age.
- Short-term and casual employees.
- Employees affected by national security; and
- Employees in police service and members of the armed forces.

Continuity of employment

Continuity of employment is important if you are seeking to bring an employment claim based upon your statutory right not to be unfairly dismissed because the right is only available to employees who have been 'continuously employed' for one year or more. Continuity of employment is also used to compute the amount of any redundancy payment and of a basic award of compensation for unfair dismissal.

The date at which the employee must have the minimum period of employment is the 'effective date of termination'. This is defined as either the date when the notice given to the employee expires or, in the case of a summary dismissal, the date of the summary dismissal. The starting date for the calculation is the day on which he or she started work. That means the day on which the employment under the contract began, which need not be the day on which the employee started to perform the duties.

14.4.2 What is unfair dismissal?
The statutory definition of "dismissal" is as follows:
> '. . . an employee is dismissed by his employer if (and ... only if) -
> (a) the contract under which he is employed is terminated by the employer (whether with or without notice),
> (b) he is employed under a contract for a fixed term and that term expires without being renewed under the same contract, or
> (c) the employee terminates the contract under which he is employed (with or without notice) in circumstances such that he is entitled to terminate it without notice by reason of the employer's conduct.'

Reason for dismissal
Once it has been established that the employee has been dismissed, an *unfair* dismissal claim will fall to be decided in two stages. The first stage consists of establishing what was the reason for the dismissal (i.e. was it potentially fair?); at the second stage the Tribunal must be satisfied that the employer acted reasonably in dismissing for the given reason.

In a complaint of unfair dismissal involving the so-called 'potentially fair' reasons, it is for the employer not only to show the reason (or, if there was more than one, the principal reason) for the dismissal but also to show that the reason falls within one of the following five categories:

WORK

- Capability or qualifications
- Employee's conduct
- Redundancy
- Statutory requirements
- 'Some other substantial reason'

Capability

The statutory definition of 'capability' here is 'capability assessed by reference to skill, aptitude, health or any other physical or mental quality', and 'qualifications' means 'any degree, diploma or other academic, technical or professional qualification relevant to the position which the employee held'.

Misconduct

There is no statutory definition of 'conduct'. Apart from the overlap between conduct and capability, conduct itself has been held to embrace a wide range of actions. Its scope includes gross misconduct, such as theft, violence, negligence and working in competition with the employer, and lesser matters, such as violence or swearing. What may be called 'off-duty' conduct will be considered, if it in some way bears upon the relationship between the employer and the employee, particularly where criminal offences are involved.

Examples here are:
(a)   X was sacked for not obeying his line manager's orders;
(b)   Y was dismissed for stealing from the works canteen.
(c)   A and B had a fight in the firm's car park.

All of these warrant instant dismissal, provided thorough investigation and disciplinary procedures have been adhered to.

Some other substantial reason

The fifth category of reason referred to above is 'some other substantial reason of a kind such as to justify the dismissal of an employee holding the position which the employee held'. This is a fairly wide category of reasons. The most common examples relate to the business needs of the employer and have tended to involve a refusal by the employee to agree to a change in contractual terms or a refusal to agree to a reorganisation falling short of redundancy.

14.4.3 Procedures

Once a potentially fair reason has been established, it is then necessary to consider whether the employer acted fairly in dismissing for that reason. The law states:

'. . . the determination of the question whether the dismissal is fair or unfair (having regard to the reason shown by the employer) –

(a) depends on whether in the circumstances (including the size and administrative resources of the employer's undertaking) the employer acted reasonably or unreasonably in treating it as a sufficient reason for dismissing the employee, and

(b) shall be determined in accordance with equity and the substantial merits of the case.'

The effect of this is that there is no burden of proof on either the employer or the employee. It is therefore wrong for an Employment Tribunal to place the burden on the employer of satisfying the Tribunal that he or she acted reasonably.

The statutory procedures

There are "standard" and "modified" statutory procedures which apply to dismissal as well as to disciplinary action short of dismissal (such as suspension). There are common features in both procedures that must be adhered to:

- Each step and action under the procedure must be taken without unreasonable delay.
- Both the timing and location of any meetings must be reasonable.
- Meetings must be conducted in a manner that enables both employer and employee to explain their cases.
- In the case of appeal meetings which are not the first meeting, the employer should, so far as is reasonably practicable, be represented by a more senior manager than attended the first meeting (unless the most senior manager attended that meeting).

Under the **standard procedure**:

1. The employee must be informed in writing of the reasons why the employer is contemplating dismissing or taking disciplinary action against him, and should be invited to a meeting to discuss the matter further.
2. No action should be taken prior to the meeting, except where the disciplinary action taken is suspension. The employee must take all reasonable steps to attend.
3. Following the meeting the employee must be informed of the employer's decision, and made aware of any appeal procedures available in the result that they are unsatisfied by the outcome.
4. In the event of an appeal, the employee must inform the employer of their intention to do so. Consequently the employer must invite the employee to attend a further meeting, with which the employee must take all reasonable steps to attend.
5. The disciplinary action or dismissal can take place before the appeal meeting.
6. After the appeal, the employer must inform the employee of his final decision.

The procedure is modified where an employee's alleged misconduct has led to the dismissal, requiring only that the employer gives the employee a written statement of the alleged misconduct and informs the employee of the right to appeal, with stages 4 and 6 of the standard procedure applying in the event of an appeal.

Grievance

There are also statutory grievance procedures, once more comprising a 'standard' and a 'modified' procedure. The standard procedure mirrors that found in the Discipline and Dismissal Procedure, except for the first stage, where in this case it is for the employee to write a letter notifying the employer of his the grievance, as opposed to the employer writing to inform the employee of reasons for the discipline or potential dismissal.

The 'modified' statutory grievance procedure again is only used in certain circumstances, and is to be utilised when the person raising the grievance is a former employee, and is as follows:

- The employee must inform the employer in writing of his grievance;
- The employer must set out his response in writing and send this to the former employee.

14.4.4 Automatically unfair dismissals

The following types of dismissal will be treated as automatically unfair:

- dismissals in connection with trade union membership and activities, or trade union recognition;
- dismissal for participation in official industrial action;
- dismissal of an employee in connection with leave for family reasons (including paternity and adoption leave);
- dismissal for reasons connected with health and safety;
- dismissal of a shop or betting worker for refusing Sunday work;
- dismissal in connection with an employee's rights under the Working Time Regulations;
- dismissal for reasons relating to an employee's performance of his or her duties as an occupational pension fund trustee;
- dismissal for reasons relating to an employee's performance of his or her duties as an employee representative;
- dismissal for making a 'protected disclosure';
- dismissal for assertion of a statutory right;
- dismissal of an employee in connection with the national minimum wage legislation;
- dismissal of a worker in connection with the statutory right to be accompanied at a disciplinary or grievance hearing.

14.4.5 Remedies

The remedies available to an employee whose complaint of unfair dismissal succeeds before a Tribunal or Court are a re-instatement or re-engagement order or compensation.

Reinstatement and re-engagement orders

A reinstatement order is an order to the employer to treat the applicant as if he or she had not been dismissed. In deciding whether to make an order, the Tribunal must take into account the following factors: the complainant's wishes; the practicability for the employer of compliance with the order; and, where the complainant caused or contributed to some extent to the dismissal, whether it would be just to order reinstatement. The effect of an order of reinstatement is to give the employee his or her old job back; it will include an ancillary order for arrears of pay between the date of dismissal and the date of reinstatement. There is no statutory maximum to the amount which may be ordered to be paid. The effect of a re-engagement order will be to give the employee a job similar to the one from which he or she was dismissed. The Tribunal is required when making the order to specify the terms of re-engagement, again including arrears of pay.

Compensation

In practice, re-instatement orders are far less common than an award of compensation, which an Employment Tribunal will make if it makes no order for re-employment, or if it makes such an order but the employer fails to comply with it. Compensation may consist of the following elements: a basic award, a compensatory award and an additional award.

The *basic award* is calculated in the same way as a redundancy payment (as discussed in the next section). It is necessary to take into account the complainant's age, length of continuous employment on the effective date of termination and the amount of gross weekly pay. Reductions in the basic award may be made where the employee is near retirement, where the employee unreasonably refuses an offer of reinstatement, where the employee's conduct before dismissal makes it just and equitable to make a reduction, where the employee has already received a redundancy payment, and where the employee has received an ex gratia payment from the employer.

The *compensatory award* should be 'such amount as the Tribunal considers "just and equitable" in all the circumstances having regard to the loss sustained by the complainant in consequence of the dismissal in so far as that loss is attributable to action taken by the employer'. The maximum amount of compensatory award that may be awarded is £60,600 as from 1 February 2007 The "heads of loss" which the compensatory award may cover are: (1) immediate loss of wages; (2) manner of dismissal; (3) future loss of wages; (4) loss of protection in respect of unfair dismissal or dismissal by reason of redundancy, and (5) loss of pension rights.

14.5 Redundancy

14.5.1 What is redundancy?

Redundancy is different from other forms of dismissal because the employer is removing the post rather than the individual employee.

14.5.2 The three-stage test

There is a three-stage test to determine whether an employee has been dismissed by reason of redundancy:

1) has the employee has actually been dismissed? If so,

2) have the requirements of the employer's business for employees to carry out work of the particular kind carried out by the dismissed employee ceased or diminished (or are they expected to cease or diminish)? If so

3) is the dismissal of the employee caused wholly or mainly by the state of affairs identified in the second stage?

If the answer to the questions posed at all three stages is yes, then we can conclude that the employee has been dismissed by reason of redundancy, and is entitled to redundancy payment rights, as we discuss further below.

14.5.3 Offer of alternative employment

Before we consider redundancy payments, we ought to consider the situation where an employee who is under notice of redundancy (or who has been constructively dismissed) is offered alternative employment.

If there is no dismissal, there can be no entitlement to redundancy payment. On the other hand, if, the employee has been dismissed, he may not be entitled to receive the redundancy payment which would otherwise be payable if he makes an unreasonable refusal of a suitable offer of alternative employment.

14.5.4 Redundancy payment

The calculation of a redundancy payment is based on the following factors:

- the employee's age at the relevant date (in most cases, the same date as the effective date of termination in unfair dismissal cases);
- the number of years of continuous employment; and
- the amount of gross weekly pay at the effective date.

The calculation is subject to the following limits:

- the number of years used in the calculation may not exceed 20; and
- the amount of a week's pay may not exceed a figure set annually by the Government, (currently £290).

The method of calculation is to work backwards from the relevant date, looking at the employee's age at the beginning of each year of continuous employment:

- for each year in which the employee was aged 41 or more (but not more than 64), one and a half week's pay is payable;
- for each year in which he or she was between 22 and 41, one weeks' pay;
- for each year over the age of 18 between the time he or she started work and 22, half a week's pay.

Thus, an employee employed for 20 years and made redundant at 62 will receive a redundancy payment reckoned on the basis of the years of continuous employment from 62 going back to 42. The maximum redundancy payment that can be awarded at present is thus £8,400. Employment before the age of 18 is not counted. The employee's period of continuous employment will be treated as starting on his or her 18th birthday if that date is later than the actual starting date.

A redundancy payment may be subject to reduction in certain cases, such as misconduct or where employees are near retirement age. Social security benefits paid to the redundant employee whilst unemployed are not deductible from the redundancy payment.

Tax position of redundancy payments
These are discussed in section 7.5.

15 Unions

The purpose of this section is to describe the nature and legal powers of unions in the workplace.

On starting work, you may find you are eligible to join a trade union. Membership of a trade union is voluntary; you cannot be required to join a union; nevertheless, even if you decide not to join a union it is helpful to have at least a basic knowledge of trade unions and their activities.

A trade union is defined as:

> 'an organisation (whether temporary or permanent)…which consists wholly or mainly of workers of one or more descriptions and whose principal purposes include the regulation of relations between workers of that description or those descriptions and employers or employers' associations.'

Similarly, employers' associations are defined as organisations (whether or not they are temporary or permanent) consisting wholly or mainly of employers or individual owners of undertakings and having amongst their principal purposes the regulation of relations between those employers and workers or trade unions.

An employers' association can be either an incorporated body (e.g. a company) or unincorporated body. Where an association is unincorporated, it has the same rights and obligations as a trade union.

In contrast, trade unions are unincorporated associations, but they are given quasi-corporate status by statute. The effect of this is that unions are able to make contracts, sue and be sued in relation to contract, tort or other matters, hold property via trustees, and have criminal proceedings taken against them, but for all other purposes they are treated as unincorporated associations.

In order to exist legally a trade union must obtain a certificate of independence. The test of independence requires that a union 'is not under the domination or control of an employer'.

The Certification Officer certifies and makes periodic checks that a union is maintaining its independence and he may withdraw a certificate of independence if the nature of the union changes (although any such decision may be appealed against).

Every member of the principal executive committee of a trade union has to be elected every five years by an election in which all members of the union are entitled to vote. Unions are subject to strict rules in relation to elections, as follows:

- balloting must be held in secret and preferably by postal voting;
- there should be non-interference by 'the union or any of its members, officials or employees'; and
- unions should finance all elections.

15.1 Trade union rights

The exact scope of activities of trade unions is open to interpretation. However, it is generally recognised that legitimate trade union activities can include:

(a)   seeking union recognition;

(b)   discussing union matters;

(c)   seeking advice from union officials; and,

(d)   seeking to recruit new members.

Reasonable time should be given by employers to employees who are trade union members in relation to such activities, including the holding of meetings during the employer's time. The appropriate time for trade union activities is defined both as occasions 'outside the employee's working hours' and time 'within working hours at which, in accordance with arrangements agreed with, or consent given by his employer, it is permissible for him to take part in those activities'.

The ACAS Code of Practice on Time Off gives some indication of the duties for which time off should be granted:

(a)   collective bargaining with the appropriate level of management;

(b)   informing constituents about negotiations or consultations with management;

(c)   meetings with other lay officials or with full-time officials;

(d)   interviews with and on behalf of constituents on grievance and disciplinary matters;

(e)   appearing on behalf of constituents before an outside body.

15.2 Collective agreements

You may sometimes hear the phrase "collective agreement". A collective agreement is any agreement or arrangement made by or on behalf of one or more trade unions and one or more employers or employers' associations and relating to one or more of the following matters:

*   machinery for negotiation or consultation relating to the collective agreement, including recognition;
*   terms and conditions of employment;
*   engagement or non-engagement, or termination or suspension of employment or the duties of employment, of one or more workers;
*   matters of discipline;
*   a worker's membership or non-membership of a trade union;
*   facilities for trade union officials;
*   pay (including pensions).

15.3 Trade union recognition

When we talk about "trade union recognition", we mean recognition of the union by an employer (or a group of associated employers) for the purposes of collective bargaining. Historically, union recognition by employers was purely voluntary, and employers could not (legally) be obliged to recognise a trade union. However, in 1999, the Government passed new legislation which introduced a "statutory recognition procedure" whereby an employer could be obliged to recognise a union (or unions) where a majority of the (relevant) workforce so required. Under this statutory procedure, an independent trade union may apply to an employer for recognition in relation to a particular group of workers (a 'bargaining unit'). If the employer does not agree to recognise the union, or disputes the appropriate bargaining unit for the purposes of recognition, the union may apply to the Central Arbitration Committee (CAC), the body which adjudicates where there is a dispute between the employer and employees about who represents the workplace at a particular place of work, to decide the appropriate bargaining unit and/or whether the union should be recognised. Subject to the circumstances, recognition can be automatic, or a ballot may need to be held. Where it is shown that a majority of the workers in the bargaining unit are members of the union, the CAC can declare the union recognised without a ballot; otherwise, a secret ballot of all the workers in the bargaining unit must be held. The recognition procedures do not apply where the employer employs fewer than 21 workers.

Two or more unions can apply jointly for recognition under the statutory procedure, but in such a case it must be shown that the unions will co-operate effectively in collective bargaining.

Any request for recognition must be in writing, must specify the union or unions and the bargaining unit in respect of which recognition is claimed. The request will not be valid unless the union (or each of the unions) has a certificate of independence, and the employer (together with any associated employers) employs at least 21 workers on the day of the request, or an average of at least 21 workers in the 13 weeks leading up to that day.

Where an application is made to the CAC, it has 10 days to decide whether the application is valid and admissible. The CAC cannot consider an application unless, in addition to the requirements already noted, it is satisfied that at least 10 per cent of the proposed bargaining unit are members of the union, and that a majority of workers in the proposed bargaining unit would be likely to favour recognition. If the CAC has been asked to decide on the appropriate bargaining unit, it must initially give the parties a further 28 days to agree the bargaining unit. If the parties are still deadlocked, the CAC must determine the appropriate bargaining unit within 10 days, taking into account the need for the bargaining unit to be compatible with effective management, and, so far as is consistent with that need, the following factors:

(a)   the views of the employer and the union (or unions);

(b)   existing national and local bargaining arrangements;

(c)   the desirability of avoiding small fragmented bargaining units within an undertaking;

(d)   the characteristics of the workers falling within the bargaining unit and of any other employees of the employer whom the CAC considers relevant;

(e)   the location of the workers.

The main rights accruing to an independent, recognised trade union in relation to consultation and the provision of information are:

(a)   to receive relevant information for the purposes of collective bargaining;

(b)   to be consulted in respect of collective (i.e. large scale) redundancies; and

(c)   to be consulted in relation to a transfer of an undertaking.

The CAC comprises a Chairman, assisted by lay panel members, representing both employers and employees. Further information can be found at www.cac.gov.uk.

15.4 Consultation at work

In some countries, such as Germany and the Netherlands, there is a well-established mechanism for worker consultation, through works councils for example. This is sometimes referred to as the 'social partnership approach', and has been introduced into domestic laws across the European Union through The National Consultation and Information (NIC) Directive. It requires that workers should have the basic right to consultation, and a mechanism for bargaining should be agreed between the parties. Companies are required to inform regularly on the business's economic situation and to consult with workers on key decisions regarding the organisation's future. These include situations where jobs are threatened and where any anticipatory measures, such as training, skill development and other measures increasing the adaptability of employees, are planned. Consultation is also compulsory for decisions that are likely to lead to substantial changes in work organisation or in contractual relations. The rules apply to those businesses/organisations with over 100 workers (and from 2008 for those with more than 50 workers), so do not affect very small businesses.

15.5 Industrial Action

At some time in your career, you may be called upon to participate in industrial action or may otherwise encounter industrial action in the workplace. 'Industrial action' is a strike or withdrawal of labour. In most, if not all, strike action, contracts of employment are affected. However, neither employer nor employee gives notice to terminate the contract, even though strike action amounts to a breach of contract by the striking employees.

In theory, an employer is not obliged to pay the striking workers during an industrial action. In practice, deductions from pay are regulated by agreement between employers and employees (or more typically, employee representatives, usually in the form of trade unions).

Strike action is not the only form of industrial action. Other forms include work-to-rule and go-slow, as well as overtime bans. In addition, employees may work normally but refuse to perform the particular duty about which they are protesting. An employer may also resort to industrial action, since an employer holds the right to make changes in their business. Consequently, employers may have cause to 'lock-out' their workforce.

Industrial action is lawful where:

(a)   the employers have a potential claim for breach of contract; and,

(b)   those taking industrial action are acting in 'contemplation or furtherance of a trade dispute against the employer'.

In such cases, legislation gives immunity from legal proceedings in respect of any action which:

- induced a person to breach a contract of employment;
- threatened that a contract of employment will be breached;
- interferes with the trade, business or employment of a person; or
- constitutes an agreement by two or more persons to procure the doing of any such act.

However, the statutory immunities will be removed in the following situations:

(a)   secondary action;

(b)   unlawful picketing;

(c)   action to enforce union membership;

(d)   action to impose union recognition;

(e)   action in support of dismissed unofficial strikers;

(f)   action without proper notice to an employer;

(g)   action without a valid strike ballot.

16 Employment Tribunals

What are these?
  what happens?
  what can they do?
  what remedies are available?

16.1 Employment Tribunals

Should you ever find yourself pursuing (or defending!) a legal employment-related claim through the Courts, you may well encounter Employment Tribunals. Employment claims are generally initiated in an Employment Tribunal, although it is by no means uncommon for cases to be appealed to higher courts as we will discuss in due course. Employment Tribunals consist of a three-member panel: a legally-qualified Chairperson, and two lay members (sometimes called 'wing members'), who are not legally qualified. The Chairperson, who is appointed by the Judicial Appointments Commission as either full-time or part-time, must be a barrister or solicitor of at least seven years' standing, while the lay members (who are all part-time) are chosen after consulting organisations representing employees and those representing employers. This means that the lay members have experience of each side of industry, i.e. management and employees, and together provide what is sometimes called an 'industrial jury'.

16.1.1 The organisation of Employment Tribunals

The Employment Tribunal Service (ETS), which is part of the DTI, has responsibility for the overall administration of Employment Tribunals. It has a Director appointed by and who reports to the Secretary of State for Trade and Industry.

16.1.2 Procedure

Only an outline of the procedure of the Employment Tribunals can be given here. Essentially, Employment Tribunals have an overriding objective which is 'to deal with cases justly'. This means dealing with cases, 'so far as practicable', so as to ensure that the parties are on an equal footing, saving expense (legal aid is not available in cases heard before an Employment Tribunal), dealing with cases in ways proportionate to their complexity, and ensuring that they are dealt with expeditiously and fairly. There is no requirement to use any special form to commence proceedings in the Tribunal, although there is a standard form, called an ET1, which may be lodged as the originating application within the relevant time limit. In unfair dismissal and discrimination cases, for example, the relevant time limit is three months, whereas it is six months in redundancy payments claims and equal pay claims. The Tribunal has discretion to extend this limit.

Employment Tribunals have the power to strike out a 'misconceived' claim (or defence – known as the Notice of Appearance). This is defined as claims (or defences) with 'no reasonable prospect of success'. The idea is that hopeless claims (or defences) are not and should not be allowed to proceed to the hearing. Similarly, the Tribunal may strike out 'scandalous... or vexatious' claims. A copy of the claim is sent to the respondent employer, together with form ET3 on which the employer may set out its response, which must be made within 21 days, although the Tribunal may extend this limit where it was not reasonably practicable to respond in the time stipulated. A copy of the ET1 is also sent to ACAS, with a view to possible settlement before the hearing with the assistance of an ACAS conciliation officer.

Employment Tribunals may make orders for disclosure. Broadly speaking this is the process whereby one party can be obliged to provide the other with any (relevant) information within its possession and/or inspection of documents, further particulars of the claim or the notice of appearance, or to provide written answers to any question. They may also order a pre-hearing review (PHR), either on the application of one of the parties, or on their own application, where it appears that an aspect of the claim or defence is unlikely to succeed. PHRs may be heard by a Chairperson sitting alone. Where the Employment Tribunal decides that the aspect of the claim in question is unlikely to succeed, it can impose a condition that a party pays a deposit of up to £500 within 21 days before being allowed to continue with the proceedings, with a warning to that party that an order for costs could be made against them at the full hearing, together with forfeiture of the deposit.

16.1.3 The Hearing

Although Employment Tribunals are allowed to regulate their own procedure, their proceedings tend to be quite formal, similar to civil court proceedings. Quite often, parties attend with barristers or solicitors in attendance, although this is *not* mandatory. If possible, the parties should agree in advance of the hearing the documents to be used before the Tribunal, usually contained within a bundle of documents, for ease of reference. The party with the burden of proof begins. In an unfair dismissal case, where the employer accepts that a dismissal has taken place, the burden of proof will be on the employer, who will start. However, in a constructive unfair dismissal case, where the fact of dismissal is in dispute, it is the employee who starts. Witnesses give evidence on oath and are "examined" (i.e. asked questions by each side). When all witnesses have given their evidence, closing submissions are made by each side, and the Tribunal retires to consider its decision.

The Employment Tribunal may reserve its decision until a later date or give its decision orally at the conclusion of the hearing, with the written decision setting out summary reasons being sent out some time later. However, the parties may request full written reasons either at the hearing or within 21 days of dispatch of the summary reasons. In discrimination and equal pay cases, full written reasons are always provided.

16.1.4 Representation

There are no rules requiring that parties are formally represented by lawyers before Employment Tribunals. Therefore, anyone can appear and litigants can represent themselves. Employment Tribunals, like all Tribunals, are supposed to be informal and have relaxed rules of evidence. In fact, the Chairman of the Tribunal controls all the rules, within discretionary limits and the realms of fairness to all parties.

Do I have to use a solicitor /barrister?

As stated above, the simple answer is no! However, legal representation is advised in all but the simplest of cases. Moreover, since most employers are legally represented (not least because their insurers usually insist on it), it is generally advisable to seek out legal representation. If you are in a union – don't forget to ask your union for help. Or, if the issues concerned involve discrimination law, why not contact one of the agencies – EOC, CRE or Disability Rights Commission. ACAS are also there to give advice, but not assistance nor representation. Further details of all these organisations are in Appendix 1.

16.1.5 Costs

As we all know, legal proceedings can be very expensive. The general rule is that upon the conclusion of a civil (i.e. non-criminal) legal action, it is the losing party who is responsible all (or most) of the legal costs of both sides (although there are exceptions to this general rule, depending upon the exact circumstances of each case). This general rule of "costs being awarded in favour of the victor" does not however, normally apply in cases brought before Employment Tribunals, which do not (generally speaking) award costs. Having said this, we should note that an Employment Tribunal does have power to make a costs order against a party (or a party's representative) where, in bringing the proceedings, the party or the representative has 'acted vexatiously, abusively, disruptively or otherwise unreasonably, or the bringing or conducting of the proceedings by a party has been misconceived', up to a maximum of £10,000.

16.1.6 Reviews and appeals

Employment Tribunals may review their decisions, either of their own volition or at the request of one of the parties, within 14 days of announcing their decision. There are very limited grounds for review, e.g. a clerical error, or that the decision was made in the absence of one party. An appeal may be made to the Employment Appeal Tribunal ("EAT") on a point of law within six weeks of the decision being given.

16.1.7 Remedies

At the end of a Tribunal hearing, the Tribunal must give its decision on the merits of the case (other than in rare circumstances where it might instead remit the case for a re-hearing by another Tribunal) and its reasons for that decision.

The judgment and reasons may be communicated to the parties in one of three ways:

- The Chairman may announce both the judgment and reasons together, by dictating into a recording machine in the presence of the parties, after the end of the hearing.
- The Chairman may announce the judgment only, reserving the reasons to be set out in writing at a later date.
- The Tribunal may reserve both its judgment and reasons, and give these out at a later date.

16.1.8 Reasons

The Tribunal (or a Chairman) is able to issue a judgment which is the final determination of the proceedings on a particular issue, and make orders which are issued in relation to interim matters and require a person to do or not to do something.

If the judgment is reserved and sent to the parties later it must also contain the reasons for the judgment. The following information must be included in written reasons for a judgement:

- The issues which were identified as being relevant to the claim;
- If issues were not determined, what those issues were and why they were not determined;
- Findings of fact relevant to the issues which have been determined;
- A concise statement of the applicable law;
- How the relevant findings of fact and applicable law have been applied in order to determine the issues; and
- Where the judgment includes an award of compensation or a determination that one party make a payment to the other, a table showing how the amount or sum has been calculated or a description of the manner in which it has been calculated.

Whenever a Tribunal awards compensation or reaches a determination whereby a party is required to pay a sum of money to another (excluding an award of costs or allowances), then the decision must contain a statement of the amount of compensation awarded or of the sum to be paid. This statement must be followed by a table or description explaining how it has been calculated. This rule applies to all decisions, regardless of whether they are in summary or extended form.

WORK

The tribunal clerk will then send the judgment and reasons to the Secretary of the Tribunals who enters the document in the Register at the Central Office of Employment Tribunals and sends a copy to each of the parties and to any other person who made an appearance in the case.

16.2 Employment Appeals

The EAT hears appeals from the Employment Tribunals on points of law (not fact). A President is appointed for a term of three years from the ranks of High Court judges. The EAT's composition is similar to that of Employment Tribunals, in that it has two lay members drawn from employers' and employees' organisations, but the Chairperson is a High Court judge or circuit judge. A judge sitting alone in the EAT may hear appeals from a single-member Employment Tribunal, and the EAT may consist of the Chairperson and one lay member where the parties agree to this. Unlike the Employment Tribunal, legal aid is available in the EAT. As appeals are made to the EAT on points of law, it is much more usual for the parties to have legal representation in this forum. Although proceedings are not quite as formal or legalistic as in the High Court, they are more formal than in the Employment Tribunal.

The EAT is a court of record, so its decisions must be followed by Employment Tribunals. However, different divisions of the EAT are not obliged to follow their own decisions, which can lead to confusion at Employment Tribunal level about what is the correct legal analysis to be applied. The English EAT sits in London (the Scottish EAT sits in Edinburgh). Appeals from the EAT are to the Court of Appeal and then to the House of Lords.

16.2.1 Time limits

Different claims are subject to different time limits; that is, they have different deadlines within which they must be brought. Examples include:

Claim	Time limit
Unfair dismissal for official industrial action	6 months from date of dismissal
Redundancy payment	6 months starting with the relevant date
Equal pay	6 months from the date employment ceased
Interim relief pending complaint of unfair dismissal	7 days immediately following termination
Contract counter-claim by employer	6 weeks from receipt of details of an employee's contractual claim

17 Human rights

What are they?
how do they apply?
what help do they provide?

It would be wrong of us to discuss employment rights and obligations without at least mentioning the issue of human rights. The Human Rights Act 1998 ("HRA") incorporates the main provisions of the European Convention on Human Rights into UK law.

As a result a number of fundamental rights and freedoms now underpin the UK legal system. This affects many areas of UK law, including employment. However, while the HRA is an important piece of legislation and much reported in the media, its impact on employment law has not (yet) been as great as some commentators predicted.

17.1 The European Convention on Human Rights

The European Convention is a Treaty which was drawn up in 1950 by the Council of Europe. It reflects the aspirations of post-war Europe and therefore contains a number of provisions (known as 'Articles') which aim to protect the fundamental rights of citizens against abuse by the state or its institutions. These are more concerned with civil liberties in a political context than with economic rights; for example, there is no right to work.

17.1.1 Relevant articles

The Articles which are most relevant in the employment context include:
- the right to a fair trial (Article 6)
- the right to respect for private and family life (Article 8)
- the right to freedom of thought, conscience and religion (Article 9)
- the right to freedom of expression (Article 10)
- the right to freedom of assembly and association (Article 11)
- the prohibition of discrimination (Article 14).

Despite the importance of these rights the Convention recognises that they are not absolute and that legitimate restrictions can be placed on them in a democratic society.

For example:
The Convention states that the right to freedom of expression can be subject to such restrictions

'as are prescribed by law and are necessary in a democratic society in the interests of national security ... for the prevention of disorder or crime, for the protection of health or morals, for the protection of the reputation or rights of others, for preventing the disclosure of information received in confidence, or for maintaining the authority and impartiality of the judiciary'.

As a result a balancing exercise has to be performed when determining if a Convention right has been breached.

17.2 Incorporation of the European Convention on Human Rights into UK law

When the Government ratified the Convention in 1951 it assumed that the existing UK law offered sufficient protection against human rights abuses and decided there was therefore no need to incorporate the Convention into UK law. This meant that anyone wishing to bring a claim for breach of a Convention right had to do so before the European Court of Human Rights ("ECHR") in Strasbourg, which was a long and expensive process.

The Government's confidence in the existing law turned out to be overly optimistic and over the years the ECHR has found the UK to be in breach of Convention rights on a number of occasions.

One of the best-known examples in the employment context is the case of *Halford v UK*. The case concerned a senior police officer whose calls on a private line in her office were intercepted by her employers. She claimed this action breached Article 8 which specifically protects 'private life and correspondence'. The ECHR agreed, taking the view that, in the absence of any warning to the contrary, the police officer had a reasonable expectation that her calls would be private.

Cases such as this increased the pressure on the UK Government to incorporate the Convention into UK law so that individuals could enforce Convention rights against the state and its institutions in British Courts, rather than having to go to Strasbourg. This was finally achieved by the Human Rights Act and so today a police officer could bring proceedings against his or her employer for a breach of Article 8 directly in the UK Courts.

17.3 Key provisions of the Human Rights Act

The most important provisions of the HRA are as follows:

17.3.1 New cause of action against public bodies (section 6)

The HRA makes it unlawful for public bodies to act in a way which is incompatible with the Convention.

However, this obligation is more onerous for some public bodies than others. This is because the HRA distinguishes for these purposes between "pure" public bodies (which include the police and Government departments) and "hybrid" bodies (such as Railtrack and the BBC) which have a mixture of public and private functions.

A pure public body must comply with the Convention in every aspect of its dealings, including its role as employer. If it does not it can be sued by the aggrieved employee directly in the ordinary courts for breach of Convention rights.

On the other hand, an individual can only sue a hybrid public body for failing to act in accordance with the Convention in respect of its public functions. As employment activities have generally been regarded by English law as private in nature, this means that such hybrid bodies are unlikely to be directly liable to employees for breaches of Convention rights (unless the breach gives rise to some other liability, e.g. in contract).

17.3.2 Role of UK Courts and Tribunals

UK Courts and Tribunals have to act consistently with the Convention when deciding cases, even in cases between private persons, such as an unfair dismissal claim brought by an employee against a private employer.

17.3.3 Interpretation of legislation

Employment Tribunals are under an obligation, so far as is possible, to interpret and give effect to legislation in a way which is compatible with the Convention rights.

This obligation applies irrespective of whether the employer is a public, hybrid or private body. Where an employee brings a claim under existing employment protection legislation (e.g. for unfair dismissal or unlawful discrimination) then the Employment Tribunal will have to take into account any possible infringement of Convention rights.

In an unfair dismissal case, where an employee's Convention rights have been breached during the dismissal process then an Employment Tribunal would have to take this into account when determining whether the employer had acted reasonably in all the circumstances in dismissing the employee.

Similarly, where the reason for a dismissal relates to the exercise by an employee of a Convention right then the Employment Tribunal would have to take this into account when assessing fairness.

17.3.4 Declaration of incompatibility

If it is impossible to interpret an Act of Parliament in accordance with Convention rights the senior courts (i.e. the High Courts, Court of Appeal and the House of Lords) can make a declaration that the relevant Act is incompatible with the Convention. This does not amend the Act but is a clear signal to Parliament that amendment is necessary. Neither Employment Tribunals nor the Employment Appeal Tribunal have the power to issue a declaration of incompatibility.

17.4 Most commonly encountered articles in the workplace

The Convention rights which are most likely to be relevant in the employment context are the right to respect for family and private life (Article 8), the right to freedom of expression (Article 10) and the right to peaceful assembly and the freedom to associate (Article 11).

17.4.1 Right to respect for private and family life

This may have an impact on the following situations:

Monitoring and surveillance: in *Halford v UK* (discussed above), the European Court of Human Rights held that an employee has a 'reasonable expectation of privacy' in the workplace. In carrying out any telephone tapping, e-mail monitoring or other surveillance, an employer must respect this expectation in addition to other relevant legislation such as the Data Protection Act and the Regulation of Investigatory Powers Act.

Searches and drug tests: these would infringe an employee's Article 8 rights unless the employer could rely on one of the "derogations" to the right (e.g. the employer could show that a search was necessary for the prevention of crime or for the protection of the rights and freedoms of others).

Office relationships: a policy prohibiting office relationships may infringe Article 8. If a private sector employer dismissed an employee for failing to abide by this policy then the Employment Tribunal would have to take account of any possible infringement of Article 8 when deciding whether the dismissal was unfair.

17.4.2 Right to freedom of expression

Freedom of expression does not simply encompass free speech. It also covers other forms of self-expression and could affect workplace dress codes, for example.

In the public sector, employers would have to rely on one of the derogations to justify the imposition of a dress code. The most relevant would appear to be that the code was necessary 'for the protection of the reputation or rights of others'.

Employment Tribunals would have to take Article 10 into account if considering the fairness of a dismissal for failure to comply with the code. It would also be relevant if an employee brought a sex or race discrimination complaint relating to the imposition of a dress code. Most commentators believe that the HRA will make it easier for an employee successfully to claim that a dress code is discriminatory.

17.4.3 Right to peaceful assembly and freedom to associate

There has been some debate as to whether a number of provisions of UK collective labour law, including those regarding picketing, the right to be a member of a particular trade union and the right to strike, are fully compatible with the provisions of Article 11.

17.5 Remedies

Act of public authority only

This section covers the remedies available where an individual exercises the right of action introduced by the Act and claims directly against a public authority for breach of Convention rights.

Just and appropriate remedy

A Court may grant such relief or make such order, within its powers, as it considers just and appropriate. In doing so, it will balance the rights of the individual and the public interest.

As a result the three traditional remedies for unlawful conduct by public authorities – declaration (confirms which rights were violated, publicly), injunction (stops it happening, i.e. prevents it recurring/occurring if pre-emptive in the first instance) and damages (monetary compensation to cover your losses) – will be available in human rights cases. In addition, if the claim is brought by way of judicial review the remedies of quashing, prohibiting or mandatory orders would be available.

Damages

Damages may only be awarded if, taking into account the other remedies granted, the Court is satisfied that the award is necessary to "afford just satisfaction" to the claimant, in other words, to demonstrate the success of their claim.

The Court must take into account the principles applied by the European Court of Human Rights when determining whether to make an award, and how much to award. These principles are difficult to discern clearly. The overriding principle is that of 'just satisfaction', which may result in no award of damages if the Court considers that the declaration that the individual's human rights have been infringed of itself affords the individual just satisfaction.

Compensation may be awarded for financial loss, non-financial matters, such as anxiety and distress, and costs and expenses. In the past awards by the ECHR have not been particularly high (e.g. in the Halford case £10,000 was awarded). It remains to be seen if UK courts follow this approach.

Private law claims

As we have seen, there can be no direct claim for breach of Convention rights against a private body or a hybrid public body acting in its private capacity.

However, if such a body is sued under existing employment laws the Courts must interpret those laws as far as possible in accordance with the Convention. This will not affect the remedies available. So, for example, if an applicant claims unfair dismissal against a private employer then, even if human rights arguments are used in the course of the claim, the remedies available will still be reinstatement, re-engagement or compensation.

Appendix 1: Useful sources

Advisory, Conciliation and Arbitration Service
www.acas.org.uk

The Advisory, Conciliation and Arbitration Service (ACAS) was established in 1974. Its head office is in London and it has 11 regional offices across the UK. It is an independent (but Government-funded) organisation. It is governed by a Council, consisting of a Chair appointed by the Secretary of State for Trade and Industry, and nine members representing employers, trade unions, and independent members (usually lawyers and/or academics).

Arbitration is a voluntary process at the collective level whereby the parties to a dispute agree to submit to the decision of an arbitrator, although the decision itself is not legally binding (it is expected, however, that having agreed to submit to this process, the parties will observe the terms of any decision arising from it). Where there is, or is likely to be, a trade dispute ACAS may, at the request of one or more of the parties to the dispute and with the consent of all parties, refer the matters in dispute to arbitration. Arbitration should be considered by ACAS only after conciliation or negotiation have been attempted to resolve the dispute. Arbitration is carried out through the Central Arbitration Committee (see below) or by an arbitrator selected from a panel of names kept by ACAS.

ACAS has a statutory role to encourage the settlement of Tribunal claims. As soon as a Tribunal claim is made, ACAS is informed and an ACAS officer is sent copies of all correspondence between the parties and the Tribunal. The parties can use the ACAS officer as a useful intermediary for the purposes of any settlement negotiation, in the confidence that any discussions through ACAS cannot be reported to the Tribunal and that they will remain confidential.

The duty of the ACAS officer to promote settlement is also useful because the ACAS officer has powers to document settlements without needing lawyers, through the use of a special settlement agreement called a 'COT3' (and it's free!). The ACAS officer will help in negotiating the terms of the COT3, finalise the COT3, and withdraw the claim on the party's behalf once settlement has been reached.

The Commissions – EOC, CRE & DRC

www.eoc.org.uk; www.cre.gov.uk; www.drc-gb.org

There are currently three commissions in the field of discrimination law: the Equal Opportunities Commission (EOC); the Commission on Racial Equality (CRE); and the Disability Rights Commission (DRC). The EOC covers sex discrimination and equal pay, the CRE deals with race discrimination and the DRC covers disability discrimination. Recently, the Government has announced that these three bodies will merge in 2007 to form a new consolidated body overseeing equal opportunities and human rights at work.

Equal Opportunities Commission (EOC)

www.eoc.org.uk

The EOC was established under the Sex Discrimination Act 1975. It has a statutory duty to work towards the elimination of discrimination and to promote equal opportunities. Further it has a duty to keep the working of the relevant legislation under review, i.e. the SDA and the Equal Pay Act 1970. The EOC can assist in bringing cases to Employment Tribunals and the courts. It can also undertake and/or fund research and educational activities, as well as issue codes of practice. Examples are the Codes of Practice on Sex Discrimination, Equal Opportunity Policies and the Code of Practice on Equal Pay. The EOC also has the power to conduct a formal investigation "for any purpose connected with the carrying out of [its] duties".

Commission for Racial Equality (CRE)

www.cre.org.uk

The CRE, which is similar to the EOC, was created by the Race Relations Act 1976. It has similar powers and duties to that of the EOC. It can issue codes of practice. Examples include: the Code of Practice for the elimination of racial discrimination, and the Code of Practice on the Duty to Promote Racial Equality). These codes do not have statutory force but they are admissible in evidence and may be taken into account by tribunals and courts in determining any question under the relevant statutes. Like the EOC, the CRE can instigate formal investigations "for any purpose connected with the carrying out of [its] duties", but only where they have reasonable suspicion that unlawful acts of discrimination are taking place. If, following a formal investigation, the CRE become satisfied that a person is committing or has committed any unlawful discriminatory acts or practices, they may issue a non-discrimination notice to employers.

The Disability Rights Commission (DRC)

www.drc.org.uk

The DRC was established under the Disability Rights Commission Act 1999. The DRC's main duties have been to work towards eliminating discrimination against disabled people; to promote equal opportunities for disabled people; to keep the DDA under review; to provide information and advice to disabled people, employers and service providers. It has the power to issue codes of practice and to support individuals seeking to enforce their rights. It has similar powers to the other two Commissions in terms of conducting investigations and issuing non-discrimination notices, similar to the other two Commissions.

The Commission for Human Rights and Equality

The government has indicated its intentions to integrate the three relevant Commissions discussed above into a single body. The new unified body will have the task of promoting diversity whilst protecting equality and human rights.

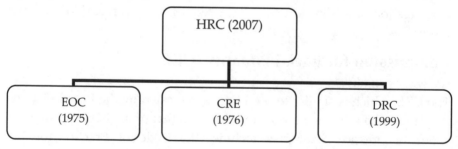

Business Debtline
Provides a free telephone debt counselling service for self-employed and small businesses, partly funded by banks. Tel: 0800 197 6026

Consumer Credit Counselling Service
Funded entirely by the credit industry, the service offers advice to people in debt. Tel: 0800 138 1111

Citizens Advice
Offers free, independent and confidential advice from more than 700 locations throughout the UK

HMRC
www.hmrc.gov.uk
The website of HM Revenue & Customs. The pensions pages provide detailed guidance as regards the tax treatment of pension schemes and the benefits they provide.

Motley Fool UK
www.fool.co.uk
A wideranging website addressing a variety of financial matters.

National Debtline
A free, confidential and independent service funded by the Department of Trade and Industry and the credit industry. Tel: 0808 808 4000

The Pensions Advisory Service
www.pensionsadvisoryservice.org.uk
An independent non-profit making organisation which can provide free advice and guidance on a range of pensions problems.

The Pensions Ombudsman
www.pensions-ombudsman.org.uk
The Ombudsman appointed by the Government to supervise the operation of pension schemes, with widespread powers to intervene when necessary.

APPENDIX 1

The Pensions Regulator

www.thepensionsregulator.gov.uk

The Pensions Regulator is the UK regulator of work-based pension schemes.

The Pensions Tracing Service

The Pensions Tracing Service maintains a register of occupational and personal pension schemes, to assist people to trace their pension rights. More information about the Pensions Tracing Service may be found at www.thepensionservice.gov.uk.

Appendix 2: Further Information
Books

ARNHEIM, Michael. *The handbook of human rights law: an accessible approach to the issues and principles.* London, Kogan Page.

BARNETT, Daniel *and* SCROPE, Henry. *Employment law handbook.* London, Law Society.

CIPD. *CIPD employment law for people managers.* London, Chartered Institute of Personnel and Development.

CIPD. *Religious discrimination : an introduction to the law.* London, Chartered Institute of Personnel and Development.

DEPARTMENT OF TRADE AND INDUSTRY. *A guide for employers and employees;* London, Department of Trade and Industry: *Redundancy consultation and notification; The working time regulations : workers and employers.*

EDWARDS, Martin *and* MALONE, Michael. *Tolley's equal opportunities handbook.*

GAINES, Robert (Executive Editor). *The Pensions Factbook,* Gee Publishing Limited (loose leaf publication)

GILLOW, Elizabeth; HOPKINS, Martin *and* WILLIAMS, Audrey. *Harassment at work.* Bristol, Jordans. Chartered Institute of Personnel and Development.

LEWIS, David *and* SARGEANT, Malcolm. *Essentials of employment law.* London, Chartered Institute of Personnel and Development.

PITT, Gwyneth. *Employment law.* London, Sweet and Maxwell.

SELWYN, Norman M. *Law of employment.* London, LexisNexis.

Tolley's health and safety at work handbook. Croydon, Tolley.

STANLEY, Thomas J and DANKO, William D. *The Millionaire Next Door,* 1996, Pocket Press . ISBN - 0-671-01520-6. A popular study of the American wealthy, its lessons have applications in the United Kingdom.

WADHAM, John; MOUNTFIELD, Helen *and* EDMUNDSON, Anna. *Blackstone's guide to the Human Rights Act 1998.* 3rd ed. Oxford, Oxford University Press.

APPENDIX 2
Useful Websites

GOVERNMENT AND EXECUTIVE AGENCIES	WEB ADDRESSES
Advisory, Conciliation & Arbitration Service (ACAS)	www.acas.org.uk
Commission for Racial Equality	www.cre.gov.uk
Department for Constitutional Affairs	www.dca.gov.uk
Department of Trade and Industry	www.dti.gov.uk
Disability Rights Commission	www.drc.org.uk
Employment Appeal Tribunal (EAT)	www.employmentappeals.gov.uk
Equal Opportunities Commission	www.eoc.org.uk
Government Information Service	www.ukonline.gov.uk
Health and Safety Executive	www.hse.gov.uk
Her Majesty's Treasury	www.hm-treasury.gov.uk
Information Commissioner	www.informationcommissioner.gov.uk
Home Office	www.homeoffice.gov.uk
Department of Constitutional Affairs	www.dca.gov.uk
The Stationary Office	www.tso.co.uk
COURTS AND COURT DECISIONS	**WEB ADDRESSES**
Court service: one of the best Government sites for lawyers	www.courtservice.gov.uk
Employment Appeal Tribunal	www.employmentappeals.gov.uk
House of Lords judgments since 14 November 1996	www.publications.parliament.uk
The Incorporated Council of Law Reporting for England and Wales	www.lawreports.co.uk

EUROPEAN COURTS, INSTITUTIONS AND INFORMATION	WEB ADDRESSES
Agencies of the European Community	http.europa.eu.int/agencies/index_en.htm
EU Commission	www.europa.eu.int/comm/index.htm
EU recent developments	www.europa.eu.int/geninfo/whatsnew.htm
European Court of Human Rights	www.echr.coe.int/
European Court of Justice	www.curia.eu.int/en/index.htm
European Foundation for the Improvement of Living and Working Conditions	www.europa.eu.int/agencies/efound/index_en.htm
European Industrial Relations Observatory	www.eiro.eurofound.ie
European Trade Union Confederation	www.etuc.org
The Federation of European Employers	www.fedee.com/index.shtml
ORGANISATIONS	**WEB ADDRESSES**
Bar Council	www.barcouncil.org.uk
Confederation of British Industry	www.cbi.org.uk/home.html
International Labour Organisation	www.ilo.org/public/english/index.htm
Law Society	www.lawsoc.org.uk
Local Government Management Board	www.lgmb.gov.uk
Low Pay Commission	www.dca.gov.uk/consult/confr/htm
Office for National Statistics	www.statistics.gov.uk
The Law Commission	www.lawcom.gov.uk
TUC	www.tuc.org.uk

Index

INDEX

INDEX

INDEX